Air Fryer Cookbook

The

1000 Flavorful Air Fryer Recipes for Any Taste and Occasion

Written By

Jennifer Newman

Legal & Disclaimer

The information contained in this book and its contents is not designed to replace or take the place of any form of medical or professional advice; and is not meant to replace the need for independent medical, financial, legal, or other professional advice or services, as may be required. The content and information in this book have been provided for educational and entertainment purposes only.

The content and information contained in this book have been compiled from sources deemed reliable, and it is accurate to the best of the Author's knowledge, information and However, the Author cannot guarantee its accuracy and validity and cannot be held liable for any errors and/or omissions. Further, changes are periodically made to this book as and when needed.

You agree that by continuing to read this book, where appropriate and/or necessary, you shall consult a professional (including but not limited to your doctor, attorney, or financial advisor or such other advisor as needed) before using any of the suggested remedies, techniques, or information in this book.

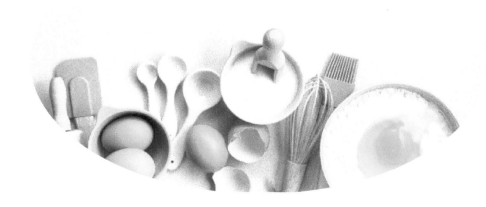

Contents

Part 1: Air Fryer Cookbook

Part 2: The Complete Air Fryer Cookbook

PART – I

Air Fryer Cookbook

The

600 Best Healthy and Deliciously Simple Recipes for Your Air Fryer

Jennifer Newman

Introduction

Healthy food should not be a fad or an option to choose, it should be part of your life. Of course, this does not mean that you have to give up enjoying cooking. Nor of the many dishes that can be prepared healthy. To achieve this there are certain appliances that can help you a lot. For example, an Air Fryer.

An oil-free fryer is an appliance that is used to cook different foods without this ingredient. Therefore, it saves a good amount of money and, above all, it reduces your caloric intake.

With an air fryer you will cook different foods in a similar way to a traditional one. But thanks to its special operation, you will do it without using a single drop of oil. In this way, you will prepare exquisite dishes without added fat and with a considerably lower caloric intake.

In this book, you are going to learn everything about an air fryer. That is, the benefits, the tips and especially recipes that will help you make your experience with a unique air fryer.

Enjoy it!

Chapter 1

Introduction To Air Fryer

An oil-free fryer works similar to an oven, based on hot air. When you turn it on, an electrical resistance is activated that will heat the internal air, then fans will start to move to distribute all the air over the food. The result will be a triple action: fry, broil, and cook with hardly any oil. Or for some dishes, without any oil.

They may have different aesthetics and sizes, but all models of air fryers have 3 elements in common: a container for placing food, a thermostat and a timer to control cooking time. Some designs include a basket in the container to facilitate the introduction and extraction of ingredients.

Do you need to use oil in an air fryer?

A traditional oven or deep fryer recipe may require the use of oil to help cook and texture food ingredients. However, the oil is optional, since the hot air circulation of the device allows the food placed inside to cook completely.

Air-fried foods cook perfectly without oil. If you are using oil for any reason, I would recommend using an oil spray to limit the amount of oil used.

What should you avoid cooking?

Experts warn about using an air fryer to prepare foods that contain a liquid dough, as they will not cook pancakes or homemade cakes like the oven would.

Similarly, it is not recommended to cook rice and pasta in an air fryer, since these elements must be cooked beforehand so that the oven gives them that good texture.

Advantages of oil fryers

Reducing oil consumption is not your only advantage. Here we leave you others just as remarkable:

- *Simple cleaning*: Forget about oil splashes, catchy debris, etc. Simply wipe it with a damp cloth and wash the removable basket if required.
- *Healthier food*: Using less oil also implies that there will be fewer calories and harmful fats in your body.
- *Oil-free fryers take much less cooking time than an oven*: Which means greater energy savings!

- They have different ways of cooking food
- Its use is not complicated at all
- They have LCD screen

Is it worth buying an air fryer?

These appliances are a great, hassle-free appliance to have on hand in your kitchen if you want to grill vegetables or cook simple meat dishes quickly. This is the result of the appliance's hot air circulation, which helps speed up the preheat and cook times associated with traditional ovens, making it a must-have for any beginner and cook master.

However, they are not exactly ideal appliances for those with larger families and people who like to prepare meals in large batches, as there is a limited amount of space inside many air fryer baskets.

Chapter 2

Air Fryer Breakfast Recipes

Minced Pork Burger

Servings: 2

Preparation time: 5 minutes

Cook time: 10 minutes

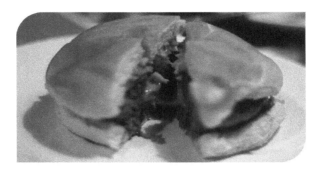

Ingredients	Steps to Cook

Ingredients

- ½ lb minced pork
- 1 tbsp grated Parmesan
- Herbs
- Salt to taste

Steps to Cook

1. First, place a glass of water in the bottom of the fryer, under the basket.
2. The presence of water prevents the escape of "smoke" and the smell of burning, as it has the great utility of preventing the fat, dripping from the meat, from ending up in the lower parts and burning, causing a bad smell.
3. Obviously, in case you forget to put the water before you start cooking, you can add it later (you will remember to smell the meat ...) but always turn off the air fryer first.
4. Cook at 350°F for 10 minutes.

Nutritional Information

- Calories: 333.8
- Carbohydrates: 13.6g
- Fat: 18.4g

- Protein: 24.1g
- Sugar: 2.3g
- Cholesterol: 126.7mg

Scrambled Eggs

Servings: 1

Preparation time: 2 minutes

Cook time: 1 minute

Ingredients	Steps to Cook

- *2 large eggs*
- *2 butter spoons*
- *salt and pepper*

1. Add a small aluminum tray to the basket of an air fryer.
2. Add butter and heat to 350°F to melt (about 1 minute)
3. Break both eggs on the aluminum tray.
4. Return to the fryer and cook at 325°F until ready. ** Note: For overly hard boiled eggs, this takes approximately 8 minutes.

Nutritional information

- Calories: 263
- Carbohydrates: 1g
- Fat: 33g

- Protein: 14g
- Sugar: 2g
- Cholesterol: 482mg

Mint Frittata

Servings: 2

Preparation time: 5 minutes

Cook time: 15 minutes

Ingredients

- 6 small eggs
- 2 sprigs of fresh mint
- 2 tbsp of milk
- ½ oz. grated cheese
- salt and pepper to taste

Steps to Cook

1. Wash the mint and remove the leaves from the twig, insert them into the glass of the immersion blender.
2. Add all other ingredients and mix until you get green dough.
3. Cut a piece of parchment paper large enough to line the fryer basket, wrinkle it with your hands to make it easier to fit, make sure it also covers a bit of the edge, like a frying pan. Remove and preheat fryer to 350°F for 3 minutes.
4. Put the parchment paper back in the basket and pour half of the dough over it. Close the fryer and cook for 12 minutes at 350°F.

Nutritional Information

- Calories: 134
- Carbohydrates: 3g
- Fat: 10g

- Protein: 8g
- Sugar: 2g
- Cholesterol: 181mg

Frittata With Sausage

Servings: 2

Preparation time: 5 minutes

Cook time: 18-20 minutes

Ingredients

- ¼ pound breakfast sausage, fully cooked and mashed
- 4 eggs, lightly beaten
- ½ cup shredded cheese mixture
- 2 tbsp chopped red bell pepper
- 1 green onion, chopped
- 1 pinch of cayenne pepper (optional)
- Cooking spray

Steps to Cook

1. Combine sausages, eggs, Cheddar cheese, bell peppers, onion and cayenne in a bowl and mix to combine.
2. Preheat the fryer to 360°F. Spray a 6x2-inch nonstick cake pan with cooking spray.
3. Place the egg mixture in the prepared cake pan.
4. Cook in fryer until frittata is ready, 18-20 minutes.

Nutritional information

- Calories: 152.7
- Carbohydrates: 3.1g
- Fat: 10.1g
- Protein: 12.8g
- Sugar: 0.8g
- Cholesterol: 165.3mg

Breakfast Cookies

Ingredients	Steps to Cook

Ingredients

- 1 cup ripe banana puree
- ½ cup peanut butter
- ½ cup of honey
- 1 tsp of vanilla extract
- 1 cup old fashioned oatmeal
- ½ cup whole wheat flour
- ¼ cup skimmed milk powder
- 2 tsp ground cinnamon
- ½ teaspoon salt
- ¼ tsp baking soda
- 1 cup dried cranberries°

Steps to Cook

1. Preheat fryer to 600°F. Beat banana, peanut butter, honey, and vanilla until well combined. In another bowl, mix together oatmeal, flour, milk powder, cinnamon, salt, and baking soda; gradually add the banana mixture. Mix dried cranberries.
2. In batches, drop dough into ¼ 2-inch cup. Away in the greased tray in the fryer basket; flatten to ½ in. thickness.
3. Cook until lightly browned, 6 to 8 minutes. Let cool in the basket for 1 minute. Remove to the racks.
4. Serve warm or at room temperature. Freezing Option: Freeze cookies in freezer containers, separating layers with parchment paper. To use, defrost before serving or, if desired, heat in a preheated fryer at 600°F until heated through, about 1 minute.

Nutritional information

- Calories: 146.9
- Carbohydrates: 26.5g
- Fat: 3.5g
- Protein: 3.4g

- Sugar: 7.5g
- Cholesterol: 20.3mg

Crusty Bread

Servings: 2

Preparation time: 1 minute

Cook time: 6 minutes

Ingredients	Steps to Cook

- Stale or baked and frozen breads (various types)
- Sufficient water

1. Distribute the loaves of bread in the bottom of the container and sprinkle a little water.
2. Close the lid, select 400^{0}F, set the time to 6 minutes.
3. Then serve the crispy bread with fresh flavor.

Nutritional information

- Calories: 68.3
- Carbohydrates: 14.3g
- Fat: 0.2g

- Protein: 1.9g
- Sugar: 0g
- Cholesterol: 0mg

Sweet Potato With Bacon And Cheddar Cheese

Servings: 4-8

Preparation time: 5 minutes

Cook time: 30-40 minutes

Ingredients	Steps to Cook

Ingredients

- 2 ¼ pounds small potatoes, cut into four and cooked
- 3 tbsp olive oil
- 2 tbsp of flour
- Salt to taste
- Bacon to finish
- Cheddar cheese sauce
- 1 jar of cheddar cheese
- 1 cheese tablet
- ½ grated onion
- 1 tbsp of margarine
- ½ box of sour cream
- Salt to taste

Steps to Cook

1. Preheat the fryer to 400°F for 4 to 6 minutes. Place the potatoes cut in four in a bowl with the olive oil and mix to cover all the potato pieces. With the help of a sieve, sprinkle with the wheat flour mixed with the salt. Bring to the fryer for about 30 minutes, stirring gently a few times, so they are uniform in color.
2. Place in a baking dish and cover with cheddar cheese sauce and sprinkle pieces of fried bacon. Then serve as an accompaniment to baked goods or as an appetizer.

Cheddar Sauce:

3. In a saucepan, melt the butter and fry the onion until golden. Add cheddar cheese and thumb cheese. When it begins to melt, add the cream and beat well with a platter until very creamy. If you prefer, transfer it to a blender and blend until creamy. Put the salt. If the sauce is very thick, add a little milk.

Nutritional information

- Calories: 460
- Carbohydrates: 78g
- Fat: 13g

- Protein: 17g
- Sugar: 6g
- Cholesterol: 30mg

Empanadas Mini Sausages

Servings: 20

Preparation time: 2 minutes

Cook time: 10-11 minutes

Ingredients	Steps to Cook

- ½ lb mini sausages
- 3 ½ oz. puff pastry already prepared (refrigerated or frozen, thawed)
- 1 tbsp of mustard powder

1. Preheat the fryer to 400°F. Drain the sausages completely and pat dry lightly on a layer of paper towels.
2. Cut the puff pastry into 5 x 1½ cm strips and cover the strips with a thin layer of powdered mustard. Wrap each sausage in a spiral strip of dough.
3. Place half of the sausages wrapped in batter in the basket and slide them into the fryer.
4. Set the timer for 10-11 minutes. Bake the breaded sausages until golden brown. Roast the remaining sausages in the same way. Serve the sausages on a tray accompanied by a bowl of mustard.

Nutritional information

- Calories: 290.3
- Carbohydrates: 39.6g
- Fat: 11.5g

- Protein: 11.2g
- Sugar: 2.1g
- Cholesterol: 57.5mg

Tomato Stuffed With Creamy Chicken

Servings: 3

Preparation time: 5 minutes

Cook time: 20 minutes

Ingredients

- 3 medium tomatoes
- 3 tbsp of chopped onion
- 3 cloves garlic, crushed
- 6 tbsp grated cooked chicken breast
- 3 tbsp sliced mushroom
- 3 tbsp of cream cheese
- Salt and pepper to taste

Steps to Cook

1. Cut off the top of the tomatoes, remove the seeds and set aside.
2. To make the filling, brown the garlic and onion in a pan, then add the mushroom and minced chicken, season with salt and pepper to taste, and finally add the creamy curd.
3. Fill the tomatoes and take them to the fryer for 20 minutes at 360°F.

Nutritional information

- Calories: 177.7
- Carbohydrates: 4.2g
- Fat: 4.2g
- Protein: 29.9g
- Sugar: 1.7g
- Cholesterol: 67.5mg

Tapioca Dice

Servings: 2-4

Preparation time: 5 minutes

Cook time: 30 minutes

Ingredients	Steps to Cook

Ingredients

- *½ lb of grated rennet cheese*
- *½ lb of granulated tapioca*
- *2 cups of hot milk*
- *Salt, pepper and oregano to taste.*

Steps to Cook

1. In a bowl, add the grated rennet cheese, the tapioca, the salt, the pepper and the oregano to taste, mix. After that, add the milk and continue mixing, until everything is incorporated.
2. Transfer the mixture to a film-lined form and leave it in the refrigerator for about 3 hours.
3. After that, simply cut them into small cubes and place them in the electric fryer for about 30 minutes at 400°F. Ready!

Nutritional information

- Calories: 544.2
- Carbohydrates: 134.8g
- Fat: 0g

- Protein: 0.3g
- Sugar: 5.1g
- Cholesterol: 10mg

Ricotta Balls With Basil

Servings: 6

Preparation time: 10 minutes

Cook time: 15 minutes

Ingredients

- 1 egg, separated ½ lb ricotta
- 2 tbsp of flour
- and clear yolk
- Freshly ground black pepper
- ½ oz. fresh basil, finely chopped
- 1 tbsp chives, finely chopped
- 3 slices of stale white bread

Steps to Cook

1. Mix the ricotta in a bowl with the flour, the egg yolk, 1 tsp of salt and freshly ground black pepper. Add the basil, chives, and orange zest to the mixture. Divide the mixture into 20 equal portions and form the balls with wet hands. Let the balls rest for a while. Grind the bread slices until obtaining a fine bread crumb with the food processor and mix with the olive oil. Put the mixture in a deep container. Lightly beat the egg white in another deep bowl. Preheat the fryer to 400°F. Carefully roll the ricotta balls into the egg whites and breadcrumbs. Place ten balls in the basket and slide it into the fryer. Set the timer for 8 to 10 minutes. Bake the balls until golden. Bake the rest of the balls in the same way. Serve the ricotta.

Nutritional information

- Calories: 150
- Carbohydrates: 19g
- Fat: 2.6g

- Protein: 14.5g
- Sugar: 3.5g
- Cholesterol: 74.4mg

Grated Potatoes

Servings: 2-4

Preparation time: 5 minutes

Cook time: 15-18 minutes

Ingredients

- 1 lb low-starch potatoes, shelled
- ¼ cup milk
- Freshly ground black pepper
- Nutmeg
- 1 ½ oz. grated cheese

Steps to Cook

1. Preheat the air fryer to 400°F. Cut the potatoes very thin.
2. In a bowl, mix the milk and cream; season to taste with salt, pepper and nutmeg. Cover the potato slices with the milk mixture.
3. Transfer the potato slices to the quiche shape and pour the rest of the cream mixture from the bowl over the potatoes.
4. Distribute the cheese evenly over the potatoes. Place the quiche in the fryer basket and slide the basket into the fryer.
5. Set the timer for 15 to 18 minutes and let it brown until golden and smooth. Serve the potatoes au gratin in squares with fish or in the oven.

Nutritional information

- Calories: 69
- Carbohydrates: 15g
- Fat: 0.1g
- Protein: 1.7g
- Sugar: 0.2g
- Cholesterol: 0mg

Shrimp Paulista

Servings: 4

Preparation time: 5 minutes

Cook time: 20-25 minutes

Ingredients

- 1 lb medium shrimp with clean, washed shell
- ½ lemon
- 1 ½ tbsp of flour
- 2 garlic cloves, squeezed
- Salt to taste

Steps to Cook

1. Preheat the fryer to 400°F for 4 to 6 minutes. Season shrimp with salt, lemon, and squeezed garlic. Let drain in a strainer.
2. Cover the bottom of a baking sheet with two layers of absorbent paper and spread the shrimp. Sprinkle the flour and mix well. Prawns should be without water when adding wheat flour, because if they are with water, they will stick together.
3. Place in the fryer basket and leave to work for 20 minutes, until golden brown, stirring occasionally for even cooking. Serve with white rice and a green salad.

Nutritional information

- Calories: 164
- Carbohydrates: 2g
- Fat: 6g
- Protein: 24g
- Sugar: 0.3g
- Cholesterol: 76mg

Falafel With Tahini

Servings: 2-4

Preparation time: 5 minutes

Cook time: 15-20 minutes

| Ingredients | Steps to Cook |

Ingredients

Falafel:

- chickpea nuggets
- 1 lb chickpeas
- Fresh mint leaves
- 2 or 3 Syrian loaves
- Milk to moisten
- 1 tbsp of pasta dessert
- crushed garlic
- Salt and pepper to taste
- Lemon drops

Tahine sauce:

- 1 tbsp of tahini
- ½ squeezed lemon
- ½ cup of water
- ½ crushed garlic clove

Steps to Cook

Falafel:

1. Preheat the fryer to 400°F for 4 to 6 minutes. Drain the chickpeas. In a bowl, combine the minced bread, mint leaves, chickpeas, and beaten garlic.
2. Add the pepper and the drops of lemon juice. Moisten the mixture with a little milk and let it rest for half an hour, so that the milk is absorbed.
3. Then mix the mixture in a processor. The consistency must be smooth, but firm to form balls. Make medium balls and flatten them out a bit.
4. Put a layer of balls in the fryer basket and leave it for about 15 minutes, turning it half the time so that it browns evenly. If necessary, leave another 5 minutes. Place them in the center of a plate. When you serve, place the garnishes around.

Tahine Sauce:

5. Mix all ingredients and serve.

Nutritional information

- Calories: 61
- Carbohydrates: 6g
- Fat: 4g

- Protein: 2g
- Sugar: 0g
- Cholesterol: 0mg

Halloween Cookie

Servings: 2-4

Preparation time: 10 minutes

Cook time: 10 minutes

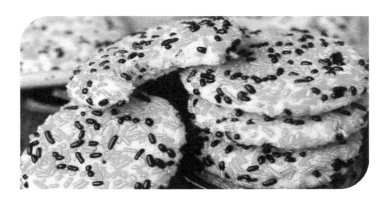

Ingredients	Steps to Cook

Ingredients

- 1 cup butter at room temperature
- 1 cup granulated sugar
- 2 eggs
- 3 tsp of vanilla
- 2 ¼ cups all-purpose flour
- 2 tsp of baking powder
- ½ tsp salt
- 1 cup black and orange granules

Steps to Cook

1. Preheat the air fryer to 350°F.
2. Using a hand mixer, beat the butter and sugar. Cream for about two minutes or until fluffy. Scrape down the sides of the bowl.
3. Add the eggs and vanilla and mix until well combined.
4. Add flour, baking powder, and salt. Mix until fully incorporated. The dough will become sticky.
5. Pour your sweets into a bowl. Remove cookie dough from bowl and place on granulated portion. Roll the dough into the drizzled part until it is completely covered. Reshape the dough into a ball before placing it on a parchment paper lined baking sheet.
6. Cookies will spread widely during cooking.
7. Bake at 350°F for 10 minutes.

Nutritional information

- Calories:150
- Carbohydrates: 18g
- Fat: 8g
- Protein: 2g

- Sugar: 8g
- Cholesterol: 34mg

Caramel Popcorn

Ingredients

- 8 cups of popcorn
- 1 butter tablet
- 1 cup of sugar
- 1/3 cup whipped cream

Note: Be sure to use a more "natural" corn, without butter or salt, so you can better taste the sauce!

Steps to Cook

1. Put a quantity of corn in a pan in put it into the air fryer. Drizzle with a little olive oil.
2. Set the temperature at 240^0F for 5 minutes.
3. When the popcorn is ready, put it in a large bowl and set aside while preparing the sauce.
4. Mix butter, sugar and cream and heat over medium heat, stirring constantly. In a few minutes the sauce should be boiling, continue boiling until the mixture reaches the soft ball stage 240^0F.
5. Remove mixture from heat and pour over popcorn, stirring until all popcorn is well coated. Be sure to serve it right away.

Nutritional information

- Calories: 120
- Carbohydrates: 25g
- Fat: 2.5g

- Protein: 1g
- Sugar: 8g
- Cholesterol: 20mg

Crunchy Strawberry

Servings: 4

Preparation time: 15 minutes

Cook time: 45 minutes

Ingredients

- 4 cups of chopped strawberries
- ¼ cup sugar
- ¼ tsp of cinnamon
- 3 tbsp all-purpose flour
- 2 tsp of lemon juice
- 2 tsp grated lemon zest

Topping:

- 1/3 cup cold butter
- ½ cup flour
- ½ cup oatmeal
- ½ cup packed brown sugar
- ¾ tsp cinnamon
- ¼ tsp of salt

Steps to Cook

1. Preheat the air fryer to 375^0F. Grease an 11 × 7-inch baking pan.
2. In a small bowl, mix together the cinnamon and sugar. In a large bowl, combine the strawberries, cinnamon mixture, and flour. Gently stir to coat.
3. Add lemon juice and lemon zest to strawberries and transfer to 11 × 7 inch greased skillet put the fritters in the Air fryer for 15 minutes at 360^0F, pulverized with a little oil. Chop the lettuce and place in a salad bowl.
4. Put a little salt on the lettuce and place the fritters on it, well distributed. Add the Cesar sauce.

Topping:

5. In a food processor, combine the flour, oats, cinnamon, sugar, salt, and butter. Press until the cover looks like thick crumbs.
6. Pour the topping over the strawberries on the baking sheet, making sure to evenly coat to the edges.
7. Bake 30 minutes at 260^0F or until frosting is golden and fruit is smooth and bubbly. Serve hot or cold.

Nutritional information

- Calories: 140
- Carbohydrates: 18g
- Fat: 6g

- Protein: 2g
- Sugar: 13g
- Cholesterol: 35mg

Roasted Carrot

Servings: 1

Preparation time: 5 minutes

Cook time: 20 minutes

Ingredients

- 1 carrot
- Salt to taste
- Black pepper to taste
- Smoked paprika to taste
- Olive oil

Steps to Cook

1. Start by cutting the carrots into small strips. Cut it in half.
2. Season well and mix with olive oil.
3. Take the air fryer at 360^0F for 20 minutes or until golden brown, this is the secret, as they are crispy on the outside and soft on the inside.
4. Serve with a little sauce.

Nutritional information

- Calories: 109
- Carbohydrates: 14g
- Fat: 5.8g

- Protein: 1.4g
- Sugar: 7g
- Cholesterol: 0mg

Toast With Garlic And Cheese

Servings: 1-2

Preparation time: 2 minutes

Cook time: 5 minutes

Ingredients	Steps to Cook

Ingredients

- Enough French loaves cut in half
- 3 tbsp olive oil
- 1 tbsp butter
- 1 pinch of salt
- 1 pinch of black pepper
- Enough sliced cheese

Steps to Cook

1. Make a paste in a small bowl with butter, olive oil, crushed garlic, and season with salt, pepper, and oregano to taste.
2. Pass this mixture over the bread slices. Top each half with sliced cheese.
3. Place in the air fryer at 360°F for about 8 minutes or until golden, as desired.

Nutritional information

- Calories: 70
- Carbohydrates: 11g
- Fat: 2.5g
- Protein: 2g
- Sugar: 0g
- Cholesterol: 0mg

Chapter 3

Air Fryer Poultry Recipes

Chicken Flounder

Servings: 1-2

Preparation time: 5 minutes

Cook time: 10-15 minutes

Ingredients	Steps to Cook
• Chicken flounder to taste • Oil to brush	1. Preheat your air fryer to 400°F for 4 minutes. Given the time, put the sausage in the fryer. 2. Set for 15 minutes at 400°F. After 5 minutes, remove from the fryer and, with a paper towel or a kitchen brush, rub a little oil over the sausage and shake or turn it over. 3. Return the sausages to the air fryer and check from time to time to see if it is already at the desired point. 4. If necessary, leave more time. Until you get the color and stitch you want.

Nutritional Information

- Calories: 113
- Carbohydrates: 0.35g
- Fat: 3.61g

- Protein: 18.71g
- Sugar: 0.08g
- Cholesterol: 48mg

Sassami chicken

Ingredients

- enough sassami to fill the fryer pan
- Salt to taste
- black pepper and oregano to taste
- 1 clove garlic, minced
- 1 drizzle of olive oil
- ½ lemon (juice)

Steps to Cook

Put the sassami in a bowl, add the spices, garlic, lemon, oil, and stir and set aside for about 15 minutes.

Place in the fryer and leave for about 30 minutes at 360°F (or until golden), stirring about every 10 minutes, to bake evenly.

Nutritional Information

- Calories: 581
- Carbohydrates: 57g
- Fat: 30g

- Protein: 24g
- Sugar: 42g
- Cholesterol: 72mg

Herbed Chicken Wings Sticks

Servings: 4-6

Preparation time: 15 mins

Cook time: 40 minutes

Ingredients	Steps to Cook
<ul><li>2 ¼ lb wing sticks</li><li>Salt to taste</li><li>Oregano to taste</li><li>Black pepper to taste</li><li>Garlic to taste</li><li>Grated onion to taste</li><li>Lemon to taste</li><li>Olive oil</li></ul>	1. Season the drumsticks, with the previous elements, marinate for about 15 min. 2. Pour oil over the drumsticks and stir well, spreading the oil over all of them. 3. Bring to a deep fryer at 400^{0}F for 40 minutes, stirring occasionally, to bake evenly.

Nutritional Information

- Calories: 200
- Carbohydrates: 3g
- Fat: 12g

- Protein: 17g
- Sugar: 1g
- Cholesterol: 110mg

Chicken Sweet Potato Balls

Servings: 4

Preparation time: 1 minute

Cook time: 20 minutes

Ingredients

- 2 sweet potatoes
- 1 chicken breast
- Salt and oregano to taste
- optional filler
- to taste of cheese or curd

Steps to Cook

1. Cook the potatoes until they are very tender.
2. Cook the chicken with salt and spices and crumble
3. Puree the potato; if it dries too much, you can put a little water in the chicken cooking.
4. Mix the shredded chicken into the puree and season to taste.
5. Make balls, you can fill with cheese or curd
6. Place in the air fryer for 25 minutes at 400°F or until golden brown.

Nutritional Information

- Calories: 110.2
- Carbohydrates: 26.5g
- Fat: 0g

- Protein: 1.9g
- Sugar: 7.7g
- Cholesterol: 0mg

Breaded Chicken, Parmesan Cheese And Roasted Vegetables

Servings: 4

Preparation time: 5 minutes

Cook time: 15-20 minutes

Ingredients

- 4 chicken breast fillet
- Preferred vegetables to taste
- 2 eggs
- Parmesan cheese to taste
- Seasonings preferably to taste

Steps to Cook

1. Season the chicken fillets to your liking, set aside for 1 hour to get the flavor of the seasoning. Then pass the egg and then the Parmesan cheese. Put in the air fryer at 400°F, until golden brown to taste.
2. Put the cut vegetables in a pan and season to taste, a tip if you can grill it with rosemary and bay leaves, it's wonderful.
3. Close with laminated paper and bake in the air fryer at 350°F for 15 minutes, then remove the laminated paper and allow it to brown completely.

Nutritional information

- Calories: 260.6
- Carbohydrates: 11.8g
- Fat: 12.5g
- Protein: 26.5g
- Sugar: 1.2g
- Cholesterol: 62.5m

Crispy Chicken

Ingredients

- 1 lb of seasoned chicken (5 pieces)
- cornstarch to bread

Steps to Cook

1. Sprinkle the chicken pieces over the cornstarch.
2. Place in fryer at 360°F for 30 minutes, or until golden. Turn half the time. Do not overlap the chicken pieces, place only what fits in the bottom of the basket, on average 5 pieces fit

Nutritional information

- Calories: 300
- Carbohydrates: 23g
- Fat: 10g
- Protein: 24g
- Sugar: 7g
- Cholesterol: 45mg

Whole Roasted Turkey

Servings: 4-6

Preparation time: 30 minutes

Cook time: 3h

Ingredients

- 1 clean turkey with about 8.8 lbs
- 2 large onions, cut into small pieces
- ½ tbsp hot sauce
- 1 tbsp French mustard
- 1 bottle of dry white wine
- 3 cups chicken broth
- 1 cup butter, melted
- salt to taste
- melted butter for injection

Steps to Cook

1. Preheat the air fryer at 360°F.
2. Place the onions, garlic, pepper sauce, mustard, 1 cup of wine, 1 cup of chicken stock, butter, salt and beat in a blender.
3. Transfer to a bowl, add the remaining wine and chicken stock, and mix well.
4. Fill the turkey and place it on an ungreased baking sheet.
5. Hold the skin of the turkey breast with one hand and remove it from the meat with the other.
6. Prick the meat with a fork and, with the help of a seasoning injector, inject the melted butter at several points on the turkey breast.
7. Rub the prepared seasoning onto the surface of the turkey and inject a little into the meat.
8. Pull the skin back, covering the turkey again, and sew with a thick thread.
9. Cover with aluminum foil and put in the air fryer for about 3 hours, basting the turkey every 20 minutes with the sauce that falls into the pan.
10. When the paper is dark, remove it and leave the turkey in the air fryer until golden.

Nutritional information

- Calories: 214
- Carbohydrates: 0.1g
- Fat: 8.4g

- Protein: 32g
- Sugar: 0g
- Cholesterol: 124mg

Stuffed Breast Turkey

Servings: 5

Preparation time: 15 minutes

Cook time: 30 minutes

Ingredients

- 3 lb of turkey breast
- ¼ lb of banana with raisins
- 1 ¼ cup of water
- 3 ½ oz. of sugar
- 5 ¼ oz. fresh tamarind
- Chopped parsley, salt and freshly ground black pepper to taste

Steps to Cook

1. Open the turkey breast and place the raisin bananas lengthwise inside. Wrap and tie with string. Wrap in foil and bake in the air fryer, preheated at 400°F for approximately 30 minutes.
2. Remove from the air fryer and, with the help of a fork; check that the inside of the turkey is hot. If not, return it to the air fryer.
3. Discard the shell and core of tamarind.
4. In a saucepan, dilute the sugar in the water, add the pulp of the fruit and simmer for at least 30 minutes or until you get a dense and shiny sauce. Remove from heat and strain.
5. Cut the turkey breast and put it on the plates with the tamarind sauce.

Nutritional information

- Calories: 152
- Carbohydrates: 0g
- Fat: 0.8g
- Protein: 34g

- Sugar: 0g
- Cholesterol: 94mg

Roast Turkey With White Wine

Servings: 4-6

Preparation time: 30 minute

Cook time: 4h

Ingredients

- 1 turkey (10-12 pound)
- ½ cup vinegar tea
- ½ bottle of dry white wine
- 1 lemon juice
- 2 tsp of red pepper sauce
- 2 tbsp of salt
- 1 onion
- 3 garlic cloves
- green smell
- 1 bay leaf
- ½ lb mayonnaise

Steps to Cook

1. The day before, clean, wash, and drain the turkey.
2. Mix all the spices with mayonnaise and rub well inside and outside the whole turkey.
3. The next day, bake in the air fryer at 360^{0}F for about 4 hours, with all the spices and covering with aluminum foil.
4. Once in a while, pick up the paper and spray the turkey with the baking dish.
5. Remove from the oven when you prick the turkey with a fork and do not release any more liquid from its meat.
6. In the pan, place the potatoes in the air fryer and let them brown.

Nutritional information

- Calories: 214
- Carbohydrates: 0.1g
- Fat: 8.4g

- Protein: 32g
- Sugar: 0g
- Cholesterol: 124mg

Turkey To The Brazilian

Servings: 4-6

Preparation time: 30 mins

Cook time: 1h30 minutes

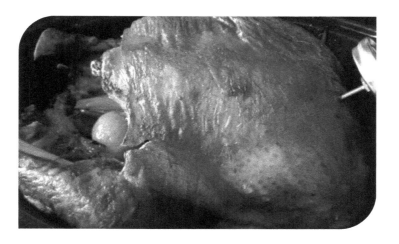

Ingredients

- 1 turkey (8.8-lb)
- 1 tbsp of mustard
- 3 cups dry white wine
- 3 cups chicken broth
- 1 cup margarine or butter
- 2 onions
- 5 garlic cloves
- Pepper mill
- Salt

Filling:

- 1 tbsp of chives
- 1 tbsp of parsley
- 1 tbsp of breadcrumbs
- 1 banana, diced
- 1 chicken broth powder
- ½ cup of oil
- ½ cup of olive oil

Steps to Cook

1. Whisk in a blender: 1 cup wine, 1 cup chicken broth, chopped onion, garlic, and mustard, hot sauce, margarine, or butter and salt. Place on an ovenproof plate and add the rest of the wine and the chicken stock, mix well and reserve.

For the filling:

2. Sautéing over low heat the corn, chicken stock, bananas, sifted flour, and pepper, stirring constantly, until a loose, moist flour forms. Remove from the heat, add green seasoning and fill the turkey. Place the turkey on the ungreased baking sheet. Prick the turkey with a fork and add the reserved sauce.
3. Close with a barbecue stick and tie the turkey legs. Cover with aluminum foil and bake in the air fryer at 600°F for about 1 ½ hours, constantly sprinkling with the pan. Remove the foil to brown for another hour and a half or so, continue to drizzle with the sauce.

- *2 cups cornmeal*
- *2 grated onions*
- *Black pepper*

Place on the serving plate and decorate with flour and green seasoning.

Nutritional information

- Calories: 214
- Carbohydrates: 0.1g
- Fat: 8.4g

- Protein: 32g
- Sugar: 0g
- Cholesterol: 124mg

Turkey Breast To Baldissara

Servings: 2-4

Preparation time: 30 mins

Cook time: 2h

Ingredients	Steps to Cook

Ingredients

- 1 turkey breast
- 1 glass of white wine
- 1 lemon juice
- 1 large onion
- Salt
- 5 garlic cloves
- White pepper
- 1 teaspoon of garlic salt
- Nutmeg
- Bay leaves

Steps to Cook

1. Place the turkey breast in the refrigerator for one day and one night.
2. The next day: season.
3. Beat everything in a blender, place in a bowl with the turkey breasts. Marinate for 24 hours in the closed container in the refrigerator.
4. Lots of butter in the pan with quality butter.
5. Place the turkey breasts, spread more butter on the breasts, and place aluminum foil so that it does not touch the turkey breasts.
6. Bake for 2 hours, then remove the paper and let it brown.
7. Serve with white rice

Nutritional information

- Calories: 152
- Carbohydrates: 0g
- Fat: 0.8g

- Protein: 34g
- Sugar: 0g
- Cholesterol: 94mg

Roasted Turkey Breast

Servings: 2-4

Preparation time: 2h

Cook time: 30 minutes

Ingredients

- 1 ¼ lb boneless turkey breast
- 1 cup orange broth
- ½ can of guarana diet salt
- Garlic and vinegar

Steps to Cook

1. Season the turkey with garlic, salt and vinegar.
2. Add the orange juice and guarana, leaving to soak for 2 hours.
3. Bake in the air fryer at 360⁰F for 30 minutes, always drizzling with the sauce.

Nutritional information

- Calories: 152
- Carbohydrates: 0g
- Fat: 0.8g

- Protein: 34g
- Sugar: 0g
- Cholesterol: 94mg

Turkey Breast With Vegetable Panache

Servings: 2-4

Preparation time: 30 mins

Cook time: 2h

Ingredients	Steps to Cook

- 1 bone-in seasoned turkey breast
- 1 cup of white wine
- 4 tbsp of margarine

Panache:

- 1 bunch of broccoli
- ½ bunch of radish
- 2 diced zucchini
- 3 carrots, sliced
- 4 tbsp of margarine
- 10 sprigs of parsley, washed and chopped
- 3 ½ oz. peas
- Black pepper and salt

1. Preheat the air fryer to 320°F for 10 minutes. Arrange the turkey breast on a baking sheet, drizzle with white wine, cover the baking sheet with aluminum foil, and bake for 2 hours.
2. Remove the foil, grease the bird with the margarine 3 to 4 times during the preparation and complete the cooking until the thermometer pops out. While the turkey is baking, prepare the panache.

Panache:

3. Boil salted water in a large saucepan and cook one vegetable at a time quickly, leaving them crispy. Heat a large skillet, melt the margarine, add 2 tablespoons of water and add the vegetables. Gently mix Season with salt and pepper, sprinkle with parsley and serve along with the turkey breast. Enjoy your meal.

Nutritional information

- Calories: 152
- Carbohydrates: 0g
- Fat: 0.8g

- Protein: 34g
- Sugar: 2g
- Cholesterol: 94mg

Tasty Fillet Of Turkey

Ingredients	Steps to Cook

Ingredients

- *1 lb turkey fillets*
- *1 package of cream*
- *1 can of rolled mushrooms*
- *3 onions*
- *1 glass of wine*
- *Enough olive oil*
- *Enough lemon*
- *Black pepper to taste*
- *Salt to taste*

Steps to Cook

1. Turkey fillets are cited into thin strips and seasoned for 1 hour with lemon juice, salts, and pepper.
2. Meanwhile, put oil in a frying pan and cut the onions into thin slices and pour the olive oil so that they turn blond. Remove and left on a plate.
3. Then put the fillets in the air fryer and fry them at 400⁰F for 30 minutes. Remove as well. Then pour the rolled mushrooms and the glass of wine and cover the pan.
4. When it's done, add the onion again on top of the cream, bring it to a boil, taste the salt. Pour on the fillets.

Nutritional information

- Calories: 156
- Carbohydrates: 0g
- Fat: 1g
- Protein: 35g

- Sugar: 0g
- Cholesterol: 300mg

Turkey Thigh

Servings: 1-2

Preparation time: 10 minutes

Cook time: 40-50 minutes

Ingredients	Steps to Cook

Ingredients

- 1 turkey leg
- 4 cloves garlic, crushed
- 1 tbsp of oregano
- 1 bay leaf
- Salt and pepper to taste
- 1 cup of rose wine
- 1.7 oz. margarine

Sauce:

- 4 apples
- 2 tbsp of lemon
- 1 tbsp of margarine
- 1 tbsp of onion
- 1 cup sour cream
- ½ cup of honey tea

Steps to Cook

1. Place the turkey drumstick in a bowl with the spices (salt, garlic, oregano, bay leaf, pepper and wine).
2. Lift up the skin a little and spread it with a little margarine, put the skin in place and pass the rest of the margarine.
3. Leave in the sauce for 2 hours.
4. Cover with foil, place in preheated air fryer at400°F for 40 to 50 minutes.
5. Then remove the paper and let it brown at 600°F.
6. Then drizzle with apple sauce and serve.

For the sauce:

7. Put the chopped apples and sour cream in a blender, add the honey and whisk. Reserve. Sauté the butter with the onion, add the reserved liquid, boil, turn off.

Nutritional information

- Calories: 156
- Carbohydrates: 0g
- Fat: 1g
- Protein: 35g
- Sugar: 0g
- Cholesterol: 300mg

Flavored Turkey Breast

Ingredients	**Steps to Cook**

Ingredients

- 1 lb smoked turkey breast
- 1 tbsp butter
- 2 cup of dry white wine
- 2 tbsp of honey
- 1 tsp of flour
- 3 stalks of chopped green onion

Steps to Cook

1. Cut the turkey breast into thick slices, about 1 cm thick. Remove the outer layer that surrounds the meat with a sharp knife.
2. Brown turkey breast slices on both sides in the air fryer at 360^0F for 20 minutes.
3. Remove and arrange the slices on the serving plate, keeping it in a warm place.
4. Heat the wine. When it boils, add the honey, previously mixing it with the flour.
5. Stir with a spatula until you have a slightly thick sauce.
6. Add the green onions and then pour, little by little, over the heated turkey slices.

Nutritional information

- Calories: 156
- Carbohydrates: 0g
- Fat: 1g

- Protein: 35g
- Sugar: 0g
- Cholesterol: 300mg

Stuffed Turkey Fillet Rolls

Servings: 2-4

Preparation time: 15 minutes

Cook time: 20-30 minutes

Ingredients

- 4 fillets of turkey breast
- 4 halves of sun-dried tomatoes
- 200 g goat cheese
- Salt
- Chile

Steps to Cook

1. Beat the fillets with the meat whisk (to soften to taste). Season with salt, pepper and oil to taste.
2. Place half a slice of tomato and 50 g of goat cheese on each of the fillets.
3. Roll them up and then wrap them in aluminum foil.
4. Arrange the rolls in a pan and bake in the preheated air fryer at 420°F for 20 to 30 minutes.
5. Remove from the air fryer, open the rollers and spread a little butter/margarine on them.
6. Put them back in the pan and back in the air fryer until golden.
7. Serve hot with rice and arugula salad or serve cold with mayonnaise-based sauces.

Nutritional information

- Calories: 152
- Carbohydrates: 0g
- Fat: 0.8g

- Protein: 34g
- Sugar: 0g
- Cholesterol: 94mg

Turkey Breast In Champagne

Servings: 2-4

Preparation time: 12h

Cook time: 20-30 minutes

Ingredients

- 1 turkey of 8.8 lb
- 1 bottle of champagne
- 6 garlic cloves
- 2 onion
- 6 tbsp Worcestershire sauce
- 1 tbsp of black pepper
- Orange juice
- Salt
- ½ lb of butter

Steps to Cook

1. Whisk the orange juice, Worcestershire sauce, onion, minced garlic, champagne, pepper, and salt in a blender. Place the turkey on a high-sided baking sheet. Drizzle with the sauce and let it taste for about 12 hours, always drizzling. Two or three hours before, drain the garlic wine and then mix it with half the melted butter. Pass this garlic wine through a sieve, and then reserve the remaining sieve.
2. Using a seasoning syringe, add almost all of the strained garlic wine mixture and melted butter.
3. Distribute this mixture over the entire turkey breast, so that the meat is well moist.
4. Two hours later, rub the bird with the rest of the reserved sieve, making small openings with the sharp knife to lift all the skin of the bird.
5. Leave 2 more hours in the seasoning and bake.
6. Before placing in the air fryer, cover with aluminum foil so that the meat cooks slowly.
7. Put in the air fryer at 400°F for 30 minutes.

Nutritional information

- Calories:292
- Carbohydrates: 10g
- Fat: 2g

- Protein: 17g
- Sugar: 3.1g
- Cholesterol: 50mg

Quail À Mont Vert

Servings: 2-4

Preparation time: 12h 15 minutes

Cook time: 90 minutes

Ingredients

- 4 large quail
- 1 bottle of dry white wine
- 1 tsp of sweet paprika
- 1 tsp of hot paprika
- ½ package fresh sage, chopped or 2 tbsp dehydrated sage
- 1 head minced garlic
- ¼ tsp of virgin olive oil
- 1.7 oz. of butter
- Salt to taste
- 4 rosemary sprigs

Steps to Cook

1. The recipe is very easy; it should only be prepared well in advance.
2. Wash the quail well. Boil salted water in a skillet enough to cover the quail.
3. When the water boils, place the quail in the pan and cover for 5 minutes.
4. Drain and let cool. Put a little minced garlic inside each quail. Place the quail in a large bowl and top with white wine. Add sweet bell pepper, hot pepper, olive oil, and sage. Marinate in the seasoning in the refrigerator for at least 12 hours. Remove the quail from the seasoning and place it in a pan with butter.
5. Take to the preheated air fryer to about 200⁰F and bake for 90 minutes.
6. Open the oven every 15 minutes and turn the quails and sprinkle with the marinade.

Nutritional information

- Calories: 227
- Carbohydrates: 0g
- Fat: 14.1g

- Protein: 25.1g
- Sugar: 0g
- Cholesterol: 86mg

Stuffed Quail

Ingredients	Steps to Cook

For filling:

- 4 quail
- ½ lb of cooked pine nuts
- 3 ½ oz. of cooked rice
- 5 dried apricots, finely chopped
- 1 orange skin peel

For the sauce:

- Juice of ½ oranges
- ½ cup of white wine
- 2 cabbage of butter soup.
- Salt and pepper.
- Thyme
- blond
- Rosemary
- 1 cabbage of sugar tea

1. Grate the pine nuts, if you use nuts or pinoli, break them thick.
2. Mix with rice, chopped dried apricots and orange zest.
3. Salt to taste.
4. Place the orange juice, white wine and a bouquet of thyme, bay leaves and rosemary in a pan and reduce for 30 minutes, turn off the heat and mix in the butter. Reserve.
5. Season the quail with salt and pepper, add the filling.
6. Brush with a generous amount of sauce in the air fryer at 400⁰F, then brush every 15 minutes until the end of cooking, about 45 minutes.

Nutritional information

- Calories: 246
- Carbohydrates: 1g
- Fat: 16g

- Protein: 23g
- Sugar: 0g
- Cholesterol: 210mg

Quail Stuffed With Pineapple Hawaii

Servings: 2-4

Preparation time: 15 mins

Cook time: 20-30 minutes

Ingredients

- 1 cup champagne
- 1 cup of water
- ½ tbsp ground black pepper
- 2 tsp of salt
- 3 tsp of curry
- 3 tsp virgin olive oil
- 3 minced garlic
- 3 ½ tsp lemon vinegar
- 4 medium size hawaii pineapple slices
- 4 very clean quails washed and dried
- 20 sliced endive leaves

Steps to Cook

1. Cut the pineapple curry slices. Reserve.
2. Heat 2 tablespoons of oil in a frying pan and brown the pineapple slices on both sides.
3. Chop them and fill the quail. Tie well Place on the baking sheet. Season with champagne, water, salt, and garlic.
4. Bake in the air fryer for 40 minutes or until golden brown.
5. Arrange the quail on the plates. Add endive and reserve.
6. Mix the vinegar, remaining oil, and pepper. Endive water. Pineapple, rosemary and thyme leaves to decorate.

Nutritional information

- Calories: 246
- Carbohydrates: 1g
- Fat: 16g
- Protein: 23g

- Sugar: 0g
- Cholesterol: 210mg

Roast Duck

Servings: 4-6

Preparation time: 20 mins

Cook time: 60 minutes

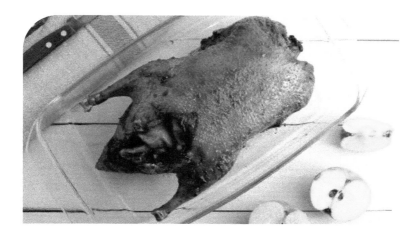

Ingredients	Steps to Cook

Ingredients

- 1 duck
- Green smell to taste
- 1 head of garlic
- Parsley August
- 1 tomato
- 1 chopped onion
- 5 large boiled potatoes

Steps to Cook

1. Separate the duck and potatoes; beat everything in a blender until a cream is formed.
2. Then pierce the duck and pour the cream over it until the cream enters it.
3. Place the sliced potatoes in the skillet with the duck, bake in the air fryer at 400°F for about 60 minutes or until golden.

Nutritional information

- Calories: 472
- Carbohydrates: 0g
- Fat: 40g

- Protein: 27g
- Sugar: 0g
- Cholesterol: 118mg

Grilled Duck To Roti

Servings: 4-6

Preparation time: 20 mins

Cook time: 60 minutes

Ingredients

- 1 duck breast
- 1.7 oz. of butter
- Beef broth or roti sauce
- ¼ cup of dry or sweet red wine
- Salt and pepper to taste
- White rice

Steps to Cook

1. Preheat the air fryer at 600°F.
2. Season the breast with your favorite herbs. Let marinate for 30 minutes.
3. Put in the air fryer for about 45 minutes.
4. Place the two halves of the grilled breast on the grill or plate.
5. For the sauce start with the butter and the broth or roti. Then put the wine.
6. While reducing the sauce, cut the grilled breast and put it in the sauce for two minutes, turn quickly, serve and pass the rice to the sauce.

Nutritional information

- Calories: 119
- Carbohydrates: 0g
- Fat: 2g

- Protein: 35.5g
- Sugar: 0g
- Cholesterol: 110mg

Stuffed Quail And Brussels Cave

Servings: 1-2

Preparation time: 20 minus

Cook time: 40 minutes

Ingredients	Steps to Cook

Quail Filled With Risoto:

- 1/3 lb boneless quail
- 1 ½ oz. rice
- 2 tsp of dry white wine
- 1 tsp whole cashews
- 1 tsp pear onion
- 1 oz. of whole butter without salt
- ½ tsp of tomato
- 1 oz. of raw ham
- 1 oz. dehydrated light background
- 1 tsp ground white pepper
- ½ oz. of fresh parsley
- ½ tsp of refined salt

Cave Of Brussels:

- 1.7 oz. brussels sprouts

Steps to Cook

1. Season the quail inside and out with salt and pepper.
2. Break and toast the cashews in sauté. Reserve.
3. Prepare and heat the transparent background.
4. In a frying pan fry the buttered onion, add the rice and wrap it in the fat, add the wine and let it reduce a little, put the bottom slightly hot little by little and mix until cooked.
5. Add tomato and cook slightly more.
6. When the beans are cooked, remove from the heat; mix with the raw ham in brunoise. Add the grated Parmesan cheese and butter. Mix
7. Adjust the seasonings. Prepare a full-bodied risotto. Add some roasted cashews.
8. Fill the quail with the risotto and wrap them in plastic wrap and then in aluminum foil.
9. Bake in the air fryer at 400^{0}F for 40 minutes or until quail is cooked.
10. Finish with chopped parsley and a little toasted chestnut.

- *½ tsp of ground white pepper*
- *30 g of whole butter without salt*
- *3 g of refined salt*

Brussels Sprouts:

11. Blanch the Brussels sprouts in boiling salted water in a pan.
12. Remove from the water. Sauté stir fry with butter. Spice with salt and pepper.

Mounting:

13. Place quail in the center of a shallow white plate.
14. Pack the cabbages in one corner of the plate.
15. Garnish with chopped parsley and roasted chestnuts.

Nutritional information

- Calories: 246
- Carbohydrates: 1g
- Fat: 16g

- Protein: 23g
- Sugar: 0g
- Cholesterol: 210mg

Wrapped Duck

Servings: 4-6

Preparation time: 20 mins

Cook time: 1h 30 minutes

Ingredients

- 1 duck of 3 lb
- 1 ½ tbsp butter
- Wise
- 1 sprig of rosemary
- Salt
- black pepper

Steps to Cook

1. Season the duck inside and out with salt and pepper, put the sage and rosemary inside and sew to keep it in shape.
2. Wrap the duck on a sheet of parchment paper greased with butter and then on a sheet of aluminum foil.
3. Place the wrapped duck in the air fryer at 400°F and bake for 1 hour and 30 minutes.
4. Serve the wrapped duck, removing the foil on the table.

Nutritional information

- Calories: 119
- Carbohydrates: 0g
- Fat: 2g

- Protein: 35.5g
- Sugar: 0g
- Cholesterol: 110mg

Duck With Orange

Servings: 4-6

Preparation time: 20 mins

Cook time: 30-40 minutes

Ingredients

- 1 duck of 3 lbs
- 2 large oranges
- 1 lemon
- 2 butter spoons
- ¾ cup sugar
- 1 bay leaf
- 1 tbsp of wheat flour
- ½ cup of vinegar
- ¼ cup dry white wine
- ½ cup of liqueur
- 2 cups chicken broth
- Petroleum
- Salt
- black pepper
- 1 tbsp of potato starch

Steps to Cook

1. Season the duck with salt, pepper, bay leaf and white wine. Place it on a baking sheet and top with oil and half of the butter. Bake in the air fryer at 400°F for 30 minutes.
2. Separately, peel the oranges, remove the white part and cut them into thin strips.
3. Caramelize the sugar, add a little water, dilute with a little vinegar, add the lemon juice, the oranges and simmer until the syrup is halved.
4. In another skillet, melt the butter, add the flour and stir until golden. Dilute the mixture in the chicken broth and mix well until the broth thickens.
5. Add to previously prepared orange sauce and cook for another 10 minutes.
6. Before removing from the heat, add the diluted potato starch to the liquor.
7. When the duck is well roasted, place it on a plate, remove the fat from the sauce that formed in the pan and dilute with white wine.

8. Pass through the sieve, add to the orange sauce, heat and place in a gravy boat.
9. Decorate the duck with orange peel and lettuce leaves.

Nutritional information

- Calories: 119
- Carbohydrates: 0g
- Fat: 2g

- Protein: 35.5g
- Sugar: 0g
- Cholesterol: 110mg

Quail To Cream

Ingredients	Steps to Cook

Ingredients

- *2 ¼ lb quail*
- *3 tbsp of margarine*
- *2 tbsp of olive oil*
- *1 large grated onion*
- *2 tbsp of wheat flour*
- *1 cup of white wine (dry)*
- *1 can of sour cream*
- *5 ¼ oz. mozzarella cut into cubes*
- *Salt and pepper to taste*
- *Parmesan to brown*

Steps to Cook

1. Cook the quail for 5 minutes in boiling water, remove it and drain it, let it warm up a bit and joke around.
2. Heat the margarine with the oil, add the onion and sauté a little, add the flour, mix with a spoon until golden, add the wine and boil until the alcohol comes out. Put the mozzarella.
3. Then add the cream, salt and pepper. When it boils, turn off the heat on an ovenproof plate and distribute the quail.
4. Add the cream on top and then the Parmesan, bake in the air fryer for 20 minutes until golden at 360°F.

Nutritional information

- Calories: 246
- Carbohydrates: 1g
- Fat: 16g

- Protein: 23g
- Sugar: 0g
- Cholesterol: 210mg

Quail To Paprika Sauce

Servings: 4-6

Preparation time: 15 minutes

Cook time: 50 minutes

Ingredients

- 5 quail tails
- 3 cloves garlic, crushed
- 1 tbsp butter
- 2 cups beef broth
- 12 small peeled potatoes
- 1 medium red bell pepper, chopped
- 1 medium green bell pepper, chopped
- 1 cup of red wine
- Salt to taste
- Hot sauce or black pepper to taste
- 1 cup sliced mushrooms
- 15 tender chives.
- 4 tbsp of olive oil
- 1 tbsp of paprika dissolved in olive oil
- 3 ½ oz. black olives

Steps to Cook

1. In a skillet brown the garlic with butter, the broth, the potatoes, the peppers, the red wine, the salt and the pepper. When the sauce is ready, set aside.
2. Preheat the air fryer at 360°F. Pour the sauce on the quail and put in the air fryer. Cook for 20 minutes.
3. Add the olives, mushrooms, onions, and paprika.
4. Simmer for another 30 minutes.

Nutritional information

- Calories: 246
- Carbohydrates: 1g
- Fat: 16g

- Protein: 23g
- Sugar: 0g
- Cholesterol: 210mg

Chicken Pizza With Coconut

Servings: 2-4

Preparation time: 15 minutes

Cook time: 35-40 minutes

Ingredients	Steps to Cook

Ingredients

- Chicken thigh
- Tomato
- Coconut milk
- Catupiri
- Oregano to taste
- Olives to taste
- Chopped onion

Steps to Cook

1. Cook the drumstick and chicken thigh in a pan with water and salt to taste for 20 min.
2. Remove and put in the pan, now with a drizzle of olive oil, add the chopped onion right away.
3. When fried, add ¼ cup of coconut milk and leave on medium heat for another 5 minutes.
4. Pour over the pizza dough; add tomato slices, catupiri, a little oregano and olives.
5. And bake in the air fryer at 400^{0}F for another 15 to 20 minutes.

Nutritional information

- Calories: 300.1
- Carbohydrates: 27g
- Fat: 7g

- Protein: 32g
- Sugar: 2g
- Cholesterol: 210mg

Quail In The Beer

Servings: 2-4

Preparation time: 5 minutes

Cook time: 15 minutes

Ingredients	Steps to Cook

Ingredients

- 2 ¼ lb of clean quail
- 4 chopped green onions
- ½ bunch of chopped parsley
- 1 tbsp minced garlic
- 1 tbsp of olive oil
- 1 glass of light beer

Steps to Cook

1. Beat the ingredients in a blender.
2. And place the quail in a deep bowl with sauce on top.
3. Leave to marinate one day in the fridge.
4. Bring it to the air fryer for 15 minutes at 400°F, always turning it.

Nutritional information

- Calories: 246
- Carbohydrates: 1g
- Fat: 16g

- Protein: 23g
- Sugar: 0g
- Cholesterol: 210mg

Chapter 4

Air Fryer Meat (Beef, Pork and Lamb) Recipes

Fried Pork Ear

Servings: 2

Preparation time: 15 minutes

Cook time: 40 minutes

Ingredients	Steps to Cook

Ingredients

- *2 very clean pig ears*
- *3 garlic cloves, crushed*
- *1 chopped onion*
- *olive oil*
- *½ lemon*
- *Salt to taste*
- *black pepper to taste*
- *Milk*
- *Bread crumbs*

Steps to Cook

1. Mash the garlic and cut the onion. Mix all.
2. Then add the pork ears, mix a little bit, add the lemon juice, salt, black pepper to taste (to add flavor) and then add water to coat.
3. Let the meat cook in the air fryer for about 25 minutes at 400°F (until the ears are tender) and then remove them from the heat.
4. Then cut the ears into strips and leave them in the freezer for at least 1 hour.
5. Then, pass the pieces in a bowl with a little milk, then on breadcrumbs and then bake in the air Fryer at 400°F for 15 minutes.

Nutritional Information

- Calories: 165
- Carbohydrates: 7g
- Fat: 9g

- Protein: 11g
- Sugar: 0g
- Cholesterol: 253mg

Pork Belly

Servings: 2-4

Preparation time: 20 minute

Cook time: 26-30 minutes

Ingredients	Steps to Cook
• 1 lb thinly sliced pork belly • Salt to taste • Lemon to taste • Black pepper to taste	1. Season the pork with salt, lemon, and black pepper and let sit for at least 20 minutes to get the seasoning. 2. Distribute in the electric fryer and rotate 360°F for 25 to 30 minutes, stirring occasionally until golden brown on all sides or to the desired point.9. 3. Slice the pork loin; then serve and enjoy it!

Nutritional Information

- Calories: 83
- Carbohydrates: 0g
- Fat: 6.1g

- Protein: 6.5g
- Sugar: 0g
- Cholesterol: 24mg

Beef Sausage

Servings: 4

Preparation time: 1 minute

Cook time: 20 minutes

Ingredients	Steps to Cook
• *4 pieces of beef sausage*	1. In each section of the sausage, make two cross "scratches" with the knife, not in depth. 2. Grease the fryer with olive oil and arrange the sausages. 3. Leave for 20 minutes at 360°F, rotating or mixing half the time. 4. They will be juicy, but if you prefer drier, add about 5 minutes on average.

Nutritional Information

- Calories: 304
- Carbohydrates: 0g
- Fat: 28g

- Protein: 12g
- Sugar: 0g
- Cholesterol: 62mg

Tuscan Sausage With Potatoes

Servings: 4

Preparation time: 1 minute

Cook time: 20 minutes

Ingredients	Steps to Cook

- 3 Tuscan sausages of your choice
- 1 large potato
- salt to taste
- oregano to taste
- black pepper to taste
- olive oil to taste

1. Peel, dice and season the potatoes with salt, oregano, the spices you want. Drizzle well with olive oil and mix to make the oil smell all the potatoes.
2. Make 3 vertical cuts on each sausage.
3. Take everything to the air fryer, set it to 400°F.
4. Follow the color and point of your choice of sausages and potatoes, opening, from time to time, to observe. The moment it opens, also shake the bowl to move the sausages and potatoes so that it is browned and roasted on all sides.
5. When it is to your liking, turn it off, remove it and serve.

Nutritional Information

- Calories: 290.3
- Carbohydrates: 43.7g
- Fat: 9.1g

- Protein: 9g
- Sugar: 2.1g
- Cholesterol: 21.5mg

Beef With Yuca Balls

Servings: 6

Preparation time: 5 minutes

Cook time: 20 minutes

Ingredients	Steps to Cook

Ingredients

- 1 lb of ground beef
- ½ lb Yuca, cooked and crushed
- 1 clove garlic
- ½ onion
- 1 tomato
- to taste green smell
- to taste Salt and pepper
- 1 tbsp of olive oil

Steps to Cook

1. Mix the meat, yucca and olive oil.
2. Put salt, pepper and the green smell mixing well.
3. When the mixture is homogeneous, add the onion, garlic and tomato cut into small pieces.
4. Make 12 balls with your hands and put it in the Air fryer for 20 minutes at 400°F.

Nutritional information

- Calories: 120
- Carbohydrates: 25g
- Fat: 2.5g

- Protein: 1g
- Sugar: 8g
- Cholesterol: 20mg

Different Meat Balls

Ingredients

- 1 lb of ground meat (duckling, flanker, soft leg)
- 1 pepperoni sausage
- 1 onion
- 3 garlic cloves
- 1 package of onion cream

Steps to Cook

1. In a processor, add the pepperoni, onion, and garlic and grind everything.
2. Add the ground beef and onion cream (powder) and mix everything well.
3. Make balls with the help of a spoon.
4. Bake in the fryer for 20 minutes at 400°F.
5. They are juicy on the inside and golden on the outside.

Nutritional information

- Calories: 300
- Carbohydrates: 19g
- Fat: 18g

- Protein: 13g
- Sugar: 6g
- Cholesterol: 35mg

Pork Rib (Type Of Outback)

Servings: 4-6

Preparation time: 15 minutes

Cook time: 50-60 minutes

Ingredients

- 2 ¼ lb of pork ribs
- ½ lemon
- 1 cup tomato sauce
- ½ cup dark mustard
- ½ cup of vinegar
- 1 spoon of sugar
- Salt and black pepper to taste.

Steps to Cook

1. Spray the basket of the air fryer.
2. Place the rib piece in half "folded" so that it fits into the pan.
3. On top, place the tomato sauce, mustard, pepper, salt, sugar and vinegar (or if you want, replace these spices with a tube of prepared barbecue sauce).
4. Add two glasses of water, cover the pan, and cook for about 50 minutes at 400⁰F.
5. Remove from the pressure cooker being careful not to disassemble it.
6. Place the piece on a greased baking sheet, drizzle with the sauce, or add more barbecue sauce.
7. Place in the air fryer until you have a crispy crust.

Nutritional information

- Calories: 250
- Carbohydrates: 39.3g
- Fat: 9.4g

- Protein: 4g
- Sugar: 15.6g
- Cholesterol: 0mg

Crocodile In Sauce

Servings: 4-6

Preparation time: 15 minutes

Cook time: 15 minutes

Ingredients	Steps to Cook

Ingredients

- 2 ¼ lb of crocodile fillet (tail, loin, back)
- 5 tsp of vinegar
- 5 tbsp chives
- 5 tbsp onion
- 5 tbsp of parsley
- Oregano to taste
- 1 glass of palm oil
- 1 can of hello garden
- 2 cups of tea
- ½ cup of white wine
- 1 tbsp of wheat flour
- 3 boiled eggs
- 25 g of salt

Steps to Cook

1. Wet the meat with vinegar and salt; let it rest for 30 minutes, turning once.
2. In a skillet, heat the palm oil, turn the onion to brown.
3. Marinate the meat and add on the air fryer at 400°F. Cook for 10 minutes.
4. Remove the meat add the water, wine, grapefruit and oregano to the pan.
5. Add flour and cook until sauce thickens.
6. Put the meat back in the sauce and simmer for 5 minutes.
7. When serving, place the meat on a plate, pour the sauce on top and garnish with boiled egg slices and green smell.

Nutritional information

- Calories: 104
- Carbohydrates: 0g
- Fat: 1g
- Protein: 21g

- Sugar: 0g
- Cholesterol: 0mg

Roasted Steak

Servings: 5

Preparation time: 5 minutes

Cook time: 40 minutes

Ingredients

- 5 fillets
- Garlic and salt to taste
- 5 tablespoons mayonnaise
- 1 package of grated cheese

Steps to Cook

1. Season the fillet and place it on a baking sheet with 2 strands of oil.
2. Put in the air fryer at 400°F for 30 minutes or until golden brown on both sides.
3. When almost everything is roasted, place a tablespoon of mayonnaise on each one and spread it on top.
4. On top of the mayonnaise, spread the grated cheese and return to the air fryer for another 10 minutes, or until the mayonnaise with the cheese is golden brown.

Nutritional information

- Calories: 200
- Carbohydrates: 39.3g
- Fat: 6.26g

- Protein: 24.45g
- Sugar: 0g
- Cholesterol: 53.10mg

Creamy Pork Ribs

Ingredients

- 3 ½ lb pork ribs
- 2 large sliced onions
- 2 tomatoes, chopped
- 2 carrots, chopped
- Olive oil, salt, garlic, lemon

Steps to Cook

1. Season the meat with lemon and salt.
2. Put the onion underneath, the other ingredients.
3. Do not add water.
4. Cover the pan and put it on the air fryer at 400°F, leave it to simmer for 30 minutes.
5. Add salt to taste.
6. Place in a pan and bake just to brown the meat for 15 minutes.
7. Serve with potato straw and the broth that formed in the bottom.

Nutritional information

- Calories: 200
- Carbohydrates: 39.3g
- Fat: 6.26g

- Protein: 24.45g
- Sugar: 0g
- Cholesterol: 53.10mg

Belly Pork Rind

Servings: 5

Preparation time: 5 minutes

Cook time: 40 minutes

Ingredients	Steps to Cook

Ingredients

- 2 ¼ lb of belly (bacon)
- Salt and black pepper to taste.
- 1 cup all-purpose flour
- ½ lemon

Steps to Cook

1. Preheat the air fryer at 600°F for a few minutes.
2. Chop the belly into small pieces, season with salt and pepper and lemon, reserve for about 15 minutes.
3. Place in the container with a lid, place the flour, cover and make sudden movements so that the flour mixes well and forms a very thin layer of lid.
4. Put the bellies in the preheated air fryer for 30 minutes stirring occasionally.

Nutritional information

- Calories: 81
- Carbohydrates: 0g
- Fat: 5g
- Protein: 9.1g

- Sugar: 0g
- Cholesterol: 20mg

Pork Leg

Servings: 5

Preparation time: 5 minutes

Cook time: 40 minutes

Ingredients	**Steps to Cook**

Ingredients

- 2 ¼ lb of Pork Leg
- 6 large onions
- 4 broth
- 1 tbsp coriander
- ½ glass of water

Steps to Cook

1. Chop the onions into slices and divide them into two portions.
2. Line the bottom of the basket of the air fryer with a portion of the onion.
3. Put the ham on the onion.
4. Crumble the broth over the ham.
5. Cover the ham with the other portion of the onion, add the water.
6. Select 600°F and set the timer to 40 minutes.
7. This is the time for the meat to cook and the onion to melt, forming a juicy broth.

Nutritional information

- Calories: 369
- Carbohydrates: 0g
- Fat: 24g

- Protein: 36g
- Sugar: 0g
- Cholesterol: 137mg

Rocambole Of Ground Meat

Servings: 5

Preparation time: 5 minutes

Cook time: 40 minutes

Ingredients

- 1 lb of ground meat
- 1 package of onion soup
- sliced ham
- sliced cheese
- green seasoning
- salt to taste

Steps to Cook

1. Season the ground beef with the onion soup, green seasoning, and salt.
2. Place the seasoned meat on a sheet of laminated paper or parchment paper and roll the dough, 1 cm thick, more or less.
3. Line the meat with the ham and cheese, you can also add green corn, peas and curd.
4. Roll the meat, using the sheet of foil or butter, into a roll.
5. Put in the air fryer at 360°F for 15 minutes.

Nutritional information

- Calories: 308
- Carbohydrates: 0g
- Fat: 20g
- Protein: 31g
- Sugar: 0g
- Cholesterol: 101mg

Picanha Red Sauce

Servings: 5

Preparation time: 10 minute

Cook time: 25 minutes

Ingredients	Steps to Cook

- 3 lbs fillet
- salt with garlic to taste
- 1 cup Worcestershire sauce
- ground black pepper to taste
- 2 tbsp of mustard
- 2 tomatoes
- 1 onion
- 1 orchard
- Salt
- green smell

1. Cut the tenderloin into 2 cm thick fillets.
2. Mix 1 cup of Worcestershire sauce in a bowl, mustard, garlic salt (to taste) and black pepper to taste.
3. Preheat the air fryer to 360°F and place fillets for 25 minutes, turning every 7 minutes.
4. Cut the 2 tomatoes and the onion into small cubes. Put them in a saucepan and mix 3 tablespoons of grapefruit.
5. Season with a green aroma and salt with garlic to taste.
6. Put the red sauce on the steak.
7. Serve with rice accompanied by red wine.

Nutritional information

- Calories: 160
- Carbohydrates: 16g
- Fat: 10g

- Protein: 2g
- Sugar: 2g
- Cholesterol: 300mg

Chapter 5

Air Fryer Seafood Recipes

Tilapia Fillet With Vegetables

Servings: 2

Preparation time: 15 minutes

Cook time: 40 minutes

Ingredients	Steps to Cook
• 2 tilapia fillets • Mushrooms to taste • 1 broccoli • 1 sweet potato • 1 carrot • Seasoning to taste	1. Grill and sauté the mushrooms in the oil. 2. Cut the vegetables, season and place on a baking sheet and close with laminated paper. 3. Baked it in the fryer at 400°F for 25 minutes. 4. Make a beautiful dish and have a good appetite.

Nutritional information

- Calories: 120
- Carbohydrates: 25g
- Fat: 2.5g

- Protein: 1g
- Sugar: 8g
- Cholesterol: 20mg

Shrimps In The Pumpkin

Servings: 4

Preparation time: 10 minutes

Cook time: 45 minutes

Ingredients

- 2 ¼ lb of medium shrimp
- 4 tbsp of olive oil
- 2 cloves of garlic
- 1 onion
- 5 seedless tomatoes
- Salt and black pepper to taste.
- 1 can of cream without serum
- ½ lb of cream cheese
- 1 strawberry
- green aroma to taste
- 3 tbsp of tomato sauce

Steps to Cook

1. Remove the top and seeds from the strawberry.
2. Wash and wrap in foil and bake in the air fryer at 360°F for 45 minutes.
3. In a saucepan, heat the oil and sauté the garlic and onion, add the shrimp and cook for 5 minutes.
4. Add the chopped tomatoes, pepper, salt, and tomato sauce.
5. Turn off the heat and add the cream and green smell.
6. Mix well and finally add the curd.
7. Pass a bit of curd inside the strawberry and pour the shrimp cream.

Nutritional Information

- Calories: 360
- Carbohydrates: 7.49g
- Fat: 21.06g
- Protein: 34.35g
- Sugar: 1.21g
- Cholesterol: 270mg

Shrimp Strogonoff

Servings: 2-4

Preparation time: 5 minutes

Cook time: 10 minutes

Ingredients

- 1 tbsp butter
- 1 medium onion, grated
- 1 lb of medium clean shrimp
- Salt and pepper
- 4 tbsp of brandy
- 3 ½ oz. minced pickled mushrooms
- 3 tbsp of tomato sauce
- 1 tbsp of mustard
- 1 can of cream

Steps to Cook

1. Clean the shrimp. Remove the peels and wash them very well with water and lemon, drain and set aside.
2. Heat the butter and brown the onion. Remove from the heat and mix with the shrimp and stir well, season with salt and pepper.
3. Put in air fryer at 320°F for 5 minutes.
4. Heat the cognac in a shell until it catches fire. And pour it over the shrimp, flaming them.
5. Add the mushroom, tomato sauce, mustard, and put back in the air fryer for about 5 minutes.
6. When serving, add the cream, stir well and heat without boiling.
7. Serve the stroganoff with white rice and straw potatoes.

Nutritional Information

- Calories: 434
- Carbohydrates: 41g
- Fat: 15g
- Protein: 32g

- Sugar: 4g
- Cholesterol: 107mg

Pumpkin Shrimp With Catupiry

Servings: 2-4

Preparation time: 10 minutes

Cook time: 45-55 minutes

Ingredients

- 1 large strawberry
- 2 ¼ lb of medium shrimp
- 1 pot of catupiry
- 1 glass of palm heart
- 1 bottle of coconut milk
- Salt
- Chile
- 1 grated onion
- 2 cloves of garlic
- 2 chopped seedless tomatoes
- 1 tbsp of wheat flour dessert

Steps to Cook

1. Remove the strawberry cap and then all the seeds. After washing, spray salt inside. Wrap the entire strawberry with aluminum foil. Bake in the air fryer for 45 minutes at 400⁰F. Reserve, but before taking with a spoon some strawberry slices to add to the stew.

Stew:

2. Fry the onion and garlic in the oil. Then the tomatoes and the strawberry slices she took out, allowing it to steep for 10 minutes. Add the chopped palm kernel and then the shrimp, which should not cook for more than 10 minutes, because if you cook them longer, it will be totally hard. Add the coconut milk and 1 tablespoon of flour dissolved in water, so that it is slightly thick. And add half the catupiry box to the prepared stir fry and turn off, incorporating it well into the stir fry and salt.

Mounting:

3. With the strawberry still hot, take catupiry balls with your hands and place them on the bottom and sides (the catupiry must be very cold to stick more easily).
4. Pour the hot stir fry into the strawberry and serve.
5. Put parsley to taste or coriander, (it depends on the flavor of each one).

Nutritional Information

- Calories: 241
- Carbohydrates: 12g
- Fat: 10g

- Protein: 25g
- Sugar: 2g
- Cholesterol: 128mg

Fricassee Of Jamila Shrimps

Servings: 2-4

Preparation time: 10 minutes

Cook time: 30-40 minutes

Ingredients

- 2 ¼ lb clean shrimp
- Salt and pepper to taste
- olive oil
- 1 large grated onion
- Chopped garlic
- 3 tomatoes, chopped
- parsley and chives
- 1 can of vegetable
- 1 can of sour cream
- 1 can of corn
- grated cheese to taste
- 2 glasses of curd
- ½ lb mozzarella cheese
- potato sticks

Steps to Cook

1. Wash the shrimp and season with salt, pepper and lemon. Allow time for the seasoning to soak in.
2. Sauté the grated onion, minced garlic, tomatoes, parsley, and chives in olive oil.
3. Add the shrimp and the garden. Mix and cook for about 5 minutes or until shrimp are pink. Reserve.
4. Whisk the corn with sour cream and grated cheese in a blender.
5. Spread the creamy curd, shrimp sauce on a plate, and then pour the whipped cream on top.
6. Cover with mozzarella.
7. Take to the air fryer to brown at 360°F for 30 minutes.
8. Serve hot with white rice and straw potatoes.

Nutritional Information

- Calories: 241
- Carbohydrates: 12g
- Fat: 10g

- Protein: 25g
- Sugar: 2g
- Cholesterol: 128mg

Fried Beach Shrimps

Servings: 2-4

Preparation time: 5 minutes

Cook time: 15 minutes

Ingredients

- 2 ¼ lb of clean and washed gray shrimp
- ½ lemon
- Salt
- 1 ½ tbsp of flour
- 2 garlic cloves, squeezed

Steps to Cook

1. Season shrimp (must be very dry) with salt, lemon, and squeezed garlic.
2. Sprinkle the flour and mix well.
3. Take to the air fryer at 360°F for 15 minutes and fry until golden. Serve well with a leafy salad and white rice.

Nutritional Information

- Calories: 38
- Carbohydrates: 2.7g
- Fat: 2.3g

- Protein: 1.5g
- Sugar: 0.1g
- Cholesterol: 11mg

Fried Shrimp Without Flour

Servings: 2

Preparation time: 5 minutes

Cook time: 10 minutes

Ingredients

- ½ lb small shrimp without shell
- 2 tbsp of olive oil
- 2 garlic cloves, crushed
- ½ large onion, chopped
- 2 tbsp soy sauce
- salt to taste
- black pepper to taste
- parsley to taste
- grated fresh parmesan cheese to taste

Steps to Cook

1. In a pan add a little olive oil, crushed garlic, and onion, marinate for 5 minutes.
2. Add the shrimp, salt, black pepper, and soy sauce.
3. Take to the air fryer at 360^0 F. Let it cook for 10 minutes.
4. Let shrimp fry until golden brown, then sprinkle with Parmesan cheese.

Nutritional Information

- Calories: 38
- Carbohydrates: 2.7g
- Fat: 2.3g
- Protein: 1.5g
- Sugar: 0.1g
- Cholesterol: 11mg

Shrimps With Garlic And Oil

Servings: 4-6

Preparation time: 5 minutes

Cook time: 2 minutes

Ingredients	Steps to Cook

Ingredients

- 3 lbs medium shrimp
- 10 cloves of garlic
- Salt to taste
- Olive oil to taste

Steps to Cook

1. Wash the shrimp in the shell, removing the head.
2. Peel the garlic cloves, cutting them in half.
3. Fry the garlic well in the oil (well done).
4. Place the shrimp in a pan, sprinkling with a little salt.
5. Take to the air fryer at 320°F for 5 minutes.
6. Place the oil with the garlic in a bowl, pouring it over it.
7. Serve with snowy beer.

Nutritional Information

- Calories: 38
- Carbohydrates: 2.7g
- Fat: 2.3g

- Protein: 1.5g
- Sugar: 0.1g
- Cholesterol: 11mg

Breaded Pawns

Ingredients

- 12 large prawns
- 3 tablespoons butter, melted
- 6 eggs
- Wheat flour to the point
- Salt to taste
- 1 tbsp of virgin olive oil

Steps to Cook

1. Cook the prawns in the air fryer at 320^0F, being careful not to cook them for about 10 minutes. Remove.
2. Then peel the prawns and place them in the melted butter, resting.
3. Separate the whites from the yolks of the 6 eggs, beating the whites in the snow, then add the wheat flour until it sighs, season with salt and the spoon of oil.
4. Then place the prawns in this pasta and with a spoon, remove each shrimp, accompanied by a little pasta.
5. Put back in the air fryer for 5 minutes.

Nutritional Information

- Calories: 38
- Carbohydrates: 2.7g
- Fat: 2.3g

- Protein: 1.5g
- Sugar: 0.1g
- Cholesterol: 11mg

Shrimp Pancakes

Servings: 1-2

Preparation time: 5 mins

Cook time: 15 minutes

Ingredients	Steps to Cook

- 1 cup all-purpose flour
- 1 glass of water
- 3 beaten eggs
- 1 tablet chicken broth

1. Boil the water and dissolve the chicken broth, let it cool and place the beaten eggs and the wheat flour, stir well until everything dissolves and a smooth mass fry the tablespoons and a little oil in the tefal pan and keep the part in a baking dish.
2. Make the prawns to taste and leave with a little sauce.
3. Top with pancakes and shrimp sauce and sprinkle with grated cheese. Do this until the last layers of grated cheese are ready.
4. Bake in the air fryer at 360°F for 15 minutes. Serve with white rice and salad.

Nutritional Information

- Calories: 38
- Carbohydrates: 2.7g
- Fat: 2.3g

- Protein: 1.5g
- Sugar: 0.1g
- Cholesterol: 11mg

Shrimps With Palmito

Ingredients

Steps to Cook

White Sauce:

- 1 cup grated Parmesan cheese
- 1 tbsp butter
- 4 ½ lb shrimp
- ½ cup of olive oil
- Very minced garlic
- Striped onion
- 1 can of sour cream
- 1 can of sliced palm heart
- Grated Parmesan cheese for sprinkling

For White Sauce:

- 1 onion, sliced
- Margarine and butter
- 2 cups milk
- 2 tbsp of flour
- Salt to taste

Preparation of the white sauce:

1. Lightly brown the onion with the margarine and butter.
2. Put the milk and wheat flour in a blender.
3. Add the stewed onion.
4. Beat everything very well.
5. Bring this mixture to the fire and cook until it forms a thick cream. Remove the white sauce from the heat and add the Parmesan cheese and butter. Reserve.
6. Sauté the shrimp in olive oil, with garlic and onion.
7. Add the sautéed shrimp to the white sauce and gradually add the palm kernel and cream, mixing everything very well.
8. Arrange in a greased refractory shape, sprinkle plenty of Parmesan cheese on top.
9. Bake in the air fryer at 360°F for 15-20 minutes.

Nutritional Information

- Calories: 362
- Carbohydrates: 47g
- Fat: 9g

- Protein: 22g
- Sugar: 5g
- Cholesterol: 157mg

Gratinated Pawns With Cheese

Servings: 4

Preparation time: 15 mins

Cook time: 20 minutes

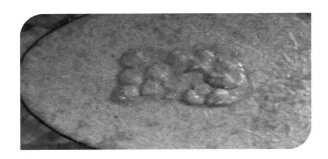

Ingredients	Steps to Cook

Ingredients

- 2 ¼ lbs clean, chopped prawns
- 1 tbsp of fondor
- 1 tbsp of oil
- 1 tbsp butter
- 1 grated onion
- 5 tomatoes, beaten in a blender
- 1 tablet of crumbled shrimp broth
- 1 glass of light cream cheese
- 1 tbsp of breadcrumbs
- 1 tbsp Parmesan cheese

Steps to Cook

1. Season the prawns with the fondor and reserve for 1 hour.
2. Fry them in the oil and butter mixture.
3. Put them in a refractory container and set aside.
4. Brown the onion in the shrimp fat, add the tomatoes, the shrimp broth tablet and a cup of boiling water.
5. Bring to a boil in a covered skillet until just a little.
6. Add curd and stir until melted.
7. Pour over the prawns, sprinkle the breadcrumbs mixed with the grated Parmesan cheese and place them in the air fryer at 400°F for 20 minutes or until brown.

Nutritional Information

- Calories: 52
- Carbohydrates: 0g
- Fat: 0g

- Protein: 11g
- Sugar: 0.1g
- Cholesterol: 0mg

Crab

Servings: 20

Preparation time: 5 mins

Cook time: 5 minutes

Ingredients	Steps to Cook

- 1 pound of crab meat
- 20 crab cones
- 2 onions
- 2 tomatoes
- 3 garlic cloves
- 1 bell pepper
- ½ glass of white vinegar
- 1 head of black pepper
- 1 head of cumin
- 1 small salt
- Olive oil to taste

1. Place the chopped onion until golden. Then add the remaining spices (pepper, cumin, minced garlic) with ½ glass of vinegar.
2. Put the green smell, the crushed tomatoes, the pepper cut into pieces. When the seasoning is well cooked, add the olive oil to taste (at least 3 tablespoons).
3. Then add the crab meat and boil for 5 minutes.
4. Fill the crab cones, drizzle with grated Parmesan cheese and bake in the air fryer at 320° for 5 minutes to melt the cheese.

Nutritional Information

- Calories: 119
- Carbohydrates: 0g
- Fat: 2.08g

- Protein: 23.64g
- Sugar: 0g
- Cholesterol: 117mg

Crab Balls

Servings: 2-4

Preparation time: 5 mins

Cook time: 25 minutes

Ingredients

- 1 lb of crab
- Salt to taste
- Olive oil
- 2 cloves garlic, minced
- 1 chopped onion
- 3 tbsp of wheat flour
- 1 tbsp of parsley
- 1 fish seasoning
- 2 lemons
- 1 cup milk

Tarnish:

- 1 beaten egg
- Bread crumbs
- Oil for frying

Steps to Cook

1. Wash the crab in the juice of 1 lemon.
2. Season with the juice of the other lemon, along with the salt and the prepared fish seasoning.
3. In a frying pan, sauté the onion and garlic with the sweet oil.
4. Mix the crab meat with the stir fry.
5. Let cook in this mixture for another 5 minutes.
6. Add the parsley.
7. Dissolve the flour in the milk and add it to the crab.
8. Stir constantly, until this mixture begins to come out of the pan.
9. Let cool, shape the meatballs, go through the beaten egg and breadcrumbs.
10. Fry in the air fryer at 400°F for 25 minutes.

Nutritional Information

- Calories: 119
- Carbohydrates: 0g
- Fat: 2.08g

- Protein: 23.64g
- Sugar: 0g
- Cholesterol: 117mg

Crab Empanada

Servings: 4-8

Preparation time: 15 mins

Cook time: 25 minutes

Ingredients

- 1 small onion
- 1 tomato
- 1 small green pepper
- 1 lb of crab meat
- Seasoning ready for fish
- 1 tbsp of oil
- Pastry dough

Steps to Cook

1. Sauté the chopped onion, tomato, and pepper in oil.
2. Add the crab meat and seasoning.
3. Cook until very dry, without stirring, so that it does not stick to the bottom of the pan.
4. Fill the cakes with the prepared crab meat.
5. Fry in the air fryer at 400°F for 25 minutes.

Nutritional Information

- Calories: 119
- Carbohydrates: 0g
- Fat: 2.08g

- Protein: 23.64g
- Sugar: 0g
- Cholesterol: 117mg

Crab Meat On Cabbage

Servings: 2-4

Preparation time: 20 mins

Cook time: 5 minutes

Ingredients	Steps to Cook

Ingredients

- 1 pound shredded crab meat
- 1 pound cooked and minced dogfish
- 2 cups of cooked rice
- 1 small green cabbage
- Parsley and coriander
- Chile
- 2 tbsp of palm oil
- 2 tbsp cornstarch
- Tomato sauce
- Bread crumbs
- Garlic

Steps to Cook

1. Season and cook the dogfish in a little water.
2. When it is smooth, crush and enjoy the broth that has formed. Add the crab meat, which should already be thawed. Add the tomato sauce, palm oil, cooked rice, and pepper.
3. Dissolve the starch in warm water and pour it into the mixture. Sharpen the mixture, taste the salt and sprinkle the chopped parsley and coriander on top.
4. Cook 6 whole cabbage leaves separately in salted water until al dente.
5. In a baking dish, place the open leaves and the cream of crab with fish inside.
6. Sprinkle with breadcrumbs and bake in the air fryer at 320°F for 5 minutes to brown..

Nutritional Information

- Calories: 318
- Carbohydrates: 0g
- Fat: 18g

- Protein: 33g
- Sugar: 0g
- Cholesterol: 300mg

Gratinated Cod

Servings: 4-8

Preparation time: 20 minutes

Cook time: 30 minutes

Ingredients

- 2 ¼ lb cod
- 1 red bell pepper
- 1 green bell pepper
- 1 onion
- 3 ripe tomatoes
- 2 cloves of garlic
- 1 cup black olives
- Oregano to taste

Mashed potatoes:

- 2 ¼ lb boiled and squeezed potatoes
- 2 butter spoons
- ½ cup milk
- Salt to taste

Cream:

- 1 cup catupiry cheese

Steps to Cook

1. Prepare the mashed potatoes first, squeeze the potatoes and add the butter and milk with the potatoes still very hot, just stir well and add salt to taste.
2. Place this puree on a high ovenproof plate. And organize like a pie crust. Make the stir fry with the cod that has already been desalted (soak the day before and change the water at least 5 times).
3. Bring to a boil briefly, 5 minutes in boiling water.
4. Then crush the cod into chips.
5. Put enough oil in a frying pan and fry the onion and garlic. Then add the chopped bell peppers and tomatoes and cook for about 10 minutes.
6. Then add the olives and cod and let it cook for another 10 minutes.
7. Without letting it dry out too much. And add oregano to taste. Usually, you don't need to add salt, as the cod already contains enough.
8. But, if you need to put a little.

- 1 can of cream
- ½ cup coconut milk

9. Play this braised cod over mashed potatoes.

Cream:

10. Beat all the ingredients in a blender and pour over the cod.
11. Take to the previously heated air fryer at 600°F for 30 minutes or until it brown.
12. Serve with white rice and a leafy salad.

Nutritional Information

- Calories: 90
- Carbohydrates: 0g
- Fat: 1g

- Protein: 20g
- Sugar: 0g
- Cholesterol: 0mg

Gratinated Cod With Vegetables

Servings: 2-4

Preparation time: 20 mins

Cook time: 20 minutes

Ingredients

- 2 ¼ lb cod
- 1 pound of potato
- 1 pound carrot
- 2 large onions
- 2 red tomatoes
- 1 bell pepper
- 1 tbsp of tomato paste
- Coconut milk
- Garlic, salt, coriander and olive oil to taste.
- Olives

Sauce:

- 2 cups milk
- 1 ½ tablespoons all-purpose flour
- 1 tbsp butter
- 1 egg
- ½ cup sour cream
- Nutmeg, black pepper and salt

Steps to Cook

1. Soak the cod for 24 hours, always changing the water. Blanch at a rapid boil, removing skin and pimples. Strain the water where the cod was cooked and reserve.
2. Season the cod in French fries, with garlic, salt and coriander. Besides, put a saucepan on the fire with olive oil and sliced onions. Add the skinless and seedless tomatoes, pepper, and chopped olives. Add the cod, tomato extract, coconut milk, and a little of the water where the cod was cooked. Let everything cook a lot. It gets a lot of sauce. Test the salt. Cook sliced potatoes and carrots.
3. Whisk together milk, wheat, and melted butter in a blender. Bring to the fire and stir until the mixture thickens. Finally, add the cream, nutmeg, black pepper, salt and beaten egg.
4. Grease a plate with olive oil after rubbing a clove of garlic inside. Arrange the cod, potato, and carrot in alternate layers. Cover everything with sauce and bake in the air fryer at 380°F for 20 minutes.

Nutritional Information

- Calories: 152.8
- Carbohydrates: 3.3g
- Fat: 3.3g

- Protein: 26.3g
- Sugar: 1.4g
- Cholesterol: 62.4mg

Salmon Fillet

Servings: 2-4

Preparation time: 20 mins

Cook time: 5 minutes

Ingredients	Steps to Cook

Ingredients

- 1 lb salmon fillet
- Sliced pitted olives
- Oregano
- 3 tbsp soy sauce
- Salt to taste
- Olive oil to taste
- Lemon
- Aluminum foil
- ½ sliced onion

Steps to Cook

1. Wash the salmon with lemon juice.
2. Heat the oil and add the sliced onion, leaving on the fire until it becomes transparent. Reservation.
3. Cover a baking sheet with aluminum foil so that leftovers can cover all the fish.
4. In the foil on the baking sheet, place the fish already seasoned with salt, drizzle with olive oil and soy sauce.
5. Garnish with sliced olives and a little oregano. Pour the onion on top. Wrap with aluminum foil so that the liquid does not spill when it starts to heat up.
6. Bake in the air fryer at 400°F for about 30 minutes.
7. Serve with vegetables and green salad.

Nutritional Information

- Calories: 468
- Carbohydrates: 0g
- Fat: 28g

- Protein: 50g
- Sugar: 0g
- Cholesterol: 143mg

Hake Fillet With Potatoes

Servings: 2-4

Preparation time: 20 mins

Cook time: 5 minutes

Ingredients

- 8 fillets of hake
- 4 raw potatoes
- 1 bell pepper
- 2 tomatoes
- 1 onion
- Good quality tomato sauce.
- Oregano
- Oil for greasing

Steps to Cook

1. Season the fillets as desired and reserve for 10 minutes. Grease an ovenproof dish with olive oil and make a layer of potato, then place the fillets on the potato. Add onion, tomato, bell pepper, oregano to taste, drizzle with tomato sauce (½ can).
2. Cover with the rest of the potatoes. Cover with foil and bake until potatoes are tender. Wash the salmon with lemon juice. Heat the oil and add the sliced onion, leaving on the fire until it becomes transparent. Reservation.
3. Cover a baking sheet with aluminum foil so that leftovers can cover all the fish.
4. In the foil on the baking sheet, place the fish already seasoned with salt, drizzle with olive oil and soy sauce.
5. Garnish with sliced olives and a little oregano. Pour the onion on top. Wrap with aluminum foil so that the liquid does not spill when it starts to heat up.
6. Bake in the air fryer at 400⁰F for about 30 minutes.
7. Serve with vegetables and green salad.

Nutritional Information

- Calories: 468
- Carbohydrates: 0g
- Fat: 28g

- Protein: 50g
- Sugar: 0g
- Cholesterol: 143mg

Cod Pie With Palmit

Servings: 4-6

Preparation time: 5 minutes

Cook time: 40 minutes

Ingredients

- 2 ¼ lb cod
- 4 ½ lb of natural heart previously grated and cooked
- 12 eggs
- 1 ½ cup olive oil
- 7 oz. of olives
- Tomato
- Chopped garlic, paprika and sliced onion
- Green seasoning to taste
- Salt to taste

Steps to Cook

1. Cook the cod in a frying pan and, after cooking, destroy it.
2. Drain well heart of palm. Reservation.
3. Sauté the cod and palm hearts in olive oil for 20 minutes along with tomatoes, garlic, paprika, onion, green seasoning and part of the pitted olives.
4. Pour 6 eggs and mix for 5 minutes.
5. Grease the trays with olive oil and pour the mixture.
6. Beat the remaining eggs and pour evenly over the top.
7. Garnish with onion and olives.
8. Bake in the air fryer at 380°F for 40 minutes.

Nutritional Information

- Calories: 91
- Carbohydrates: 0g
- Fat: 1.9g
- Protein: 18.5g
- Sugar: 0g
- Cholesterol: 50mg

Simple And Yummy Cod

Servings: 4-6

Preparation time: 5 minutes

Cook time: 20 minutes

Ingredients

- 2 ¼ lb of desalted cod
- 1 ½ lb of boiled and squeezed potatoes
- 1 can of sour cream
- 2 large onions, sliced
- 1 pot of pitted olive
- ½ cup of olive oil
- Butter for greasing

Steps to Cook

1. Sauté the onions in the oil until they wilt.
2. Put the cod to sauté for another 5 minutes.
3. Add the potato and sour cream and stir for another 5 minutes.
4. Turn off the heat and add a little more oil.
5. In a refractory greased with the butter, place the cod and pass the margarine over it again so that it is golden.
6. Bake in the air fryer at 400°F for about 20 minutes or until golden brown.
7. Serve with rice, it is fast and delicious.

Nutritional Information

- Calories: 91
- Carbohydrates: 0g
- Fat: 1.9g

- Protein: 18.5g
- Sugar: 2g
- Cholesterol: 50mg

Roasted Tilapia Fillet

Servings: 4-6

Preparation time: 5 minutes

Cook time: 20 minutes

Ingredients

- 2 ¼ lb tilapia fillet
- ½ lemon juice
- 4 sliced tomatoes
- 4 sliced onions
- ½ cup chopped black olives
- 1 pound of boiled potatoes
- 1 tbsp butter
- ½ cup sour cream tea
- ½ lb grated mozzarella
- Olive oil
- Salt

Steps to Cook

1. Season the fillets with lemon and salt.
2. On an ovenproof plate, place a layer of onion and tomato. Place the fillets on top of the layers.
3. Top with another layer of onion and tomato and then the olives and drizzle with olive oil.
4. Bake in the air fryer at 360°F for 15 minutes. Reserve.
5. In another bowl, squeeze the potatoes.
6. In a saucepan melt the butter. Place the potatoes and the cream.
7. Then place this puree on top of the fillets, place the mozzarella.
8. Bake in the air fryer at 360°F for another 5 minutes and serve.

Nutritional Information

- Calories: 182.7
- Carbohydrates: 11.2g
- Fat: 5.1g
- Protein: 23.5g
- Sugar: 2.2g
- Cholesterol: 55mg

Cod 7-Mares

Servings: 4-6

Preparation time: 5 minutes

Cook time: 20 minutes

Ingredients

- 1 lb cod in French fries
- 4 large potatoes, peeled and diced
- 1 can of cream without serum
- 1 cup of coffee with coconut milk
- 3 ½ oz. of mozzarella cheese in strips
- 3 ½ oz. cheese in pieces
- 100 g3 ½ oz. grated Parmesan cheese
- Aromatic herbs and salt to taste.
- 1 tbsp of curry
- Salt to taste

Steps to Cook

1. Cook the peeled and diced potatoes and set aside.
2. Remove the salt from the cod (leave it in the water overnight and change the water at least 3 times to remove the salt).
3. Place in a glass container and cook the potatoes in the microwave for 5 minutes and reserve.

Sauce:

4. In a bowl, mix the cream, coconut milk, curry, mozzarella cheese, and herbs.

Mounting:

5. On a plate, place a layer of boiled potatoes on top, place the cod fries, and pour the sauce on top.
6. Season with salt to taste.
7. Sprinkle with Parmesan cheese and cook for 7 minutes in the air fryer at 360°F.
8. When done, toss the chives over the top and serve immediately.

Nutritional Information

- Calories: 91
- Carbohydrates: 0g
- Fat: 1.9g

- Protein: 18.5g
- Sugar: 2g
- Cholesterol: 50mg

Roasted Hake With Coconut Milk

Servings: 4-6

Preparation time: 5 minutes

Cook time: 20 minutes

Ingredients

- 2 ¼ lb hake fillet
- ½ lb sliced mozzarella
- 1 can of sour cream
- 1 bottle of coconut milk
- 1 onion
- 1 tomato
- Salt and black pepper to taste.
- Lemon juice

Steps to Cook

1. Season the fillets with salt, pepper and lemon.
2. Let stand for 10 minutes.
3. Arrange the fillets and place the mozzarella slices in the middle of each and roll it up like a fillet.
4. After all the fillets rolled up.
5. Get a tray.
6. Place the tomato and onion slices (sliced) on top.
7. Top with the sour cream and coconut milk mixture.
8. Bake in the air fryer at 400⁰ covered with aluminum foil for 20 minutes.
9. Then remove it to finish baking.

Nutritional Information

- Calories: 347.4
- Carbohydrates: 5.3g
- Fat: 22.1g
- Protein: 32g
- Sugar: 0.1g
- Cholesterol: 86.4mg

Catfish

Servings: 4-6

Preparation time: 15 mins

Cook time: 1h

Ingredients	Steps to Cook

- 3 pounds sliced dogfish
- 1 pound boiled and sliced potatoes
- 1 package of onion cream
- 3 tomatoes cut into slices
- 3 bell peppers cut into slices
- 3 onions cut into slices
- Olive oil
- 2 garlic cloves, crushed
- Salt to taste
- 1 lemon juice

1. Season the fish slices with garlic, salt and lemon and reserve.
2. Place the potatoes on a baking sheet, forming a kind of bed to receive the slices, drizzle with plenty of oil.
3. Spread half of the onion cream on the potatoes.
4. Lay the slices on top.
5. Place the tomato, bell pepper and onion on top, spreading well, covering the slices. Drizzle again with olive oil and finally pour the rest of the onion cream on top.
6. Heat the air fryer at 360°F for about 15 minutes and then bake for 1 hour.

Nutritional Information

- Calories: 26.9
- Carbohydrates: 0g
- Fat: 0.8g

- Protein: 4.6g
- Sugar: 0g
- Cholesterol: 16.4mg

Squid To The Milanese

Servings: 4-6

Preparation time: 5 mins

Cook time: 10 minutes

Ingredients

- 2 ¼ lb clean squid
- Salt, pepper and oregano to taste.
- 3 beaten eggs
- 1 cup of wheat flour
- 1 cup breadcrumbs
- 1 cup chopped green chives

Steps to Cook

1. Season the squid, after cleaning and cutting into rings, with salt, pepper and oregano.
2. Pass the squid over the beaten eggs, then the wheat flour mixed with the breadcrumbs.
3. Fry in the air fryer at 400°F for 10 minutes.
4. Sprinkled with green onions.

Nutritional Information

- Calories: 26
- Carbohydrates: 0.9g
- Fat: 0.4g

- Protein: 4.4g
- Sugar: 0g
- Cholesterol: 66m

Portugal Codfish With Cream

Servings: 4-6

Preparation time: 5 minutes

Cook time: 10 minutes

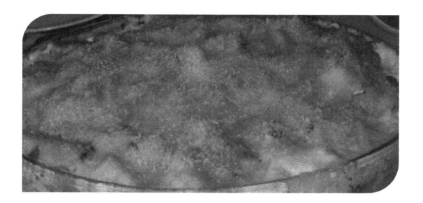

Ingredients

- 2 ¼ lbs of cod
- 1 chopped onion
- 2 cloves of garlic
- 4 medium potatoes
- 1 leek stalk (Portugal leek)
- 2 cups of cream
- 1 egg
- Parmesan
- Coriander (optional)
- Olive oil
- Black olives

Steps to Cook

1. Soak the cod in water until the salt is to your liking, approximately 24 hours.
2. In a frying pan put the oil, brown the garlic, the onion, the leek, then place the cod and let it brown.
3. Take the diced potatoes and fry separately.
4. Then put the potatoes together with the golden cod. Then put the coriander to your liking along with the cream or sour cream. Mix all.
5. Beat 1 whole egg and brush the cod, spread a little Parmesan on top and decorate with black olives.
6. Place it in the air fryer for 30 minutes at 360°F, or until it turns into a crispy cone.
7. Serve with a beautiful lettuce salad, nothing more.

Nutritional Information

- Calories: 91
- Carbohydrates: 0g
- Fat: 1.9g

- Protein: 18.5g
- Sugar: 2g
- Cholesterol: 50mg

Roasted Salmon With Provencal

Servings: 2-4

Preparation time: 5 mins

Cook time: 15 minutes

Ingredients

- 4 slices of fresh salmon
- basil
- thyme
- Rosemary
- oregano
- salt and pepper
- olive oil
- 4 tablespoons of butter
- ½ lemon juice

Steps to Cook

1. Place the salmon slices on a hot plate and sprinkle with the 4 herbs.
2. Then add salt, pepper to taste and a few drops of olive oil.
3. Bake in the air fryer for 15 minutes at 400^0F (check every 5 minutes).
4. Serve with potatoes, a fresh salad, and herb butter.

Butter with herbs:

5. Whip the butter until it is creamy.
6. Add the same herbs described above and the lemon juice.

Nutritional Information

- Calories: 468
- Carbohydrates: 0g
- Fat: 28g

- Protein: 50g
- Sugar: 0g
- Cholesterol: 143mg

Breaded Fish With Tartar Sauce

Servings: 2-4

Preparation time: 5 mins

Cook time: 25 minutes

Ingredients	Steps to Cook

Ingredients

- 1 lb of hake fillet
- 4 garlic cloves, crushed
- Juice of 2 lemons
- Salt and black pepper
- Beaten eggs
- Wheat flour
- Vegetable oil for frying

Tartar sauce:

- ½ lb chopped pickles
- 3 oz. green olives
- 3 tbsp chopped onion
- 1 garlic clove, crushed
- Parsley and chives
- 5 tbsp soy sauce
- ½ can of cream
- 3 tbsp of dijon mustard
- 1 tbsp of tomato sauce
- 4 tbsp mayonnaise

Steps to Cook

1. Season the fillets with salt, pepper, garlic, and lemon juice, let them taste for at least 30 minutes.
2. Pass the wheat, egg and wheat again.
3. Fry them in the air fryer at 400°F for 25 minutes.

Sauce:

4. Mix all the ingredients in a bowl.
5. Serve with the fillets.

Nutritional Information

- Calories: 347.4
- Carbohydrates: 5.3g
- Fat: 22.1g

- Protein: 32g
- Sugar: 0.1g
- Cholesterol: 86.4mg

Milanese Fish Fillet

Servings: 2-3

Preparation time: 5 mins

Cook time: 25 minutes

Ingredients

- 1 lb of fish fillet of your choice
- Salt
- 2 garlic cloves, crushed
- 3 eggs
- Wheat flour
- Oil for frying

Steps to Cook

1. Wash and season the fish fillets with garlic and salt.
2. If you want, you can add the juice of a lemon.
3. Beat the egg whites until stiff and add the egg yolks.
4. Pass the fish fillets, one at a time, in the wheat flour and then pass them over the beaten eggs in the snow.
5. Fry in the air fryer at 400°F for 25 minutes or until they are golden brown.

Nutritional Information

- Calories: 26.9
- Carbohydrates: 0g
- Fat: 0.8g

- Protein: 4.6g
- Sugar: 0g
- Cholesterol: 16.4mg

Sole With White Wine

Servings: 4-6

Preparation time: 5 mins

Cook time: 20-25 minutes

Ingredients

- 3 lbs of sole fillets
- 5 ¼ oz. of butter
- 1 glass of white wine
- Wheat flour
- Salt
- black pepper
- thyme

Steps to Cook

1. Season the fillet and pass the wheat flour.
2. Put in the air fryer at 400°F for 20 minutes or until brown. Reserve this fish in a preheated clay pan.
3. Toast a tablespoon of flour in the butter.
4. Add the wine, with salt, pepper and thyme to taste. Let cook for another 3 minutes, stirring continuously. Pour over the sole and serve.

Nutritional Information

- Calories: 347.4
- Carbohydrates: 5.3g
- Fat: 22.1g

- Protein: 32g
- Sugar: 0.1g
- Cholesterol: 86.4mg

Golden Fish With Shrimps

Servings: 2-3

Preparation time: 5 mins

Cook time: 35 minutes

Ingredients	Steps to Cook

Ingredients

- *1 large golden fish*
- *1 lb of shrimp*
- *onion*
- *tomato*
- *Pepper*
- *lemon*
- *olive oil*
- *Butter*
- *green smell*
- *parsley*

Steps to Cook

1. Clean the whole golden and season with lemon, black pepper to taste and salt, the same with the prawns.
2. Leave in seasoning for 1 hour.
3. Line a plate with aluminum foil and grease with butter, place the fish on this plate, add the shrimp to the belly of the fish and tie with a line.
4. Place the onion rings, tomatoes and peppers and the green smell with the parsley on top of the gold, and use it with plenty of oil.
5. Cover the plate with aluminum foil and bake in the air fryer for 35 minutes at 400°F.
6. Serve with white rice.

Nutritional Information

- Calories: 26
- Carbohydrates: 0.9g
- Fat: 0.4g

- Protein: 4.4g
- Sugar: 0g
- Cholesterol: 66mg

Stroganoff Cod

Ingredients

- 1 lb of cod
- 3 tbsp olive oil
- 2 garlic cloves, minced
- 2 ¼ lb of chopped onion
- 4 ½ lb of skinless tomatoes
- Salt to taste
- ½ cup of brandy
- Oregano, rosemary and black pepper to taste.
- 1 package of chopped green aroma
- 1 cup grated cheese
- 2 ¼ lb of fresh mushrooms cut into chips
- 1 can of sour cream1 large golden fish

Steps to Cook

1. The day before, soak the cod in water, boil and crumble all the meat. Reserve.
2. Sauté the onion and garlic in olive oil. Add the chopped tomatoes and simmer until separated. Remove.
3. Mix with the cod, add the brandy, season with salt, oregano, rosemary and black pepper. Add the green smell and the mushrooms.
4. Put in the air fryer at 320⁰ for 10 minutes. Remove from the air fryer; add grated cheese and sour cream.
5. Mix well and serve with white rice.

- *1 lb of shrimp*
- *onion*
- *tomato*
- *Pepper*
- *lemon*
- *olive oil*
- *Butter*
- *green smell*
- *parsley*

Nutritional Information

- Calories: 91
- Carbohydrates: 0g
- Fat: 1.9g
- Protein: 18.5g
- Sugar: 2g
- Cholesterol: 50mg

Cod Balls

Servings: 2-3

Preparation time: 5 mins

Cook time: 30 minutes

Ingredients

- ½ lb salted and grated cod
- 3 cups boiled and squeezed potatoes
- 1 tbsp of wheat flour
- Salt and black pepper to taste.
- 3 eggs
- 2 tbsp chopped green aroma

Steps to Cook

1. In a bowl, mix all the ingredients well.
2. Form the balls with your hands.
3. Fry in the air fryer at 400°F for 30 minutes or until golden brown.

Nutritional Information

- Calories: 80
- Carbohydrates: 0g
- Fat: 1g

- Protein: 7g
- Sugar: 1g
- Cholesterol: 275mg

Chapter 6

Air Fryer Vegetables Recipes

Aubergine Salad

Servings: 4

Preparation time: 5 minutes

Cook time: 45 minutes

Ingredients	Steps to Cook

Ingredients

- 3 aubergines
- 1 green pepper
- 1 red pepper
- 1 yellow bell pepper
- 1 large onion
- ½ cup of olive oil
- ¼ cup vinegar
- 3 tbsp black olives
- 2 cloves garlic, minced
- 1 bay leaf
- 2 tbsp of oregano
- 2 tbsp chopped parsley
- salt to taste

Steps to Cook

1. Remove some of the skin from the eggplant, cut it into thin slices lengthwise, and then cut it into strips.
2. Soak the sliced eggplants in salted water for half an hour, then rinse with water to remove the salt and squeeze.
3. Cut the onion and bell pepper into strips, place them on a baking sheet, add the eggplant, garlic, bay leaf, parsley, oregano, olives, and salt.
4. Sprinkle with half the vinegar and place in the preheated air fryer at 320°F for 45 minutes.
5. Remove from the oven and drizzle with olive oil and the remaining vinegar.

Nutritional Information

- Calories: 268
- Carbohydrates: 5g
- Fat: 27g

- Protein: 1g
- Sugar: 0g
- Cholesterol: 242mg

Vegan Balls

Ingredients

- 2 ¼ lb Yuca
- 2 cups of wheat flour
- Salt
- 2 cups crushed light soy protein
- 2 tbsp soy sauce
- 1 onion
- 2 cloves of garlic
- 1 cup of green seasoning coffee
- 1 tsp of baking powder
- 3 cups breadcrumbs
- Water

Steps to Cook

1. Cook the Yuca and puree, season with salt and sprinkle the dough with the wheat flour. Reserve.
2. Prepare the famous sautéed with the aforementioned spices, without leaving it moist.
3. Make the drumsticks: with water, moisten your hands, put 1 generous tablespoon of puree in one of them. Spread over the entire surface of your palm.
4. Put 1 tablespoon of sautéed PS in the center, close your hand and shape it.
5. In the second or third coxinha your work will be perfect. When the coxinha is formed, pass it in the water, it will not crumble and in the breadcrumbs.
6. Grease a pan with oil and breadcrumbs, place the drumsticks and bake in the air fryer for 30 minutes in at 600°F.

Nutritional Information

- Calories: 51
- Carbohydrates: 10g
- Fat: 0g
- Protein: 4g
- Sugar: 2g
- Cholesterol: 300mg

Roasted Vegetables

Servings: 2-4

Preparation time: 10 minutes

Cook time: 15 minutes

Ingredients

- 1 large carrot, chopped
- 3 large potatoes cut into thick slices (sweet potato)
- Salt to taste
- Lemon pepper to taste
- Hot paprika to taste (or sweet)
- Herbs to taste
- 1 tablespoon of olive oil (or coconut oil)

Steps to Cook

1. Cut the carrot and potato into slices of 1 cm each.
2. Soak in a container with water for 10 minutes.
3. Then remove all the water, add the spices and oil.
4. Mix well, put everything in the basket, drizzle with olive oil.
5. Set the fryer to 400°F for 15 minutes.
6. In half the time mix everything to bake evenly.
7. Then just remove and serve.

Nutritional Information

- Calories: 80
- Carbohydrates: 7g
- Fat: 6g
- Protein: 1g
- Sugar: 4g
- Cholesterol: 0mg

Roasted Rainbow Vegetables

Servings: 4

Preparation time: 10 mins

Cook time: 20 minutes

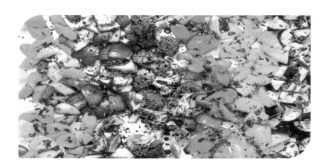

Ingredients	Steps to Cook

- 1 red bell pepper, seeded and cut into small pieces
- 1 carrot
- 1 yellow squash, cut into small pieces
- 1 zucchini, cut into small pieces
- Broccoli
- ½ purple Onion, cut into small pieces
- 1 tbsp of olive oil
- Salt and pepper to taste

1. Preheat the air fryer at 400°F for a few minutes.
2. Place the red pepper, summer squash, zucchini, broccoli, carrot, and onion in a large bowl. Add the olive oil, salt and black pepper and mix.
3. Place the vegetables in the basket on the air fryer.
4. Fry the vegetables in the open air until they are roasted, about 20 minutes, stirring halfway through the cooking time.

Nutritional Information

- Calories: 66.7
- Carbohydrates: 7.3g
- Fat: 3.6g
- Protein: 1.3g

- Sugar: 3.5g
- Cholesterol: 0mg

Roasted Broccoli

Servings: 3-4

Preparation time: 5 minutes

Cook time: 5-8 minutes

Ingredients

- 3-4 cups fresh broccoli florets
- 1 tablespoon olive oil or cooking oil spray
- 1 teaspoon optional Herbs de Provence seasoning

Steps to Cook

1. Drizzle broccoli with olive oil or drizzle with cooking oil.
2. Sprinkle seasonings everywhere.
3. Spray the fryer basket with cooking oil.
4. Take to the air fryer and cook for 5-8 minutes at 360°F.
5. Once broccoli has cooked for 5 minutes, open the fryer and examine the broccoli.

Nutritional Information

- Calories: 123.2
- Carbohydrates: 8.3g
- Fat: 9.6g

- Protein: 4.4g
- Sugar: 0.1g
- Cholesterol: 0mg

Eggplant Chips

Ingredients

- *1 aubergine*
- *Salt*

Steps to Cook

1. Slice the aubergine
2. Place scattered salt on a tray
3. Place scattered salt on a tray
4. Place scattered salt on a tray
5. Place the eggplants on absorbent kitchen paper or napkins
6. Place absorbent paper towels or napkins on top of the eggplants
7. Place aubergines in the air fryer for 10 minutes at 400°F

Nutritional Information

- Calories: 85
- Carbohydrates: 0g
- Fat: 0g

- Protein: 3.5g
- Sugar: 0.5g
- Cholesterol: 0mg

Zucchini Sticks

Ingredients

- 1 zucchini
- 2 eggs
- With flour
- 1 lemon

Steps to Cook

1. Cut the zucchini into sticks (taking off their tips but with the shell!)
2. Have a bowl with flour, another with the seasoned eggs and a last one with the lemon zest, grated cheese and breadcrumbs all together and mixed
3. Pass all the zucchinis by flour, then by the eggs and finally by the mixture of lemon, cheese and breadcrumbs.
4. Take to deep fryer without oil for approximately 20 minutes at 360°F.
5. Eat with soy sauce or ketchup!

Nutritional Information

- Calories: 174.1
- Carbohydrates: 33.5g
- Fat: 2.1g
- Protein: 6.4g

- Sugar: 5.7g
- Cholesterol: 0mg

Sweet Potato Chips

Ingredients	Steps to Cook

- *half sweet potato (sweet potato)*
- *1 tbsp of extra virgin olive oil (preferably spray)*
- *spices*
- *Salt*

1. With a mandolin or sharp knife, cut very thin.
2. Cover the slices very lightly with olive oil, place them on a plate so that they do not overlap.
3. Put them in the air fryer at 400⁰F for 20 minutes.
4. Watch them so they don't burn. Put them on a rack to cool and season them

Nutritional Information

- Calories: 151
- Carbohydrates: 16g
- Fat: 9.2g

- Protein: 0.8g
- Sugar: 2.5g
- Cholesterol: 0mg

Radish Chips

Servings: 4-8

Preparation time: 5 minutes

Cook time: 25 minutes

Ingredients

- 10-15 *radishes*
- 1 *tbsp of olive oil*
- ½ *tbsp of molasses*
- 1-2 *tbsp of cinnamon sugar*

Steps to Cook

1. Preheat the air fryer to 360°F. Cut the radishes into very thin slices and put them in the basket of the air fryer.
2. Microwave 30 seconds at full power to soften. Drain the liquid and put them in a larger bowl.
3. Add the olive oil, molasses and sugar. Mix well and spread them on a baking sheet with baking paper on top, being careful not to overlap them.
4. Put them in the air fryer for 15 minutes and turn them over. Reduce the temperature to 220°F and bake them for another 20 minutes.
5. You will see that they are wrinkled and crispy. Take them out of the air fryer and let them cool down.

Nutritional Information

- Calories: 4.3
- Carbohydrates: 0.9g
- Fat: 0g
- Protein: 0.2g
- Sugar: 0.6g
- Cholesterol: 0mg

Taro Chips

Ingredients	Steps to Cook
• 1 *large taro (yam)* • *½ tsp salt* • *1 tbsp of olive oil.*	1. Preheat the air fryer to 380°F for a few minutes. Wash, peel and cut the taro into very thin slices. Brush them with olive oil on both sides (very little). 2. Put each separate slice on a cookie sheet with a sheet of baking paper. 3. Sprinkle a little salt on top and bake them 10 minutes on each side until golden and crisp (watch them).

Nutritional Information

- Calories: 141
- Carbohydrates: 19.31g
- Fat: 7.06g

- Protein: 0.65g
- Sugar: 1.08g
- Cholesterol: 0mg

Chapter 7

Air Fryer Snacks And Appetizers Recipes

Open Esfiha

Servings: 2-4

Preparation time: 10 minutes

Cook time: 5 minutes

Ingredients	Steps to Cook

Ingredients

- 1 cup milk
- 1/3 cup warm water
- ¼ cup olive oil or olive oil
- 1 and ¾ teaspoon of salt
- 2 tablespoons of sugar
- 2 and ½ teaspoons of yeast
- 4 cups of flour

To open and shape the dough:

- ½ cup flour

Steps to Cook

1. Prepare the dough by mixing all the ingredients in a bowl until the dough is completely homogeneous. Let stand for 10 minutes covered with a cloth or film paper.
2. Prepare the fillings of your choice. The preparation of everything is very simple and equal to the dough: mix everything so that it is well seasoned and homogeneous.
3. When ready, mix the flour and cornmeal and spread on the counter. Divide the dough into thirty servings. Make balls and with your finger press in the middle to put the filling. Place the filling in the gap and keep pressing to take the shape of the knife.

- 1 tablespoon of cornmeal

Filling:

- **Meat**: 1 lb of raw ground meat, juice of 1 lemon, ½ tomato, seedless, ½ onion, 1 clove of garlic, parsley, salt and pepper to taste;
- **Cheese**: ½ lb of white cheese, ricotta or semi-cured cheese, 1 cup of creamy curd, parsley to taste;
- **Pepperoni**: 1 lb of smoked pepperoni sausage, ½ onion, parsley to taste;
- **Chicken**: ½ lb of cooked and shredded cooked chicken and ½ cup of creamy curd.

4. Organize Esfiha every four years on Air Fry and program for 5 minutes at 400°F

Nutritional Information:

- Calories: 293
- Carbohydrates: 15g
- Fat: 22g
- Protein: 5g
- Sugar: 5g
- Cholesterol: 300mg

Bolognese-Style Lasagna

Servings: 4

Preparation time: 15 minutes

Cook time: 20 minutes

Ingredients

- 1 lb lasagna pasta
- 1 lb of ground meat
- 2 boxes of cream
- 3 tbsp of butter
- 3 tbsp of wheat flour
- 1 lb of ham
- 1 lb of mozzarella
- salt to taste
- 2 cups milk
- 1 grated onion
- 3 oil tablespoons
- 1 box of tomato sauce
- 3 garlic cloves, crushed
- 1 package of grated cheese

Steps to Cook

Lasagna:

1. Cook the dough according to the manufacturer's guidelines, pour it into a baking dish with ice water so it doesn't stick, and set aside.

Bolognese sauce:

2. Sauté garlic, onion, ground beef, tomato sauce, cook 3 minutes and set aside.

White sauce:

3. Melt the margarine, add the 3 tablespoons of all-purpose flour and stir.
4. Pour the milk gradually and continue stirring.
5. Finally, add the cream, stir for 1 minute and turn off the heat.

Mounting:

6. Pour a portion of the Bolognese sauce on a plate, half the dough, half the ham, half the mozzarella, all the white sauce and the rest of the dough.
7. Repeat layers up to the edge of the container.
8. Finish with the grated cheese and place it in the air fryer at 400°F, preheated, for about 20 minutes.

Nutritional Information:

- Calories: 630
- Carbohydrates: 27g
- Fat: 40g

- Protein: 36g
- Sugar: 5g
- Cholesterol: 300mg

Salty Brazilian Peanut

Servings: 04

Preparation time: 60 minutes

Cook time: 40 minutes

Ingredients	Steps to Cook

Ingredients

- ½ lb large peanuts
- 2 ½ cup of water
- 2 tbsp of coarse salt

Steps to Cook

1. Dissolve the salt in the water and reserve.
2. Adjust the pan for 5 minutes at 360°F.
3. Put the peanuts, stirring every 2 minutes.
4. After 5 minutes, immediately pour the peanuts into the brine.
5. Leave in the solution for 1 minute, strain the peanuts and return them to the pan.
6. At 360°F, adjust another 10 minutes, stirring every 2 minutes.
7. After 10 minutes, transfer the peanuts to a dishwasher container to cool.
8. Before tasting, wait until it has completely cooled down as they wilt slightly as they heat up.

Nutritional Information:

- Calories: 189.9
- Carbohydrates: 4g
- Fat: 19g

- Protein: 4g
- Sugar: 0g
- Cholesterol: 0mg

French Style Toast

Servings: 1

Preparation time: 60 mins

Cook time: 40 minutes

Ingredients	Steps to Cook
• *salt to taste* • *2 eggs* • *2 stale breads*	1. Mix the 2 eggs with the salt in a deep plate. 2. Cut the loaves into cross halves. 3. With the help of a fork, dip the halves. 4. Drain and place them in the air fryer at 360^{0}F for 5 minutes.

Nutritional Information:

- Calories: 219
- Carbohydrates: 23g
- Fat: 11g

- Protein: 7.3g
- Sugar: 4g
- Cholesterol: 129mg

RISOLIS

Servings: 2

Preparation time: 15 mins

Cook time: 30 minutes

Ingredients

- 2 cups milk
- 1 tbsp of butter or margarine
- 1 tbsp of salt
- 2 cups flour

Steps to Cook

1. Boil the milk, butter and salt.
2. When it boils, pour the 2 cups of flour at once.
3. Knead the dough well. Roll out the dough over the sink (can be with your hands), cut the slices with the rim of a glass and fill them to taste. Close the risolis and pass the beaten egg and breadcrumbs.
4. Fry in the air fryer at 600^{0}F for 30 minutes.

Nutritional Information:

- Calories: 87
- Carbohydrates: 5g
- Fat: 4g

- Protein: 6g
- Sugar: 0g
- Cholesterol: 300mg

Yuca Catupiry

Ingredients

- 2 cups of leche
- 2 bowls of margarine
- 1 cube of broth of chicken
- 2 bowls of flour
- 1 lb of cooked Yuca

Filling:

- Dried meat upholstered with green onion and green, grated

Steps to Cook

1. Bring to the fire: milk, margarine, broth.
2. When it boils add all the flour.
3. Stir until well cooked. Remove.
4. Mix the yuca and knead to add.
5. Shape the drumsticks by placing the filling.
6. Pass the egg, breadcrumbs.
7. Fry in the air fryer for 30 minutes at 600°F.

Nutritional Information:

- Calories: 330
- Carbohydrates: 78g
- Fat: 0.6g
- Protein: 2.8g
- Sugar: 3.5g
- Cholesterol: 0mg

Pasta Snacks For Party

Servings: 10

Preparation time: 10 mins

Cook time: 25 minutes

Ingredients

- 4 ¼ cups of hot water
- 6 broth tablets
- ½ cup oil
- 4 cloves garlic, crushed
- ½ lb of wheat flour

Tarnish:

- 2 cups milk
- wheat flour
- Bread crumbs
- Salt

Filling options:

- balls (cheese or cheese with ham)
- Chicken
- Risoles

Steps to Cook

1. In a saucepan, place the oil and garlic to brown.
2. After sautéing, add the dissolved hot water with the broth of your choice and then gradually add the flour.
3. Let it cook, stirring until it comes out of the bottom of the pan. Set aside and let cool.
4. Prepare the filling you like.

Tarnish:

5. Pass the sandwiches into the salt-seasoned wheat flour.
6. Then put the balls in the milk, remove and place in the bread crumbs.
7. Then, after breading the sandwiches, put them in the air fryer preheated at 400°F and fry for 25 minutes.

Nutritional Information:

- Calories: 267.1
- Carbohydrates: 20.1g
- Fat: 11.8g
- Protein: 18.5g

- Sugar: 0.5g
- Cholesterol: 47mg

Onion Cookie

Servings: 4-6

Preparation time: 10 mins

Cook time: 45 minutes

Ingredients	Steps to Cook

Ingredients

- *1 lb margarine*
- *2 sachets of onion cream soup*
- *½ glass of mayonnaise*
- *2 lbs of wheat flour*

Steps to Cook

1. Mix everything dry, add the wet and knead well, make balls or shapes to taste and brush the yolk.
2. Take to the air fryer at 600°F for 45 minutes or until lightly browned.

Note: You can roll out the dough and use a cookie cutter with the desired shape. If you don't want to model the balls in your hand.

3. Store in tightly closed glasses or cans.

Nutritional Information:

- Calories: 515
- Carbohydrates: 66g
- Fat: 24g

- Protein: 6g
- Sugar: 16g
- Cholesterol: 300mg

Easy Chicken Balls

Servings: 2-4

Preparation time: 10 mins

Cook time: 45 minutes

Ingredients	Steps to Cook

Ingredients

- 2 cups milk
- 2 cups of water
- 1 cup of oil
- 1 knor chicken tablet
- 2 tbsp of parsley
- 1 pinch of salt
- 1 lb flour and chicken

Steps to Cook

1. In a saucepan put all the above ingredients and bring to a boil.
2. When it starts to boil, remove the pan from the heat and put 550 g of wheat flour and return to the fire to cook, stirring constantly until it comes out and put about 15 minutes in a plastic bag to cool.
3. To make the drumsticks, remove a little of the dough and shape the drumsticks by hand, placing the filling that must be done with 1 braised breast.
4. Drumsticks ready to go in milk and breadcrumbs.
5. Take to the preheated air fryer at 400°F for 45 minutes.
6. Don't forget to make the drumsticks small.

Nutritional Information:

- Calories: 294
- Carbohydrates: 15g
- Fat: 16g
- Protein: 12g
- Sugar: 2.7g

- Cholesterol: 16m

Corn Ball With Cheese

Servings: 10

Preparation time: 10 mins

Cook time: 35 minutes

Ingredients	Steps to Cook

Ingredients

- 1 can of green corn
- 1 ½ cups chicken broth
- 1 grated onion
- 3 tbsp olive oil
- 2 cups of water
- 2 cups of wheat flour
- 2 beaten egg whites
- Diced mozzarella
- Bread crumbs

Steps to Cook

1. Put the corn, the broth, the onion, the oil and the water to beat in the blender.
2. Then pour into a pan and heat, stir until it boils.
3. When it boils pour the flour until it forms a ball and release from the pan.
4. Remove from the heat and let cool.
5. Meanwhile, beat the egg whites, wrap into a ball and fill with the mozzarella.
6. Pass the egg whites and then the breadcrumbs.
7. Fry in the air fryer at 400^{0}F for 35 minutes or until golden.

Nutritional Information:

- Calories: 274
- Carbohydrates: 29g
- Fat: 16g

- Protein: 3g
- Sugar: 2g
- Cholesterol: 300mg

Chapter 8

Air fryer Desserts Recipes

Layered Apple Pie

Servings: 3-4

Preparation time: 5 minutes

Cook time: 20 minutes

Ingredients	Steps to Cook

Ingredients

- *3 apples, peeled, thinly sliced;*
- *1 cup of wheat flour;*
- *1 cup of sugar*
- *1 tbso of cinnamon powder;*
- *1 cup of milk;*
- *1 tbsp butter, melted without salt;*
- *1 egg;*
- *1 tbsp of vanilla essence.*

Steps to Cook

1. Mix the flour, sugar and cinnamon. Reservation.
2. Lightly beat the egg with a fork, add the milk, vanilla and melted butter. Reserve.
3. In the container that comes with Air Fry, make thin layers, alternating apple slices and dry ingredients. Finish with a dry coat. Finally, carefully pour the liquid mixture over everything and take it to Air Fry for 20 minutes at 360°F.

Nutritional Information

- Calories: 525.1
- Carbohydrates: 100.9g
- Fat: 11.8g

- Protein: 5.5g
- Sugar: 30.1g
- Cholesterol: 0.5mg

Coffee Cake

Servings: 2-4

Preparation time: 5 minutes

Cook time: 15 minutes

Ingredients	Steps to Cook

Ingredients

- 7 tbsp of flour
- 5 tbsp of oil
- 4 tbsp of milk
- 1 tbsp of yeast
- 1 egg

Options:

- Strawberries
- Bananas
- Chocolate syrup (or melted chocolate)
- Edible essence of the desired flavor

Steps to Cook

1. Add all ingredients in a bowl and stir until smooth;
2. Preheat air frying for 3 to 35 minutes at 360°F;
3. Divide the dough evenly into two cups;
4. Place the cups and bake for 15 minutes at 360°F.
5. When 3 minutes are left open and check if the cake has baked. This process may be faster due to the thickness of the cups.
6. When ready, remove it with a glove or cloth and garnish with the fruit and syrup.

Nutritional information

- Calories: 189
- Carbohydrates: 30.3g
- Fat: 5.96g

- Protein: 3.51g
- Sugar: 16.62g
- Cholesterol: 55mg

Caramelized Banana

Servings: 2-4

Preparation time: 5 mins

Cook time: 15 minutes

Ingredients

- 3 ½ oz. of flour
- 1 egg
- ½ cup of water
- 4 sliced bananas
- 1/3 lb of sugar

Steps to Cook

1. Beat the flour, water and egg until it reaches a homogeneous and not very firm point;
2. Wrap the banana pieces with the dough and place them in the Air Fry basket;
3. Fry for 15 minutes at 400°F.
4. While the plantains are frying, prepare the caramel by heating it with little sugar. Stir well to avoid burning;
5. Once the bananas are done, remove them from the Air Fry with tongs or a fork and roll them into the caramel.
6. Place the bananas on a plate and wait for the caramel to cool to form a crispy crust.

Nutritional Information

- Calories: 101
- Carbohydrates: 18.24g
- Fat: 2.01g

- Protein: 2.66g
- Sugar: 0.53g
- Cholesterol: 0mg

Bread Empanada

Ingredients	Steps to Cook

- 10 slices of bread without peel
- ½ lb of chopped cheese
- ½ lb minced ham
- oregano to taste
- 4 eggs
- Bread crumbs

1. Use the rolling pin and noodles to make the bread slices thinner or flatter;
2. Beat the eggs and reserve to be able to bread
3. Add a tablespoon of cheese, a tablespoon of ham and oregano;
4. Using a culinary brush, brush the beaten egg over the edges of the bread;
5. Using another slice of bread, cover the first and press the edges with a fork to close the cakes;
6. Repeat the procedure with the other cakes;
7. For bread, roll the pastries first over the beaten egg and then over the breadcrumbs;
8. Place the cakes in the Air Fryer and fry them for 15 minutes at 360°F.

Nutritional information

- Calories: 250
- Carbohydrates: 39.3g
- Fat: 9.4g
- Protein: 4g

- Sugar: 15.6g
- Cholesterol: 0mg

Rolled Pizza

Servings: 2

Preparation time: 10 mins

Cook time: 40 minutes

Ingredients	Steps to Cook

- 1 ½ cups warm milk
- 1 egg
- 1 tablet of yeast for bread
- 1 spoon of sugar
- 1 tbsp of salt
- ½ cup of oil
- 2 ½ cup all-purpose flour

1. In the blender glass, place the warm milk, egg, crumbled yeast, sugar, salt, and oil. Blend.
2. Transfer to a bowl.
3. Add the flour gradually, whisking each time it is added, if necessary add more wheat.
4. Open very large and thin and fill it as you like.
5. Then roll it up like a roll, brush it with egg yolk, and put it on a pizza plate smeared with margarine.
6. Take to the air fryer at 600°F for 40 minutes or until the dough is golden.
7. If the dough breaks open when baked, no problem.

Nutritional Information:

- Calories: 220
- Carbohydrates: 24g
- Fat: 10g

- Protein: 7g
- Sugar: 3g
- Cholesterol: 10mg

Quick Sardine Pizza

Servings: 4

Preparation time: 15 mins

Cook time: 30 minutes

Ingredients	Steps to Cook

Ingredients

- 4 eggs
- ½ cup milk
- ¼ cup olive oil
- 50 g of grated cheese
- 1 ½ cup flour
- 1 tbsp of baking powder
- 2 cans of sardine without scales and spine
- 1 tomato chopped
- ½ cup of chopped olives
- 1 small grated onion
- Salt to taste
- 2 tbsp green aroma
- Oil to grease and breadcrumbs to sprinkle
- Mozzarella to coat
- oregano

Steps to Cook

1. Beat the eggs, milk, oil and cheese in a blender.
2. Add the sifted flour with the yeast and mix well.
3. Mix together the sardines, olives, tomatoes, onions, salt and green aroma.
4. Grease the pan (of your choice) with oil and sprinkle with flour and put sardine mixture on the dough and the mozzarella.
5. Bake in the air fryer at 400⁰ for 30 minutes.

Nutritional Information:

- Calories: 125
- Carbohydrates: 7g
- Fat: 7g

- Protein: 14.8g
- Sugar: 2g
- Cholesterol: 10mg

Homemade Pizza

Servings: 4

Preparation time: 30 mins

Cook time: 25-35 minutes

Ingredients	Steps to Cook

Ingredients

- *2 double cups of wheat flour*
- *2 tbsp of oil*
- *1 tsp salt*
- *1 tsp of sugar*
- *Warm water*
- *2 loaves of bread yeast*

Steps to Cook

1. Put the flour in a bowl and add the oil to the warm water, the two tablets of bread dissolved in sugar and salt.
2. Stir with a wooden spoon and then knead the dough well with your hands without sticking in your hands.
3. Let stand for about 30 minutes. Grease the pan with butter, and then roll out the dough onto it.
4. Let it brown in a preheated air fryer at 600°F for 25 to 35 minutes.

Nutritional Information:

- Calories: 206
- Carbohydrates: 33g
- Fat: 4.7g
- Protein: 7.5g
- Sugar: 1.3g
- Cholesterol: 9.6mg

Sweet Potato Pizza

Servings: 2-6

Preparation time: 20 minutes

Cook time: 10 minutes

Ingredients	Steps to Cook

Ingredients

- 3 ½ oz. mashed boiled potatoes
- ½ lb of wheat flour
- 1 egg
- 2 butter spoons
- Salt to taste
- a pinch of sugar
- ¼ cup of warm milk
- 0.7 oz. organic yeast (for bread)

Steps to Cook

1. Put in the milk to dissolve the yeast, then the other ingredients.
2. Knead well.
3. Put in a pizza dish, greased with butter and flour, letting it rest for 20 minutes.
4. Filling to taste.
5. Bake in the air fryer at 360°F for 10 minutes.

Nutritional Information:

- Calories: 230.3
- Carbohydrates: 25.9g
- Fat: 8.2g
- Protein: 14.2g
- Sugar: 1.4g
- Cholesterol: 37.6mg

Pizza Blender Ingredients

Servings: 2-4

Preparation time: 10 mins

Cook time: 20-30 minutes

Ingredients	Steps to Cook

- 1 cup milk
- 1 egg
- 1 tbsp of margarine
- 1 ½ cup all-purpose flour
- 1 tbsp of baking powder
- 2 tomatoes
- Oregano
- Salt
- Chile
- olive oil
- ham and mozzarella to your liking

a. Whisk in a blender: milk, egg, margarine, flour, yeast and salt.
b. Place in a 30 cm frying pan and bake in the preheated air fryer at 360°F for about 20 minutes.
c. Remove from the air fryer and distribute the sliced tomatoes.
d. Sprinkle with salt, oregano, pepper and drizzle with olive oil.
e. Top with ham and mozzarella.
f. Bake again for another 10 minutes or until the mozzarella melts.

Nutritional Information:

- Calories: 315
- Carbohydrates: 38g
- Fat: 11g
- Protein: 12g
- Sugar: 4g
- Cholesterol: 275mg

Canned Sardines Empanada

Servings: 4-6

Preparation time: 15 mins

Cook time: 30 minutes

Ingredients	Steps to Cook
• 3 eggs	1. Put the sardine in the pan, mash with the fork.
• 1 cup of American oil	2. Then add the chopped tomatoes, onions, bell peppers and green smell, corn and peas.
• 1 ½ cup liquid milk	3. Let it boil a little, when it boils, turn it off and go to the dough.
• 3 cups of wheat flour	4. Beat everything in a blender, eggs, milk, wheat flour, oil and grated cheese, until the dough is light.
• 2 canned sardines	5. Grease the pan with oil and wheat flour; pour the dough and the filling on top.
• 1 can of corn	6. Take it to the air fryer previously preheated at 400⁰F for 30 minutes.
• 1 can of peas	
• 3 ½ oz. grated cheeses	
• Salt to taste	
• Tomato, onion, pepper	
• Green smell	

Ingredients

- 3 eggs
- 1 cup of American oil
- 1 ½ cup liquid milk
- 3 cups of wheat flour
- 2 canned sardines
- 1 can of corn
- 1 can of peas
- 3 ½ oz. grated cheeses
- Salt to taste
- Tomato, onion, pepper
- Green smell

Steps to Cook

1. Put the sardine in the pan, mash with the fork.
2. Then add the chopped tomatoes, onions, bell peppers and green smell, corn and peas.
3. Let it boil a little, when it boils, turn it off and go to the dough.
4. Beat everything in a blender, eggs, milk, wheat flour, oil and grated cheese, until the dough is light.
5. Grease the pan with oil and wheat flour; pour the dough and the filling on top.
6. Take it to the air fryer previously preheated at 400⁰F for 30 minutes.

Nutritional Information:

- Calories: 200
- Carbohydrates: 21g
- Fat: 10g
- Protein: 8g
- Sugar: 1g
- Cholesterol: 285mg

Fried Pizza

Servings: 2-4

Preparation time: 15 mins

Cook time: 20-25 minutes

Ingredients	Steps to Cook

Ingredients

- 2 oz. of yeast for bread
- 2 cups warm water curd
- 1 spoon of sugar
- 4 tbsp of oil
- 1 ½ tbsp of salt
- 2 tbsp drip
- 1 kg of wheat flour

Tomato sauce:

- Stuffing of your choice, such as mozzarella, pepperoni, tuna, heart of palm, chicken, etc.

Steps to Cook

1. Dissolve yeast in sugar, add water, oil, salt and drip, mix well.
2. Gradually add the wheat flour until the dough loosens from your hands.
3. Let the dough rest for about 1 hour and 30 minutes, with a damp cloth on top.
4. Open the very thin dough the size of your pan and fry it in the air fryer at 600^0 for 15 minutes.
5. Fry on one side, turn and remove when ready.
6. Put the tomato sauce and the filling you want on top.
7. Take to the air fryer at 320^0F for 10 minutes or until the filling is good, but be careful not to burn.

Nutritional Information:

- Calories: 200
- Carbohydrates: 21g
- Fat: 10g
- Protein: 8g

- Sugar: 1g
- Cholesterol: 285mg

Grated Coconut Balls

Servings: 2-4

Preparation time: 5 mins

Cook time: 15 minutes

Ingredients

- 1 cup grated coconut
- 1 egg white
- 1 ½ tbsp condensed milk
- ½ tbsp of sugar

Steps to Cook

1. In a bowl, mix all the ingredients until they form a homogeneous mass.
2. Then roll the dough into the desired size and granulate the sugar on top.
3. Grease your electric fryer with oil 360°F, place the balls and fry for 15 minutes.

Nutritional Information:

- Calories: 131.2
- Carbohydrates: 18.3g
- Fat: 5.7g

- Protein: 2.7g
- Sugar: 16.5g
- Cholesterol: 9.5mg

Sponge Cake With Natural Yogurt

Servings: 2-4

Preparation time: 10 mins

Cook time: 45 minutes

Ingredients	Steps to Cook

Ingredients

- 2 eggs
- 1 plain yogurt
- 1 cup of sugar
- 2 cups flour
- ½ cup olive oil
- ½ yeast octopus
- Lemon grid
- Icing sugar to decorate

Steps to Cook

1. Add the yogurt, sugar container, and 2 eggs in a bowl. Beat with the slotted spoon.
2. Add the flour, the yeast, the lemon zest and the oil. Beat again with the slotted spoon until everything is well mixed.
3. Preheat our fryer to 360°F.
4. In the cake pan of our air fryer put vegetable paper and pour the mixture we have made.
5. With the ingredients it carries you will need a container at least 7.5cm high by 16.5 in diameter
6. Let cook for 15 minutes.
7. Make a cross-shaped cut on the surface so that it does not continue to inflate and cooks well inside.
8. Put it back at 360°F for another 30 minutes.

Nutritional Information:

- Calories: 361.2
- Carbohydrates: 59.2g
- Fat: 10.9g

- Protein: 9.6g
- Sugar: 31.2g
- Cholesterol: 53.1mg

Cheese Empanada

Servings: 2-3

Preparation time: 1 min

Cook time: 15 minutes

Ingredients	Steps to Cook

Ingredients

- Puff pastry to taste
- Mozzarella cheese to fill to taste
- olive oil to taste
- water to taste

Steps to Cook

1. Open the dough and put the cheese filling.
2. Spread a little water on the edges of the dough with your fingers or with a brush, to seal well when closing.
3. Fold the dough in half to close.
4. With the help of a fork, press down on the edges to seal the dough well.
5. Brush a little olive oil over the dough so that it is browned.
6. Preheat your fryer for 5 minutes at 360°F.
7. Place the dough in the Air Fryer.
8. Fry for 10 minutes at 360°F.
9. Half the time, change the dough to brown on both sides.

Nutritional Information:

- Calories: 273
- Carbohydrates: 20.76g
- Fat: 10.06g
- Protein: 8.92g
- Sugar: 0.43g
- Cholesterol: 67mg

Milanese Provolone

Servings: 4

Preparation time: 5 minutes

Cook time: 5 minutes

Ingredients	Steps to Cook

- 1 lb of provolone cheese
- 4 eggs
- ½ lb of wheat flour mixed with 1 tablespoon of cornstarch
- ½ lb of toasted breadcrumbs
- Black pepper to taste

1. Peel the provolone cheese, cut it into cubes or small rings and pass them over the lightly beaten eggs. Then pass the wheat flour and cornstarch mixture. Pass the eggs again and finally the toasted breadcrumbs.
2. Once breaded, refrigerate for about an hour or more. The flour must be very dry and consistent.
3. When ready, place the pieces of provolone in air Fryer Basket, keeping a space between them. Set the fryer for 5 minutes at 400°F.

Nutritional Information:

- Calories: 100
- Carbohydrates: 0.6g
- Fat: 7.5g

- Protein: 7.3g
- Sugar: 0.2g
- Cholesterol: 20mg

Petit Gateau

Ingredients

- ½ lb dark chocolate
- ½ lb of butter
- 5 eggs
- 5 gems
- 3 ½ oz. of wheat flour
- 6 oz. of sugar

Steps to Cook

1. Melt the butter and chocolate in a refractory pan that fits in the basket for 5 minutes at 180°F, or in a water bath on a conventional stove.
2. Wait for it to cool down until it is warm to cold.
3. Add the eggs and yolks, the sugar and finally the wheat flour.
4. Put the mixture in cupcake molds, they can be silicone or iron.
5. Set the air fryer to 320°F for 6 minutes.

Nutritional Information:

- Calories: 292
- Carbohydrates: 40g
- Fat: 15g
- Protein: 4.5g
- Sugar: 30g
- Cholesterol: 17mg

Milan Banana

Ingredients	Steps to Cook

Ingredients

- 5 bananas cut in half
- cornstarch
- 1 egg
- 1 tbsp of olive oil
- toasted breadcrumbs mixed with grated parmesan cheese

Steps to Cook

1. Cut the bananas in half; pass the cornstarch, then the beaten egg, and finally the toasted breadcrumbs mixed with Parmesan cheese.
2. Preheat your air fryer for 5 minutes.
3. Place the bananas upright and place the oil on them and fry them for 10 minutes at 400°F

Nutritional Information:

- Calories: 140
- Carbohydrates: 18g
- Fat: 7g
- Protein: 1g
- Sugar: 10g
- Cholesterol: 295mg

Brigadier

Ingredients	Steps to Cook
• 1 can of condensed milk • 4 tbsp of Nescau	4. Use small pots or preferably a Ramekin. 5. Put the condensed milk and mix with the Nescau. 6. Take Air fryer for 4 minutes at 360°F. 7. Open the drawer and mix with a spoon. Repeat this cycle 2 more times.

Nutritional Information:

- Calories: 152
- Carbohydrates: 19g
- Fat: 7g

- Protein: 1g
- Sugar: 10g
- Cholesterol: 300mg

Creamy Pudding

Servings: 1-2

Preparation time: 5 minutes

Cook time: 15 minutes

Ingredients	Steps to Cook

Ingredients

- 1 can of condensed milk
- 1 can of milk
- 2 eggs
- 1 tbsp cornstarch
- syrup:
- ½ cup of sugar
- 4 tbsp of water

Containment:

- 2 cups of water

Steps to Cook

1. prepare the syrup first
2. bring water and sugar to the fire until it turns into caramel

pudding:

3. Mix all ingredients in a blender. Put the mixture in a pan. Cover the pan with foil.
4. Put in the air fryer at 360ºF for 15 minutes.
5. Put in the refrigerator and freeze for 3 hours.

Nutritional Information:

- Calories: 320
- Carbohydrates: 52g
- Fat: 12g
- Protein: 1g
- Sugar: 34g
- Cholesterol: 30mg

Squares Of Caramelized Red Berries

Servings: 2-4

Preparation time: 5 minutes

Cook time: 30 minutes

Ingredients

Red fruits:

- 3 oz. of sugar
- 1 lb of fresh red fruits
- strawberries
- raspberries
- blueberries
- currants ...

Caramelized almonds:

- 2 tbsp of sugar
- 1/3 of rolled almonds

For mass:

- 2 tbsp cornstarch
- 1 tsp of yeast
- ½ lb flour
- 2 oz. of sugar
- 1 ¼ cup milk

Steps to Cook

1. Wash and remove the small pieces of fruit, place them in a frying pan, add sugar and simmer until the water evaporates. Reservation.
2. You can use frozen fruits if you can't find them all fresh.
3. In a bowl beat the eggs with the sugar and cheese. Add milk and mix. Add flour, cornstarch, yeast and mix again. Pour the mixture into a floured square pan with butter. Put the fruit on top.
4. In a frying pan, toast the almonds, add the sugar and caramelize them quickly. Place on top of the fruit and bake in the air fryer for 30 minutes at 360°F. Let cool on a grid before cutting into squares.

- ¼ cup cream cheese or ricotta cream
- 2 eggs

Nutritional Information:

- Calories: 110
- Carbohydrates: 27g
- Fat: 0g

- Protein: 2g
- Sugar: 14g
- Cholesterol: 0mg

Quiche Lorraine

Servings: 4-6

Preparation time: 15 mins

Cook time: 20 minutes

Ingredients	Steps to Cook

- 1 puff pastry
- ½ lb Bacon
- 2 whole eggs
- 4 egg yolks
- 2 cups of fresh cream
- Salt
- black pepper and nutmeg

1. Place the dough in a mold and cover it to the edges and, with the help of a fork, make small holes throughout the dough to avoid bubbles. Preheat the air fryer and place the pan with the dough for a few minutes. Withdraw when it starts to "yellow".
2. Beat the eggs with the "fouet", add the cream and beat lightly. Let stand a few minutes. Season lightly because the bacon is usually very salty.
3. While the mixture is repeating, brown the bacon in a skillet. Spread the bacon over the dough and pour the mixture over the bacon.
4. Bake for about 20 minutes at 400°F.

Nutritional Information:

- Calories: 228
- Carbohydrates: 16.8g
- Fat: 13.8g

- Protein: 9.4g
- Sugar: 3.6g
- Cholesterol: 55.2mg

Green Corn Cake

Ingredients

- 2 cups corn
- 2 cups of sugar
- 2 cups milk
- 3 eggs
- 3 tbsp of wheat flour
- 1 tbsp of yeast

Steps to Cook

1. Beat everything in a blender, place in an air fryer and the baking sheet should be greased.
2. Bake at 400°F for 20 minutes.
3. The dough becomes soft-smooth.

Nutritional Information:

- Calories: 69.7
- Carbohydrates: 15g
- Fat: 0.4g

- Protein: 1.5g
- Sugar: 4.2g
- Cholesterol: 10mg

Conclusion

It is clear that having an air fryer is a great option. You can enjoy a healthier meal and save a good part of the oil expense. But not for that you will have to give up enjoying delicious elaborations. In the market you will find different models, many of them offer more functions than just frying.

Evaluate the capacity of the air fryer you are going to buy. It is not practical for you to be short, but neither is it too big for you. Also analyze the potency of the product. It is true that if it is high it will cook food sooner, but it will also increase electricity consumption. Try to make the chosen model easy to clean.

In this book, you've seen a lot about an air fryer. That is, its function, its advantages, etc. You have also seen a large number of recipes that you can prepare with this appliance. You can vary the methods provided to prepare those recipes. However, if you want to enjoy your dishes with an exquisite flavor, you must respect the portions provided.

PART- II

The Complete Air Fryer Cookbook

800 Foolproof, Quick & Easy Air Fryer Recipes for Beginners and Advanced Users

Jennifer Newman

Introduction

Generally, frying food involves dipping it in a bowl of boiling oil. The food becomes crispy on the outside, and it usually tastes delicious, but it's also full of oil, and that much oil isn't healthy for the human body.

With air fryers, a pulsating hot air cooking system is used, which is similar to the operation of a convection oven. This leads to results where the food is crispy on the outside and tender on the inside, without the need for oil (or perhaps just one spoonful).

It almost seems too good to be true! For those who love French fries, it is a much less oily alternative that allows you to eat more often without the adverse health effects.

Again, good news! Most models allow not only frying but also cooking, baking, and roasting food. Therefore, you can use your fryer to prepare vegetables, meats, fish, and even a whole chicken, as well as cookies or cakes. In short, an air fryer can do what a conventional oven does, but only by using little to no oil.

The Pros and Cons of the Air Fryer

Pros

There are many good things about using an air fryer. Here are some of the advantages:

- Low oil use, which makes our favorite fried foods healthier

- The air fryer doesn't smell like oil, keeping the overwhelming odor out of the house when it's used

- The ability to cook an unlimited amount of food

Cons

Among the disadvantages, the cooking time of food is generally much longer with this type of fryer than in the oven or with a conventional fryer. In addition, space is more limited, which means you must cook less food at a time.

But is it really an essential accessory?

Unless you fry a lot at home, an oven also cooks most foods, not to mention potato chips are also very good. And, above all, if we limit our consumption of fries to a few occasions, we can afford to eat those cooked in a fryer!

Tips for Using Your Air Fryer

1-Attach the Control Panel

For safety reasons, if the control panel of your semi-professional fryer is not properly connected to the appliance (on both sides), your fryer will not turn on. It is important always to press the control panel down until you hear a click. In other fryers, always check that all accessories are well fixed or recessed.

2-Adding Oil

Pour oil or grease into the fryer before turning it on. Warning: without oil, the resistance may burn and damage the device.

Pour enough oil into the fryer before turning it on. The oil level must at least reach the minimum level without exceeding the maximum level. If it exceeds the prescribed amount, the oil may spill out of the fryer as soon as you dip the basket in, which could result in burns.

3-Oil Level

Take the opportunity to renew the oil. If you prefer to wait, be sure to add the same type of oil or grease. We do not recommend mixing different oils, as they can react with each other when they heat up. Each oil has its own cooking temperature and shelf life.

Important: when you add oil or grease, it is not extending the shelf life of what is already in the fryer.

If you use solid grease, melt it according to the instructions in your user manual. Keep in mind: not all fryers are suitable for using solid fats. Opt-in this case, preferably for a model equipped with a special indicator that controls the oil melting.

4-Kinds of Oil

Oil quality is an essential element. There are two types of frying oils:

Vegetable oils such as peanut oil is very suitable for frying. In addition, they are better for health because they are less abundant in bad cholesterol.

You can also prepare your fries with lard (beef fat or pork) that gives potatoes a distinctive flavor. But as shown above, not all fryers can be used with solid fat.

5-When to Change the Oil

The oil should never be dirty. Renew the oil approximately every ten uses, or sooner if it starts to get dark, smelly, or smoky. Remember that if you also use your fryer to fry sandwiches, croquettes, or donuts, you should renew the fat more often.

In the case of cold zone fryers, you will find that the oil gets dirty less quickly and can keep longer. How does a cold zone work? Under the resistance, there is an area that does not heat directly, where the temperature remains lower. Waste and crumbs are deposited at the bottom of the fryer and do not burn. Your oil stays clean for longer, and it is better for your health! Does your fryer have no cold zone? Don't panic! Filter your oil with a special paper filter, and that's it!

6-How to Make Perfect French Fries

If you put too many fries in the fryer at the same time, the oil temperature may drop too quickly, which would not guarantee optimal results. Always read the instructions on your device carefully before using it, and do not exceed the recommended amount of potato slices.

Do you want to make crispy fries on the outside and soft on the inside? Choose floury potatoes like Bintje. Later, rinse your fries thoroughly in cold water to remove as much starch as possible, then dry them at once with a clean, dry towel. Preferably cook twice. Start by previously cooking your fresh fries for 4 to 8 minutes at 150°C, and then let them cool for half an hour. Then cook them a second time at 180-190°C.

Do you use frozen fries? The first cooking is not necessary because they are already precooked. Nor is it necessary for fries to be cooked beforehand because they are very thin.

Good to know: cooking time varies depending on the type of potato used.

7-Do you use an oil-free fryer?

In principle, you should not preheat your fryer without oil, but it will take a while for the appliance to reach the desired temperature. How do you know if the fryer is ready? An indicator light comes on, or a signal is activated which indicates that the temperature has been reached and you can now adjust the preparation time.

It is not necessary to add oil. You will only need to add a tablespoon of oil if you are preparing fresh dishes such as chicken without marinade or fresh French fries. All pre-cooked foods, such as frozen fries, croquettes, and snacks, can be cooked without oil. Use peanut oil, sunflower oil, or olive oil, but never taste bad nut oil.

On some models, you should never pour the oil directly into the bowl or basket. Pour the oil over the ingredients after placing them in the pan. For models with a basket, mix the fries and oil in advance in a bowl. For best operation, do not overload the appliance and do not forget that the capacity decreases when cooking frozen food.

Cleaning

To keep the device efficient, it requires minimum maintenance. Reading the instructions is also essential, even if not all of them offer the same quality of information, advice, and warnings.

1-Anti-Odor/Anti-Grease Filters

The covers are equipped with a filter that retains steam and grease. It is metallic and permanent (fixed or removable depending on the case) and should be changed regularly: grease activated carbon anti-odor. Some fryers have a combined filter (grease and activated carbon) and another metal and permanent. The effectiveness of the filters varies depending on the device. If you retain odors during cooking, you cannot prevent them from escaping when you soak the basket in oil and when you take it out. Ideally, use the fryer in a well-ventilated room, or make sure it is equipped with an efficient hood. Logically, oil-free devices emit less odors, and hot pulsed air is recovered in the cooking chamber. Then, the odors are trapped there.

Oil must be filtered with each use to extract the crumbs that accelerate its degradation and carry risks of inflammation. In some devices, the systems facilitate the operation (filter or box). It is recommended to keep the filtered oil cold (for example, in a bottle, in the refrigerator) and change it after eight to ten uses, or as soon as it shows certain signs. If it turns brown, become viscous, smokes during heating, if foam appears, etc..

What do you do with the used oil? Do not dispose of it in the sewer or the toilet, as it contaminates while it can be recycled (biofuels). You can deposit it in a recycling center or your trash cans (in a closed bottle).

How to Make Good French Fries

When making French fries in the air fryer, golden and crispy at will, you must choose the right materials. Several varieties of potatoes are suitable: bintje, Caesar, manon or victoria. For frozen French fries, not all of them are in the same boat.

For the oil, "special frying" should be chosen. It can be sunflower, rapeseed, or olive oil for best results.

The ideal conditions for frying range is between 160 and 190°C. Under that, it is necessary to cook the fries for an extended, which makes them absorb more oil. If you cook it at higher temps,, the oil tends to decompose and release toxic compounds, such as acrylamide, in starchy foods. To prevent fries from being too greasy and limit damage, it is better to cook small amounts and cut relatively large fries (the surface area/volume ratio counts). Remove them quickly after cooking, shake the basket, and then drain on absorbent paper. At this point, they will be crispier. Baking small amounts at a time offers a second advantage in terms of color. French fries need space, since squeezing them in the basket does not suit them.

Security Questions

The precautionary statements are not useless; about fifty accidents occur every year (oil splashes, spills, fryers fire, contact burns, etc.). Do not use the device without supervision, ensure its stability, and that the cable does not drag. Use a grounded electrical outlet. Be careful when dipping frozen potato chips in oil, as water droplets can cause splashing. Gradually introduce them and remove the basket if the bath boils too much. Keep children away, and don't forget to turn your air fryer off after use. If the oil ignites, never use water! Unplug the appliance and close the lid.

Enjoy!

Chapter 1

Breakfast Recipes

Fried Zucchini

Preparation time: 15 minutes;

Cooking time: 15 minutes; Serve: 2

Ingredients:

- 2 zucchinis cut into French fries
- ½ cup flour
- 2 beaten eggs
- 1 cup (250 ml) breadcrumbs
- ½ cup grated Parmesan cheese
- ¾ tsp salt, garlic, pepper to taste

Direction:

1. Preheat the air fryer to 390°F (200°C).

2. Put the flour, eggs and breadcrumbs in three different bowls.

3. Dip the fries in the flour, then the eggs and finally in the breadcrumbs. Work with about 10 French fries at a time and fry for 5 to 7 minutes or until crispy. Serve with a Caesar dressing.

Nutrition Value (Amount per serving):

- Calories 296
- Fat 15g
- Carbohydrates 31g
- Sugars 7g
- Protein 9.2g
- Cholesterol 134mg

Fried Pickles

Preparation time: 20 minutes;

Cooking time: 15 minutes; Serve: 8

Ingredients:

- 32 dill pickles
- 3 large beaten eggs
- 2 tbsp dill pickle juice
- ½ cup all-purpose flour
- ½ tsp salt
- ½ tsp cayenne pepper
- ½ tsp garlic powder
- 2 cups Panko breadcrumbs
- 2 tbsp fresh dill
- Oil sprayer (optional)
- Ranch dressing

Direction:

1. Preheat the hot air fryer to 425°F (220°C).
2. Let the pickles rest on paper towels until the liquid has been absorbed (about 15 minutes).
3. In a bowl, combine the flour and salt.
4. In another bowl, whisk the eggs, pickle juice, cayenne pepper and garlic powder.
5. Combine breadcrumbs and dill in another bowl.
6. Dip each pickle in the flour on both sides and shake the excess well.
7. Dip in egg mixture, then in breadcrumbs.
8. Transfer to your fryer basket and spray with oil.
9. Fry for 7-10 minutes.
10. Serve with ranch dressing if desired.

Nutrition Value (Amount per Serving):

- Calories 32
- Fat 1.2g
- Carbohydrates 4.4g
- Sugars 0.1g
- Protein 0.8g
- Cholesterol 2.5m

Onion Rings

Preparation time: 5 minutes;

Cooking time: 16 minutes;

Serve: 1

Ingredients:

- 1 large white onion
- 1 cup and ¼ flour
- 1 tsp of baking powder
- 1 beaten egg
- 1 cup milk
- ¾ cup breadcrumbs
- Seasoned salt or a mixture of paprika, salt, pepper
- 1 tbsp olive oil

Direction:

1. Spray some oil in the bottom of your fryer. If you have a temperature setting, set it to 370°F (190°C).

2. Cut the onion into rings. In a bowl, combine the flour, baking powder and add the seasoning salt (to taste).

3. Add the milk and mix well. Place the breadcrumbs on a plate.

4. Dip each slice in the dough, then in breadcrumbs and place them in the basket.

5. Add the tablespoon of oil. Cook for 8 minutes on one side, turn, and bake for another 8 minutes or until crispy.

Nutrition Value (Amount per Serving):

- Calories 580
- Fat 29g
- Carbohydrates 74g
- Sugars 19g
- Protein 8g
- Cholesterol 0mg

Potatoes + Smoked Diots Sausages

Preparation time: 10 minutes;

Cooking time: 40 minutes; Serve: 2

Ingredients:

- 800 g of potatoes
- 4 Savoy smoked diots sausages
- 2 chopped onions (or 2 shallots) +10 cherry tomatoes
- 1 sprig of thyme and rosemary+1 tbsp of parsley/chopped garlic
- 3 tbsp olive oil
- 5 ml of water + white wine
- 1 tbsp of Provencal herbs + salt 5 berries
- 4 tbsp mustard tomato

Direction:

1. Peel the potatoes and cut them into cubes.

2. In the bowl of the air fryer pour the olive oil and put the onions, with the potatoes, parsley, the herbs of Provence and the salt of 5 berries. Program the fryer manually 180°C to 15 minutes.

3. When the onions and potatoes start to brown, add the sausages, cherry tomatoes, thyme, rosemary, and white wine + water. Stir with a wooden spoon.

4. Close and continue cooking. Set to 180°C - 30 minutes.

5. With a knife, check the cooking of the potatoes; otherwise, increase the cooking time by a few more minutes.

6. Remove the dish from the fryer with the tongs.

7. Enjoy this dish with mustard tomato

Nutrition Value (Amount per Serving):

- Calories 482
- Fat 37g
- Carbohydrates 24g
- Sugars 1g
- Protein 25g
- Cholesterol 57mg

Poached Egg

Preparation time: 10-20 minutes;

Cooking time: 45-60 minutes; Serve: 6

Ingredients:

- 500g Eggplant
- 200g of celery
- ½ onion
- 90g olives
- 15g capers
- 40g pine nuts

- 300g ripe tomatoes
- 30g sugar
- 250g broth
- 60g vinegar
- 2 tsp olive oil
- Leave at discretion

Direction:

1. Cut the eggplant, celery and chop the onions.

2. Attach the mixing paddle to the tank.

3. Pour the oil and onion into the basket. Set the air fryer to 150°C and brown the onion for 4 minutes.

4. Add celery, eggplant, broth and cook for another 25 minutes.

5. Season with salt and pepper. Add the pine nuts, tomato pieces, capers and olives and cook for another 15 minutes.

6. Add the sugar and vinegar at the end and cook for another 15 minutes.

Nutrition Value (Amount per Serving):

- Calories 73
- Fat 4.95g
- Carbohydrates 0.38g

- Sugars 0.38g
- Protein 6.26g
- Cholesterol 210mg

Cheeseburger

Preparation time: 0-10 minutes;

Cooking time: 15-30 minutes;

Serve: 4

Ingredients:

- 4 chopped steak
- 4 hamburger buns
- Salad to taste
- 1 large tomato
- Mayonnaise, ketchup, or mustard to taste
- 4 slices of cheese
- Taste oil
- Salt to taste
- Pepper to taste

Direction:

1. Season the fillets and place them in the basket. Set the air fryer 180°C.

2. Cook the chopped steaks for 20 min. depending on their size turning 1-2 times during cooking.

3. Add a slice of cheese to each chopped steak and simmer for 1 minute.

4. Remove the chopped fillets from the air fryer wipe any liquid left in the basket with a cloth and heat the hamburger bread in the middle for about 1 minute.

5. Start composing the cheeseburger; spread the mayonnaise, ketchup or mustard on the bread, a salad leaf, the chopped steak with the cheese and finally the tomato slices; cover with the other slice of bread and serve.

Nutrition Value (Amount per Serving):

- Calories 343
- Fat 16.4g
- Carbohydrates 32g
- Sugars 6.7g
- Protein 17g
- Cholesterol 50mg

Strasbourg Sausage Croissants

Preparation time: 0-10 minutes,

Cooking time: 15-30 minutes;

Serve: 4

Ingredients:

- 1 round puff pastry roll
- 4 small sausages from Strasbourg
- Mustard to taste
- Poppy seeds to taste

Direction:

1. Unroll the puff pastry and define 16 triangles. Spread the mustard over the dough, place a small piece of Strasbourg sausage at the base of each triangle and roll until it reaches the tip. Press well to adhere.

2. Place the mini croissants in the pan, previously covered with parchment paper, well separated with the tip down; otherwise they may open during cooking.

3. Brush the mini croissants with water and sprinkle with poppy seeds.

4. Set the air fryer to 150°C. Simmer for 13 minutes and then turn the mini croissants half a turn.

5. Simmer for another 7 min.

Nutrition Value (Amount per Serving):

- Calories 570
- Fat 40g
- Carbohydrates 32g
- Sugar 3g
- Protein 20g
- Cholesterol 275mg

Sausage Fondues

Preparation time: 10 – 20 minutes;

Cooking time: 15 – 30 minutes;

Serve: 4

Ingredients:

- 3 large sausages from Strasbourg
- 200g of bread dough
- Mustard (optional) to taste

Direction:

1. To prepare the poached Strasbourg sausages, start by dividing the dough into 3 equal parts (or even 6 if you want to cut the Strasbourg sausages in half).

2. Spread the dough with a rolling pin so you can completely roll up the Strasbourg sausage. Spread the mustard and place the Strasbourg sausage in the center of the rectangle, rolled up completely.

3. Moisten the bread dough to make it easier to close. Remove the excess on the sides and with a small sharp knife form transverse lines on the surface of the dough.

4. Place the Strasbourg sausages in the basket covered with parchment paper.

5. Set the temperature to 180°C and simmer for 30 minutes.

Nutrition Value (Amount per serving):

- Calories 20
- Fat 0g
- Carbohydrates 4g
- Sugars 3g
- Protein 0.3g
- Cholesterol 0mg

Patty Mozzarella

Preparation time: 10 – 20 minutes;

Cooking time: 0 – 15 minutes;

Serve: 4

Ingredients:

- 12 slices of sandwich bread
- 3 eggs
- Flour to taste
- Breadcrumbs

- Leave to taste
- 12 anchovies (optional)
- 12 slices of mozzarella
- 6 slices of cooked ham

Direction:

1. Take the slices of bread and remove the crust. Cut 2 rectangles on each slice. Fill each rectangle with a slice of mozzarella, ½ slice of ham and 1 anchovy.

2. Then close everything with a slice of bread.

3. Put the eggs in a bowl, in another the flour and in a third the breadcrumbs.

4. Take the sandwiches and pass them on both sides first in the flour, then in the egg and finally in the breadcrumbs, welding well to prevent the mozzarella from coming out during cooking.

5. If you prefer, you can iron the sandwiches in the egg and in the breadcrumbs.

6. Grease the basket and preheat it for 1 minute at 150^{0}C.

7. Add mozzarella and continue cooking for 8 minutes, turning halfway through cooking.

Nutrition Value (Amount per Serving):

- Calories 290
- Fat 15 g
- Carbohydrates 24 g

- Sugars 2g
- Protein 11 g
- Cholesterol 35 mg

Strasbourg Potatoes and Sausages with Curry

Preparation time: 10-20 minutes;

Cooking time: 15-30 minutes;

Serve: 6

Ingredients:

- 750 g of fresh potatoes
- 3 Strasbourg sausages
- 2 small spoons of curry
- Salt to taste

Direction:

1. Peel the potatoes and cut them into cubes of approximately 1 cm per side. Put the Perl apples to soak in water, drain them and dry them well with a paper towel.

2. After spraying the air fryer with cooking spray, pour potatoes, salt.

3. Set the temperature to 150°C and simmer the potatoes for 20 minutes.

4. Add the Strasbourg sausages cut into small pieces, curry, and cook for another 10 minutes.

Nutrition Value (Amount per Serving):

- Calories 418.5
- Fat 17.6 g
- Carbohydrate 42.1 g
- Sugars 2.1 g
- Protein 18.0 g
- Cholesterol   44.5 mg

Treviso Chicory Sauce

Preparation time: 10-20 minutes,

Cooking time: 15-30 minutes;

Serve: 6

Ingredients:

- 400g of Treviso chicory
- 1 leek
- ½ red wine
- Salt to taste

Direction:

1. Chop the leek and place it in the basket previously greased.

2. Cook for 3 minutes at 160^{0}C.

3. Add the previously cleaned chicory cut into large pieces, pour the red wine and salt. Cook for an added 12 minutes. Ideal for filling pancakes, lasagna, savory cakes, etc.

Nutrition Value (Amount per Serving):

- Calories 20
- Fat 0g
- Carbohydrates 4g
- Protein 1g

Sausages and Peppers

Preparation time: 0-10 minutes,

Cooking time: 15-30 minutes;

Serve: 4

Ingredients:

- 4 sausages
- 2 peppers

Direction:

1. Pour the sausages and peppers cut into pieces in the basket.

2. Cook for 20 minutes at 150°C.

Nutrition Value (Amount per Serving):

- Calories 339
- Fat 27g
- Carbohydrates 5.8g
- Sugars 3g
- Protein 17g
- Cholesterol 84mg

Brioche Sausage

Preparation time: 0 – 10 minutes

Cooking time: 0 – 15 minutes; Serve: 4

Ingredients:

- 2 sausages
- 2 bread sticks

Direction:

1. Remove the crumb from the bread to obtain a hollow cylinder (make pieces of about 10 cm, otherwise it will be difficult to work them).

2. Place the sausage in half the bread, then make slices about 2 cm thick.

3. Place the slices at the bottom of the basket (6 per batch).

4. Set the temperature to 160°C.

5. Cook for 10 minutes, turning the crispy rolls on themselves after 5/6 minutes.

6. Serve while it is still hot.

Nutrition Value (Amount per Serving):

- Calories 546
- Carbohydrates 37g
- Fat 35g
- Sugars 6g
- Protein 20g
- Cholesterol 0mg

Stuffed Potato Recipe

Preparation time: 20 minutes;

Cooking time: 14 minutes; Serve: 4

Ingredients:

- 150g Potatoes
- Ham
- Cheese
- Olive oil
- Salt
- Garlic powder

Direction:

1. Cut your potato into strips but don't get to the end.

2. Paint your potato with a little oil so it doesn't burn.

3. Add salt and pepper.

4. Put the potato 35 minutes at 180°C without preheating.

5. Fill each cut with ham and cheese to taste.

6. Put the potato back 10 minutes more at 180°C.

Nutrition Value (Amount per Serving):

- Calories 379.6
- Fat 17.6 g
- Carbohydrate 40.7 g
- Sugars 4.0 g
- Protein   14.0 g
- Cholesterol 25.4 mg

Chapter 2

Snacks and Appetizers

Corn with Bacon

Preparation time: 0-10;

Cooking time: 15-30; Serve: 4

Ingredients:

- 4 Precooked corn on the cob
- 8 Sliced Bacon

Direction:

1. Roll up the corn cobs with 2 slices of bacon each.

2. Place the corn cobs inside, close the lid.

3. Set the air fryer to 180^{0}C and Cook the corn on the cob for 15 minutes.

Nutrition Value (Amount per Serving):

- Calories 90
- Sugars0g
- Fat 7g
- Protein5g
- Carbohydrate 0g
- Cholesterol 15mg

Brussels Sprouts With Bacon

Preparation time: 0-10 minutes;

Cooking time: 15-30 minutes; Serve: 6

Ingredients:

- 350g Brussels sprouts
- 100g of bacon
- 20g butter

Direction:

1. Clean the Brussels sprouts by removing the outer leaves and the base. Steam for about 20 min.

2. Place the bacon and butter in the bowl. Set the air fryer to 150°C and brown for 5 min.

3. Add the puff pastry, salt, and simmer for 10 min. additional, depending on the size of the cabbage.

Nutrition Value (Amount per Serving):

- Calories 287
- Fat 18g
- Carbohydrates 16g
- Sugars 3.8g
- Protein 18g
- Cholesterol 36m

Frozen Croissants

Cooking time: 30-45 minutes;

Serve: 4

Ingredients:

- 4 pieces of frozen croissants

Direction:

1. Preheat the air fryer at 150°C for 5 minutes.

2. Place the croissants in the basket.

3. Cook everything for 35 minutes. Turn it to 180°C (using parchment paper) after about 25 min.

Nutrition Value (Amount per Serving):

- Calories 201

- Carbohydrates 19g

- Fat 11g

- Sugars 2g

- Protein 4g

- Cholesterol 0mg

Frozen Potato Croquettes

Cooking time: 15-30 minutes;
Serve: 6

Ingredients:

- 750 g frozen potato croquette
- Fine salt to taste

Direction:

1. Preheat the air fryer at 180°C for 5 minutes.

2. Pour the potatoes in the basket. Cook everything for 24 minutes.

3. Salt and serve.

Nutrition Value (Amount per Serving):

- Calories 54
- Sugars 0g
- Carbohydrates 6g
- Protein 0.5g
- Fat 2g
- Cholesterol 0mg

Endives with Ham

Preparation time: 20-30 minutes;

Cooking time: 15-30 minutes; Serve: 6

Ingredients:

- 6 endives
- 500 ml of bechamel
- 6 slices of cooked ham
- 100g grated cheese

Direction:

1. Clean the Belgian chicory and steam for 15 min. Let them cool.

2. Separately, prepare ½ liter of bechamel and, as soon as it is ready, pour half the grated cheese and mix.

3. Pour the béchamel sauce in the bottom of the tank, roll each endive with a slice of ham, and place them too. Cover everything with the remaining bechamel and sprinkle with grated cheese.

4. Set the temperature to 150°C and cook for 15 minutes depending on the degree of gold desired.

Nutrition Value (Amount per Serving):

- Calories 106
- Fat 5.77 g
- Carbohydrates 5.69 g
- Sugars 2.67 g
- Proteins 6.2 g
- Cholesterol 0mg

4 Cheese Puffs

Preparation time: 10-20 minutes;

Cooking time: 15-30 minutes; Serve: 4

Ingredients:

- 1 rectangular puff pastry
- 250 g cheese mix
- Poppy seeds

Direction:

1. Unroll the puff pastry roll and cut it into 4 equal parts. Fill each rectangle with the cheeses cut into pieces and close the dough, welding the edges so that it does not open during cooking. This is the area of the puff pastry with water and sprinkle with poppy seeds.

2. Place 2 or 4 puff pastry (depending on its size) on the baking paper inside the basket.

3. Set the temperature to 150^0C.

4. Cook for 20 minutes or until desired browning is achieved.

Nutrition Value (Amount per Serving):

- Calories 140
- Fat 6g
- Carbohydrates 19g
- Sugars 1g
- Protein 2g
- Cholesterol 160mg

Treviso Chicory Puff Pastry

Preparation time: 0-10 minutes,

Cooking time: 15-30 minutes; Serve: 4

Ingredients:

- 1 stalk of Treviso chicory
- 1 roll of puff pastry
- Grated cheese to taste
- Salt to taste
- 1 tsp olive oil

Direction:

1. Cut the chicory of Treviso in 4 parts, wash carefully and dry.

2. Unwind the puff pastry on a work surface and cut it into small wide strips of approximately 1 cm. Roll the chicory in a spiral with the puff pastry, and more particularly outside, which would otherwise dry during cooking.

3. Cover the bottom of the basket with parchment paper. Place the chicory inside, sprinkle with grated cheese and salt.

4. Set the temperature to 180°C.

5. Simmer for 18 minutes; before serving, pour a drizzle of olive oil in each puff pastry.

Nutrition Value (Amount per Serving):

- Calories 170
- Carbohydrates 11g
- Fat 13g
- Sugars 0g
- Protein 2g
- Cholesterol 35 mg

Chocolate Muffins

Preparation time: 10-20 minutes;

Cooking time: 15-30 minutes; Serve: 10

Ingredients:

- 300g of flour 00:
- 300g of sugar
- 150g of butter
- 70g bitter cocoa powder
- 6g baking powder
- 180 ml of whole fresh milk
- 1g of salt
- Eggs
- 2g of baking soda
- 100g dark chocolate
- 1 vanilla pod

Direction:

1. In a food processor, beat the butter of the ointment with the sugar and then combine the seeds of a vanilla bean.

2. When the mixture is clear and foamy enough, add the eggs at room temperature, one at a time. Work all the ingredients for a few minutes and then add the flour, bitter cocoa, yeast, baking soda and salt (all sifted), alternating with milk at room temperature.

3. Finally, combine the dark chocolate chips

4. Fill the molds with the mixture and place them inside the air fryer (7 to 8 lots) previously preheated at 180°C.

5. Cook for about 25 minutes. In the end let cool. You can, at discretion, sprinkle with icing sugar.

Nutrition Value (Amount per Serving):

- Calories
- Fat 38g
- Carbohydrates 79.2g
- Sugars 47.9g
- Protein 9.9g
- Cholesterol 125mg

Pasticciata Pasta

Preparation time: 20 – 30 minutes,

Cooking time: 0 – 15 minutes; Serve: 6

Ingredients:

- 300g of macaroni
- 500 ml of bechamel
- 350 g minced meat
- 100 g cooked ham
- 30 g grated cheese

Direction:

1. Prepare the béchamel and cook the macaroni, making sure that they are firm when biting, once cooked, season them with separately cooked ground beef and ¾ of bechamel.

2. Pour the béchamel in the bowl, add half of the seasoned dough, cut the ham into small pieces, and pour the remaining dough. Sprinkle with grated cheese.

3. Set the air fryer to 150°C cook for about 10 min. or until the desired gold is obtained.

Nutrition Value (Amount per Serving):

- Calories 576
- Carbohydrates 58g
- Fat 25g
- Sugars 0g
- Protein 26g
- Cholesterol 0mg

Shepherd's Pie

Preparation time: 10-20 minutes;

Cooking time: more than 60 minutes; Serve: 8

Ingredients:

- 700 g of minced meat
- 350 g of tomato coulis
- 1 carrot
- 1 celery stalk
- 1 shallot
- Salt to taste
- Black pepper to taste

- 300 g of frozen peas

Ingredients for the cover:

- 1 kg of potatoes
- 200 g of milk
- 80 g butter
- 2 egg yolks
- Nutmeg to taste

Direction:

1. Divide the carrots, celery and chopped onions and then spray the basket. Brown for 5 minutes at 160°C.

2. Add the minced meat and cook for 5 minutes (during this time, using a wooden spoon, possibly separate the pieces of meat that can form). Add the tomato, salt and pepper coulis and cook for 45 minutes, mixing 3 to 4 times during cooking.

3. Finally, add the frozen peas and cook for another 10 to 15 minutes until the peas are tender.

4. Remove the blade (be careful that it is hot!) And spread the sauce with a tablespoon. Prepare the mash (according to the indicated doses) and then, using a bag of fluted puff pastry, make a lot of mash in the meat.

5. Brown everything for another 10 to 15 minutes. Let stand for 10 minutes before serving.

Nutrition Value (Amount per Serving):

- Calories 272
- Fat 8.21g
- Carbohydrate 34.46g

- Sugars 3.26g
- Protein 15.55g
- Cholesterol 34mg

Tomino With Speck

Preparation time: 0 – 10 minutes,

Cooking time: 0 – 15 minutes; Serve: 4

Ingredients:

- 4 tominos
- 8 speck slices

Direction:

1. Wrap the tominos with two slices of speck each, crossing them.

2. Cook the tominos for 5 minutes at 150^{0}C.

3. Turn them on and cook for another 3 minutes.

Nutrition Value (Amount per Serving):

- Calories 361
- Carbohydrates 2g
- Fat 30g
- Sugars 0g
- Protein 20g
- Cholesterol 0mg

Chickpeas for Snack

Preparation time: 10 minutes;

Cooking time: 25 minutes; Serve: 6

Ingredients:

- 1 can (15 ounces) unsalted chickpeas, washed and drained
- Cooking spray oil
- ½ tsp garlic powder
- ½ tsp thyme powder
- ½ tsp coarsely ground black pepper
- 1/8 tsp red pepper or to taste

Direction:

1. Pour the chickpeas in a medium bowl. Dry them with a paper towel. Spray the chickpeas with the cooking spray oil for 2 seconds and stir to cover all the chickpeas. Pour them into the fryer basket.

2. In a small bowl, mix the garlic powder, the thyme powder, the pepper, and the red pepper; Set the bowl aside.

3. Adjust the temperature to 375°F and fry in air for 10 to 15 minutes or until the chickpeas are golden and crispy. Shake the fryer basket every 5 minutes. Halfway through the cooking time, sprinkle the chickpeas with cooking spray oil for 1 second.

4. Place the hot chickpeas in a bowl. Mix them with the seasoning immediately. Serve them warm or let the crispy chickpeas cool and dry completely, then store them in an airtight container at room temperature.

Nutrition Value (Amount per Serving):

- Calories 80
- Fat 1.5 g
- Carbohydrates 13 g
- Fiber 4g
- Sugar 2g
- Protein 4g

Crispy Cauliflower Snacks

Preparation time: 5 minutes;

Cooking time: 10 minutes; Serve: 4

Ingredients:

- 3 cups small cauliflower florets
- 1 tbsp olive oil
- ¼ tsp garlic powder
- 3 tbsp whole grain breadcrumbs
- 2 tbsp wing sauce

Direction:

1. In a medium bowl, mix the cauliflower florets with olive oil, garlic powder and breadcrumbs.

2. Place the cauliflower in the fryer basket. Set the temperature to 400°F and fry in air for 3 to 4 minutes. Shake the basket. Fry in air for 2 to 4 minutes or until the cauliflower is tender and the edges are crispy.

3. Transfer the cauliflower to a bowl and mix with the wing sauce. Serve warm.

Nutrition Value (Amount per Serving):

- Calories 70
- Fat 4g
- Carbohydrates 9g
- Fiber 2g
- Sugars 3g
- Protein 4g

Profiteroles

Preparation time: 25 minutes;

Cooking time 25 minutes; Serve: 10

Ingredients:

- 100 g flour

- 100 g of butter

- 200 g of water

- 200 g large eggs

- ¼ tsp of salt

Filling:

- 1 package vanilla pudding instant mix

- 240 ml milk

- 1 cup thick cream

Direction:

1. Mix the contents of the instant vanilla pudding mixture with 240 ml of cold milk in a bowl. Beat these ingredients with the double accessory to mix for 2 minutes. Cover and refrigerate to sit for at least 5 minutes.

2. Beat the thick cream with the whisk or the double mixing accessory. Add the whipped cream to the pudding mixture. Cover and refrigerate.

3. In a large pot, place water and butter until they boil. Over medium heat, stir so that it boils. Over medium heat, add flour and salt. Stir vigorously until the dough forms a ball in the center of the pan. Transfer the dough to a large mixing bowl and let stand for 5 minutes. With the double accessory to mix, beat the eggs one by one and mix well. Pour per tablespoon, 5 cm/2 apart, on an ungreased baking sheet.

4. Bake for 25 minutes at 218°C (425°F) until it reaches a golden-brown hue. The centers must be dry.

5. When the profiteroles are cold, you can split them and fill them with the pudding mix or use a pastry bag to introduce the pudding into the profiteroles.

Nutrition Value (Amount per Serving):

- Calories 170

- Fat 13g

- Carbohydrates 11g

- Fiber 0g

- Sugars 6g

- Protein 2g

Feta Cheese Triangles

Preparation time: 20 minutes;

Cooking time: 9 minutes; Serve: 3

Ingredients:

- 1 egg yolk
- 100 g feta cheese
- 2 tbsp chopped parsley
- 1 chive in thin rings
- Freshly ground black pepper
- 5 sheets of frozen phyllo dough

Direction:

1. Beat the egg yolk in a bowl and mix it with feta cheese, parsley, and chives; Season with pepper to taste.

2. Cut each sheet of phyllo dough into three strips.

3. Take a teaspoon full of the feta mixture and place it on the inside of a strip of pasta.

4. Fold the tip of the dough over the filling to form a triangle, and then fold the zigzag tip until the filling is wrapped in a dough triangle.

5. Fill the other strips of pasta with feta in the same way. Preheat the air fryer to 200°C. Spread the triangles with a little oil and place five of them in the basket. Insert the basket in the air fryer and set the timer to 3 minutes.

6. Bake the feta triangles until golden brown. Bake the rest of the triangles in the same way. Serve the triangles on a tray.

Nutrition Value (Amount per Serving):

- Calories 89
- Fat 3.6g
- Carbohydrates 11.7g
- Sugar 0.3g
- Protein 3g

Boudin meat

Preparation time: 10 minutes;

Cooking time: 25 minutes; Serve: 4

Ingredients:

- 400 g lean minced beef
- 1 lightly beaten egg
- 3 tbsp breadcrumbs
- 50 g of salami or chorizo well chopped
- 1 small onion, well chopped
- 1 tbsp fresh thyme
- Freshly ground pepper
- 2 mushrooms in thick slices
- 1 tbsp olive oil

Direction:

1. Preheat the air fryer to 200°C.

2. Mix the minced meat in a bowl with the egg, breadcrumbs, salami, onion, thyme, 1 teaspoon of salt and a generous amount of pepper. Knead it all right.

3. Pass the minced meat to the tray or platter and smooth the top. Place the mushrooms by pressing a little and cover the top with olive oil.

4. Place the tray or dish in the basket and insert it into the air fryer. Set the timer to 25 minutes and roast the meat pudding until it has a nice toasted color and is well done.

5. Let the pudding stand at least 10 minutes before serving. Then cut it into wedges. It is delicious with chips and salad.

Nutrition Value (Amount per Serving):

- Calories 200
- Carbohydrates 10g
- Fat 15g
- Sugars 0g
- Protein 5g
- Cholesterol 0mg

Chapter 3
Seafood and Fish recipes

Grilled Sardines

Preparation time: 5 minutes;

Cooking time: 21 minutes; Serve: 2

Ingredients:

- 5 sardines
- Herbs of Provence

Direction:

1. Preheat the air fryer to 160°C.

2. Spray the basket and place your sardines in the basket of your fryer.

3. Set the timer for 14 minutes. After 7 minutes, remember to turn the sardines so that they are roasted on both sides.

Nutrition Value (Amount per Serving):

- Calories 189g
- Sugars 0g
- Fat 10g
- Protein 22g
- Carbohydrates 0g
- Cholesterol 128mg

Spicy Squids Healthy

Preparation time: 10 minutes;

Cooking time: About fifteen minutes; Serve: 2

Ingredients:

- 300 g of squid slices, about 20
- ½ cup milk or vegetable drink (me, almond)
- 2 cloves garlic, pressed
- 2 pinches of salt
- Curry lining
- 4g breadcrumbs
- 4g cornmeal (semolina no. 400, texture close to polenta)
- 4 g freshly grated Parmesan cheese
- ¼ tsp Curry powder Madras
- ¼ tsp turmeric
- 1/8 tsp of garam masala
- Salt and pepper to taste
- 2 tbsp olive oil

Direction:

1. Rinse the squids in cold water, put them in a bowl and cover them with milk. Add salt and garlic and mix well. Cover the bowl and let it rest in the fridge for 1 hour, then let it cool 30 minutes before cooking.

2. Clean the squid with paper towels without insisting. In a bowl, combine the ingredients of the coating, except the oil. Roll the squid one by one in the dry pie to cover them well. Place them on a plate and lightly apply a little oil on each washer.

3. Heat the air fryer to 400°F. As soon as it is cooked, place the squid in the fryer basket. Cook for 5 minutes, remove the basket, and shake well. Repeat these operations two or three times more, always counting 5 minutes of cooking and stirring the basket. I left yesterday 15 minutes in total; the squid would have preferred 5 more.

4. Accompanied here of fried pak-choy, rice and a small sauce made with mayonnaise and yogurt.

Nutrition Value (Amount per Serving):

- Calories 264
- Carbohydrates 18g
- Fat 9g

- Protein 20g
- Sugars 11g
- Cholesterol 0mg

Frog Thighs

Preparation time: 15 minutes;

Cooking time: 20 minutes; Serve: 2

Ingredients:

- 1 454 g bag of frog legs, thawed and dried
- 3 tsp flour
- 1 beaten egg
- 1 tbsp of neutral oil, such as grape seed
- Clementine marinade
- The juice of 2 Clementine
- ½ orange zest
- 2 tbsp neutral oil
- 1 tsp rice vinegar
- 1 tsp tamari or soy sauce, reduced in salt
- 1 tsp fish sauce
- Crunchy coating
- ½ cup panko
- ½ orange zest
- 3 tsp Parmesan
- 2 tbsp unsweetened coconut flakes

Direction:

1. On a plate that can contain frog legs, prepare the marinade by combining all the ingredients. Using a fork for fondue, pierce the skin of the thighs in several places before macerating in the refrigerator, the dish covered with a plastic wrap, between 6 and 8 hours or overnight, and not just 2 hours.

2. 30 minutes before cooking, remove the thighs from the refrigerator. Prepare three deep plates, one with the flour, one second with the beaten egg, the last with the crunchy layer.

3. Start by flouring a thigh, soak it in the beaten egg and then roll it in the crunchy layer before placing it on a plate. Do the same with the other thighs. With a pastry brush, finish with a light layer of oil on each of its two sides.

4. Heat the air fryer to 400°F, place all thighs in the basket and cook for 5 minutes. Remove the basket, shake it, and replace it for another 3 minutes, remove it and shake it, then another 2 minutes.

5. Served here with grilled bok-choy mini petals and basmati rice.

Nutrition Value (Amount per Serving):

- Calories 75
- Carbohydrates 0g
- Fat 0.3g

- Protein 16.4g
- Sugars 0g
- Cholesterol 50mg

Exquisite Shrimp

Preparation time: 10 minutes;

Cooking time: 7 minutes; Serve: 2

Ingredients:

- 20 raw shrimp 31-40, thawed and well dried
- 3 tsp flour
- 1 egg
- 2 tbsp of neutral oil, grapeseed or other
- Crunchy coating
- 2/3 cup panko (uncooked Japanese breadcrumbs)
- 3 tsp freshly grated Parmesan cheese
- 2 tbsp unsweetened coconut flakes
- ½ tsp turmeric
- ½ tsp curry powder

Direction:

1. In a small bowl, put the flour. In another small bowl, beat the egg. In a third larger bowl, for example, a deep dish, combine the ingredients for the crispy coating and mix well.

2. Press a shrimp in the flour on both sides, soak it in the egg, then press it again on both sides, this time in the crunchy layer.

3. Place on a plate and do the same with all shrimp to cook.

4. With a brush, lightly brush all shrimp with oil, turn them over and brush the other side.

5. Place them one by one in the basket of the preheated air fryer at 180ºC and replace them in the appliance. Wait 7 minutes, remove the basket, and place it on a heat resistant surface. Using a pair of silicone tweezers, remove the shrimp and serve.

Nutrition Value (Amount per Serving):

- Calories 6
- Fat 0.1g
- Carbohydrate 0.05g
- Protein 1.22g
- Sugars 0g
- Cholesterol 9mg

Shrimp Fritters

Preparation time: about 15 minutes;

Cooking time: 10 to 15 minutes; Serve: 4

Ingredients:

- 100g of flour
- 50g of cornstarch
- 50 ml of milk (to adapt to not have a paste too liquid)
- 1 sachet of baking powder
- 2 eggs
- 1 tbsp peanut or sunflower oil
- Salt and pepper
- Spices at your convenience
- 20 to 25 shrimp

Direction:

1. In a bowl, mix the flour, cornstarch, and baking powder.

2. Create a well in the middle and pour the eggs you have already beaten. Add salt, pepper, and spices if you choose to add them.

3. Mix everything while beating the dough so that it is very uniform and then let stand for 1:30.

4. Peel your shrimp while keeping your tail.

5. Once the dough is rested, dip each shrimp in it to cover it perfectly.

6. Cook:

7. Place the donuts in the fryer without oil for 10 to 15 minutes at 150°C. Check the cooking and take them out as soon as the dough is golden brown.

Nutrition Value (Amount per Serving):

- Calories 137
- Carbohydrates 8g
- Fat 9g
- Protein 4g
- Sugars 1g
- Cholesterol 32mg

Cod Meatballs with Sauce

Preparation time: 10 – 20;

Cooking time: 15 - 30, 6 people.

Ingredients:

- 350g cod heart
- 50g breadcrumbs
- 1 bunch of parsley
- Thyme to taste
- 1 egg
- 1 clove garlic
- 40g grated cheese
- Salt, pepper, flour to taste
- Tartar sauce to taste

Direction:

1. To prepare the meatballs, start by mixing the breadcrumbs in a food processor. Then add the fish, thyme, chopped parsley, garlic, grated cheese, eggs and add (at discretion) salt and pepper.

2. Collect the preparation and form balls by hand. Flour each dough ball and roll them into a skewer (3 balls of dough per skewer).

3. Place the skewers in the basket of the air fryer. Close to cook at 180°C for 10 minutes by turning the skewers while cooking.

4. Cook for an additional 10 minutes.

5. Serve with tartar sauce.

Nutrition Value (Amount per Serving):

- Calories 40
- Fat 2.9 g
- Carbohydrates 0.9 g
- Sugars 0.5 g
- Protein 2.7 g
- Cholesterol 15 mg

Cod with Cherry Tomatoes and Green Olives

Preparation time: 10-20;

Cooking time: 30-45; Serve: 4

Ingredients:

- 400g cod
- 250 g cherry tomatoes
- 350 g of potatoes in pieces
- 100 g of green olives
- Salt to taste
- 1 clove garlic
- 1 tsp olive oil

Direction:

1. Put the cod in the center. Add small tomatoes, cut in half, olives, chopped potatoes, garlic clove, oil, and salt.

2. Set the air fryer to 150°C and Cook everything for 25 min. and then mix the vegetables with a wooden spoon to homogenize the cooking.

3. Cook for an additional 15 minutes; the cooking time varies according to the size at which you will cut the potatoes

Nutrition Value (Amount per Serving):

- Calories 226.0
- Fat 2.7 g
- Carbohydrate 6.9 g
- Sugars 2.4 g
- Protein   40.6 g
- Cholesterol 99.1 mg

Breaded Cod

Preparation time: 10-20;

Cooking time: 15-30; Serve: 4

Ingredient:

- 400g cod
- 2 eggs
- Flour at discretion
- Unlimited Breadcrumbs

- Parsley at discretion
- Chives at discretion
- Leave at discretion
- 1 tsp olive oil

Direction:

1. Clean the cod and cut it into pieces according to the desired size.

2. Beat the eggs on a first plate with a pinch of salt; in a second dish put the flour and in a third mix the breadcrumbs, parsley, and chives.

3. Pour the oil into the basket of the air fryer and distribute it throughout the surface.

4. Pass each slice of cod first in the flour, then in the beaten egg and finally in the breadcrumbs; arrange the slices in the tank.

5. Set the air fryer to 150°C and cook for 10 minutes.

6. Turn the fish over and cook for another 6 minutes. Ideal accompanied by a sauce (yogurt, mayonnaise, etc.)

Nutrition Value (Amount per Serving):

- Calories 156
- Fat 2.3g
- Carbohydrates 16.4g

- Sugars 1.9g
- Protein 16.6g
- Cholesterol 0mg

Baked Scallops with Cheese

Preparation time: 10 – 20;

Cooking time: 15 – 30; Serve: 4

Ingredients:

- 4 scallops
- 40 g of breadcrumbs: 40 g
- 25 g grated cheese
- 1 tbsp parsley
- 1 tsp oil
- Salt to taste
- 1 clove of garlic (optional)

Direction:

1. Combine breadcrumbs, parsley, cheese, garlic, and salt in a bowl.

2. Place the scallops in the tank and cover them with the previously made filling, covered with a drizzle of olive oil.

3. Preheat the air fryer to 150^{0}C for 5 minutes.

4. Cook for 17 min. or until the desired cooking is obtained; before serving, add a drizzle of olive oil.

Nutrition Value (Amount per Serving):

- Calories 218.2
- Fat 14.0 g
- Carbohydrate 12.5 g
- Sugars 1.3 g
- Protein   10.0 g
- Cholesterol 35.0 mg

Zucchini with Tuna

Preparation time: 10 – 20;

Cooking time: 15 – 30; Serve: 2

Ingredients:

- 4 medium zucchini
- 120g of tuna in oil (canned) drained
- 30g grated cheese
- 1 tsp pine nuts
- Salt, pepper to taste

Direction:

1. Cut the zucchini in half lengthwise and empty it with a small spoon (set aside the pulp that will be used for filling); place them in the basket.

2. In a food processor, put the zucchini pulp, drained tuna, pine nuts and grated cheese. Mix everything until you get a homogeneous and dense mixture.

3. Fill the zucchini. Set the air fryer to 180°C.

4. Simmer for 20 min. depending on the size of the zucchini. Let cool before serving

Nutrition Value (Amount per Serving):

- Calories 389
- Carbohydrates 10g
- Fat 29g
- Sugars 5g
- Protein 23g
- Cholesterol 40mg

Caramelized Salmon Fillet

Preparation time: 0-10;

Cooking time: 15-30; Serve: 4

Ingredients:

- 2 salmon fillets
- 60g cane sugar
- 4 tbsp soy sauce

- 50g sesame seeds
- Unlimited Ginger

Direction:

1. Preheat the air fryer at 180°C for 5 minutes.

2. Put the sugar and soy sauce in the basket.

3. Cook everything for 5 minutes.

4. In the meantime, wash the fish well, pass it through sesame to cover it completely and place it inside the tank and add the fresh ginger.

5. Cook for 12 minutes.

6. Turn the fish over and finish cooking for another 8 minutes.

Nutrition Value (Amount per Serving):

- Calories 569
- Fat 14.9 g
- Carbohydrates 40 g

- Sugars 27.6 g
- Protein 66.9 g
- Cholesterol 165.3 mg

Breaded Swordfish

Preparation time: 10-20;

Cooking time: 15-30; Serve:

Ingredients:

- 500g swordfish ranches:
- Breadcrumbs to taste
- 1 tsp peanut oil
- 1 tsp olive oil
- ½ lemon juice:
- Salt to taste
- Pepper to taste
- Parsley to taste

Direction:

1. Clean and rinse the fish; grease each slice and pass it in lightly salted breadcrumbs to cover it completely.

2. Preheat the air fryer at 160°C for 5 minutes.

3. Place the breaded fish in the basket. Cook the fish for 10 minutes.

4. Turn the fish over and cook for another 8 minutes.

5. Meanwhile, prepare the marinade with olive oil, lemon juice, salt, pepper and chopped parsley; Mix with a fork.

6. Once ready, place the fish slices on the plate and pour 1 to 2 tablespoons of marinade.

Nutrition Value (Amount per Serving):

- Calories 67
- Fat 3.79g
- Carbohydrates 2.23g
- Sugars 0.22g
- Protein 5.67g
- Cholesterol 16mg

Fish and French Fries

Preparation time: 10-20;

Cooking time: 30-45; Serve: 2

Ingredients:

- 400g cod fillets
- 2 eggs
- Breadcrumbs
- Leave to taste
- Flour to taste
- 1 tsp peanut oil
- 500g of frozen French fries

Direction:

1. Clean the fish and cut it into rectangles of about 8 to 10 cm by 4 cm. Pass each slice first in the flour, then in the egg (beaten with salt) and finally in the breadcrumbs; in the end, pass them again in the egg and in the breadcrumbs to obtain a double pie.

2. Grease the basket and preheat the air fryer at 160°C for 5 minutes.

3. Cook the fish for 10 minutes.

4. Turn the fish over and cook for another 5 minutes.

5. At the end, clean the tank and insert the mixing paddle inside and then the potatoes.

6. Cook the French fries for 20 minutes or according to the desired degree of cooking.

7. At the end of cooking, remove the preparation paddle, place the previously cooked fish in the fries and reheat it for approximately 2 to 3 minutes.

Nutrition Value (Amount per Serving):

- Calories 79
- Fat 3g
- Carbohydrates 12.2g
- Sugars 0g
- Protein 0.8g
- Cholesterol 167mg

Deep Fried Prawns

Preparation time: 10 – 20;

Cooking time: 0 – 15; Serve: 6

Ingredients:

- 12 prawns
- 2 eggs
- Flour to taste
- Breadcrumbs
- 1 tsp oil

Direction:

1. Remove the head of the prawns and shell carefully.

2. Pass the prawns first in the flour, then in the beaten egg and then in the breadcrumbs.

3. Preheat the air fryer for 1 minute at 150°C.

4. Add the prawns and cook for 4 minutes. If the prawns are large, it will be necessary to cook 6 at a time.

5. Turn the prawns and cook for another 4 minutes.

6. They should be served with a yogurt or mayonnaise sauce.

Nutrition Value (Amount per Serving):

- Calories 2385.1
- Fat 23
- Carbohydrates 52.3g
- Sugar 0.1g
- Protein 21.4g

Mussels with Pepper

Preparation time: 10 - 20,

Cooking time: 0 – 15; Serve: 6

Ingredients:

- 700g mussels
- 1 clove garlic
- 1 tsp oil
- Pepper to taste
- Parsley Taste

Direction:

1. Clean and scrape the mold cover and remove the byssus (the "beard" that comes out of the mold).

2. Pour the oil, clean the mussels and the crushed garlic in the basket. Set the temperature to 200°C and simmer for 12 minutes. Towards the end of cooking, add black pepper and chopped parsley.

3. Finally, distribute the mussel juice well at the bottom of the basket, stirring the basket.

Nutrition Value (Amount per Serving):

- Calories 150
- Carbohydrates 2g
- Fat 8g
- Sugars 0g
- Protein 15g
- Cholesterol 0mg

Scallops in Butter with Leaves

Preparation time: 10 - 20,

Cooking time: 15 - 30, 4 people, Calories: 127

Ingredients:

- 400g scallops
- 20g butter
- 1 clove garlic
- Leafs to taste
- Pepper to taste
- Parsley to taste
- ½ lemon juice

Direction:

1. Clean the scallops and dry them on a paper towel.

2. Place the butter and chopped garlic inside the basket. Set the temperature to 150^0C.

3. Melt the butter for 2 to 3 minutes.

4. Add the scallops, salt, pepper and cook for 8 minutes.

5. Then add the lemon juice, parsley, and finish cooking for another 3 to 4 minutes.

6. Very good as an appetizer to serve inside the shells.

Nutrition Value (Amount per Serving):

- Calories 315.6
- Fat 13.8 g
- Carbohydrate 11.0 g
- Sugars 0.1 g
- Protein   38.7 g
- Cholesterol 114.8 mg

Scallops in Butter

Preparation time: 10 - 20,

Cooking time: 15 - 30, 4 people, Calories: 127

Ingredients:

- 400 g Scallops
- 20 g butter
- 1 clove garlic
- Salt to taste

- Pepper to taste
- Parsley to taste
- ½ lemon juice

Direction:

1. Remove the scallops by deciphering them, clean them and put them to dry on a paper towel.

2. Heat the air fryer at 150°C for 5 minutes.

3. Melt the butter for 2 to 3 minutes.

4. Add the scallops, salt, pepper and cook for 8 minutes.

5. Then add the lemon juice, parsley, and finish cooking for another 3 to 4 minutes.

6. Very good as an appetizer to serve inside the shells.

Nutrition Value (Amount per Serving):

- Calories 315.6
- Fat 13.8 g
- Carbohydrate 11.0 g

- Sugars 0.1 g
- Protein   38.7 g
- Cholesterol 114.8 mg

Monkfish with Olives and Capers

Preparation time: 10 – 20;

Cooking time: 30 – 45; Serve: 4

Ingredients:

- 1 monkfish
- 10 cherry tomatoes
- 50 g cailletier olives
- 5 capers

Direction:

1. Spread aluminum foil inside the basket and place the monkfish clean and skinless.

2. Add chopped tomatoes, olives, capers, oil, and salt.

3. Set the temperature to 160°C.

4. Cook the monkfish for about 40 minutes (depending on the size of the fish).

Nutrition Value (Amount per Serving):

- Calories 404
- Fat 29g
- Carbohydrates 36g
- Sugars 7g
- Protein 24g
- Cholesterol 36mg

Shrimp, Zucchini and Cherry Tomato Sauce

Preparation time: 0-10,

Cooking time: 15-30; Serve: 4

Ingredients:

- 2 zucchinis
- 300 shrimp
- 7 cherry tomatoes
- Pepper to taste
- Salt to taste
- 1 clove garlic

Direction:

1. Pour the oil, add the garlic clove and diced zucchini.
2. Cook for 15 minutes at 150°C.
3. Add the shrimp and the pieces of tomato, salt, and spices.
4. Cook for another 5 to 10 minutes or until the shrimp water evaporates.

Nutrition Value (Amount per Serving):

- Calories 214.3
- Fat 8.6g
- Carbohydrate 7.8g
- Sugars 4.8g
- Protein 27.0g
- Cholesterol 232.7mg

Spinach Crusted Salmon

Preparation time: 10-20,

Cooking time: 30-45; Serve; 6

Ingredients:

- 350 g salmon fillet
- 200 g bleached spinach
- 20g pine nuts
- 2 rolls of puff pastry
- 20 g butter
- 1 clove garlic
- Salt to taste
- Pepper to taste
- 1 egg

Direction:

1. Place the salmon, previously salted and spicy in the basket.

2. Cook for 15 minutes at 150°C. Once cooked, remove the salmon from the basket and let it cool. Put the butter, garlic clove, spinach (previously bleached), pine nuts, sole and pepper, and cook for 5 minutes.

3. Unwind the puff pastry on a work surface. Place the fillet in the center of the puff pastry (the skin will have been removed before the fillet has cooled) and cover with the earlier preparation.

4. Brush the 4 sides with the beaten egg and then cover with the other puff pastry. Pinch the sides to adhere the two pastes. Cut the excess puff pastry. Make a chimney on top of the puff pastry to facilitate the release of steam during cooking, then brush it with the egg.

5. Place the liner at the bottom of the basket on the baking paper (without the mixing).

6. Cook for 20/25 minutes depending on the degree of browning desired. Let cool before slicing.

Nutrition Value (Amount per Serving):

- Calories 186
- Fat 8.24g
- Carbohydrates 4.87g
- Sugars 3.22g
- Protein 23.67g
- Cholesterol 80mg

Salmon with Pistachio Bark

Preparation time: 10 - 20,

Cooking time: 15 – 30; Serve: 4

Ingredients:

- 600 g salmon fillet
- 50g pistachios
- Salt to taste

Direction:

1. Place the parchment paper on the bottom of the basket and place the salmon fillet in it (it can be cooked whole or already divided into four portions).

2. Cut the pistachios in thick pieces; grease the top of the fish, salt (little because the pistachios are already salted) and cover everything with the pistachios.

3. Set the air fryer to 180°C and simmer for 25 minutes.

Nutrition Value (Amount per Serving):

- Calories 371.7
- Fat 21.8 g
- Carbohydrate 9.4 g
- Sugars 2.2g
- Protein 34.7 g
- Cholesterol 80.5 mg

Salmon in Papillote With Orange

Preparation time: 10 - 20,

Cooking time: 15 – 30; Serve: 4

Ingredients:

- 600g salmon fillet
- 4 oranges
- Salt to taste
- 2 cloves of garlic
- Chives to taste
- 1 lemon

Direction:

1. Pour the freshly squeezed orange juice, the lemon juice, the zest of the two oranges into a bowl. Add two tablespoons of oil, salt, and garlic. Dip the previously washed salmon fillet and leave it in the marinade for one hour, preferably in the refrigerator

2. Place the steak and part of your marinade on a sheet of foil. Salt and sprinkle with chives and a few slices of orange.

3. Set to 160°C. Simmer for 30 minutes. Open the sheet, let it evaporate and serve with a nice garnish of fresh orange.

Nutrition Value (Amount per Serving):

- Calories 229
- Fat 11g
- Carbohydrates 5g
- Sugar 3g
- Protein 25g
- Cholesterol 62mg

Salted Marinated Salmon

Preparation time: 0-10,

Cooking time: 15-30; Serve: 2

Ingredients:

- 500g salmon fillet
- 1 kg coarse salt

Direction:

1. Place the baking paper on the basket and the salmon on top (skin side up) covered with coarse salt.

2. Set the air fryer to 150°C.

3. Cook everything for 25 to 30 minutes. At the end of cooking, remove the salt from the fish and serve with a drizzle of oil.

Nutrition Value (Amount per Serving):

- Calories 290
- Fiber 0g
- Fat 13g
- Protein 40g
- Carbohydrates 3g
- Cholesterol 196mg

Sautéed Trout with Almonds

Preparation time: more than 30,

Cooking time: 15 – 30; Serve:

Ingredients:

- 700 g salmon trout
- 15 black peppercorns
- Dill leaves to taste
- 30g almonds
- Salt to taste

Direction:

1. Cut the trout into cubes and marinate it for half an hour with the rest of the ingredients (except salt).

2. Cook for 17 minutes at 160⁰C. Pour a drizzle of oil and serve.

Nutrition Value (Amount per Serving):

- Calories 238.5
- Fat 20.1 g
- Carbohydrate 11.5 g
- Sugars 1.0 g
- Protein   4.0 g
- Cholesterol 45.9 mg

Stuffed Cuttlefish

Preparation time: 10 - 20,

Cooking time: 15 – 30; Serve: 4

Ingredients:

- 8 small cuttlefish
- 50 g of breadcrumbs
- Garlic to taste
- Parsley to taste
- 1 egg
- Salt to taste
- Pepper to taste

Direction:

1. Clean the cuttlefish, cut, and separate the tentacles. In a blender, pour the breadcrumbs, the parsley (without the branches), the egg, the salt, a drizzle of olive oil and the sepia tentacles.

2. Blend until you get a dense mixture. Fill the sepia with the mixture obtained.

3. Place the cuttlefish in the bowl.

4. Set the air fryer to 150°C and cook for 20 minutes. At the end of cooking, add a drizzle of olive oil and serve.

Nutrition Value (Amount per Serving):

- Calories 67.1
- Fat 0.6g
- Carbohydrates 0.7g
- Protein 13.8g
- Cholesterol 95.2mg

Sicilian Tuna Slices

Preparation time: 10 - 20,

Cooking time: 15 – 30; Serve: 4

Ingredients:

- 600 g of tuna slices
- 1 red onion stumbles
- 200 g chopped tomato
- 50 g boneless black olives
- 20 g desalted capers
- Salt to taste
- Pepper to taste
- Parsley to taste

Direction:

1. Pour sliced onion, tomato, olives, and capers in the basket.
2. Set the temperature to 150°C and cook for 10 minutes.
3. Mix the sauce with a wooden spoon and add the slices of tuna, salt, and pepper.
4. Cook the fish for 10 minutes, turning it halfway through cooking.
5. Dress with chopped parsley.

Nutrition Value (Amount per Serving):

- Calories 233
- Carbohydrates 12g
- Fat 6g
- Sugars 0g
- Protein 29g
- Cholesterol 51 mg

Fish in Air Fryer

Preparation time: 5 minutes;

Cooking time: 10 minutes; Serve: 1

Ingredients:

- 1 lemon juice
- 3 fish fillets
- 1 tbsp full seasoning with achiote
- 1 tbsp ground garlic
- 1 tbsp ground onion
- Chickpea flour needed
- Water

Direction:

1. Rinse the fish. And cut them into pieces. Dry with paper towels. Spread with lemon and season.

2. In a bowl add the chickpea flour and little water to form a thick cream.

3. Batter the fish pieces. Spread the pan of the fryer with oil and place the fish. Cook for 10 minutes at 160°C.

4. Also, the cooking time will depend on the equipment you use.

Nutrition Value (Amount per Serving):

- Calories 280
- Fat 12.5g
- Carbohydrates 0g
- Fiber 0g
- Sugars 0g
- Protein 39.2g

Rabas

Preparation time: 5 minutes;

Cooking time: 12 minutes; Serve: 4

Ingredients:

- 16 rabas
- 1 egg
- Breadcrumbs
- Salt, pepper, sweet paprika

Direction:

1. Put the rabas boil for 2 minutes.

2. Remove and dry well.

3. Beat the egg and season to taste. You can put salt, pepper and sweet paprika. Place in the egg.

4. Bread with breadcrumbs. Place in sticks.

5. Place in the fryer 5 minutes at 160^0C. Remove

6. Spray with a cooking spray and place 5 more minutes at 200^0C.

Nutrition Value (Amount per Serving):

- Calories 200
- Fat 1g
- Carbohydrates 1g
- Sugars 0g
- Protein 1g
- Cholesterol 0mg

Prawns in Ham with Red Pepper Sauce

Preparation time: 15 minutes;

Cooking time: 13 minutes; Serve: 5

Ingredients:

- 1 red bell pepper cut in half
- 10 prawns (frozen), already thawed
- 5 slices of ham

- 1 tbsp olive oil
- 1 clove garlic, minced
- ½ tbsp paprika
- Freshly ground black pepper

Direction:

1. Preheat the air fryer to 200°C. Place the pepper in the basket and place it in the air fryer. Set the timer to 10 minutes. Roast the pepper until the skin is slightly burned. Place the pepper in a bowl and cover it with a lid or with transparent film. Let stand about 15 minutes.

2. Peel the prawns, make an incision in the back, and remove the black vein. Divide the slices of ham into two halves lengthwise and roll each shrimp into a slice of ham.

3. Apply a thin layer of olive oil to the packets and place them in the basket. Insert it into the air fryer and set the timer to 3 minutes. Fry the prawns until they are crispy and ready.

4. Meanwhile, peel the halves of peppers, remove the seeds, and chop them. Beat them in the blender together with the garlic, paprika and olive oil. Pour the sauce on a plate and season with salt and pepper to taste.

5. Serve the prawns with ham on skewers and add a small plate with the red pepper sauce.

Nutrition Value (Amount per Serving):

- Calories 187
- Fat 17g
- Carbohydrates 9g

- Fiber 2g
- Sugar 2g
- Protein 2g

Chapter 4

Poultry

Chopped Chicken Olive Tomato Sauce

Preparation time: 10 minutes;

Cooking time: 30 minutes; Serve: 4

Ingredients:

- 500 g chicken cutlet
- 2 minced shallots+1 degermed garlic clove
- 75 g of tomato sauce + 15 g of 30% liquid cream
- 1 bay leaf+salt+pepper+1 tsp Provence herbs
- 20 pitted green and black olives

Direction:

1. Cut the chicken cutlets into strips and put them in the fryer basket with the garlic and the shallots. Do not put oil. Salt/pepper.

2. Set the timer and the temperature to 10-12 minutes at 200°C

3. Add the tomato sauce, the cream, the olives, the bay leaf, and the Provence herbs. Salt if necessary. Mix with a wooden spoon.

4. Close the air fryer and program 20 minutes at 180°C.

5. Eat hot with rice or pasta.

Nutrition Value (Amount per Serving):

- Calories 220.2
- Fat 7.0 g
- Carbohydrate 8.5 g
- Sugars 4.5 g
- Protein   28.9 g
- Cholesterol 114.8 mg

Chicken Thighs in Coconut Sauce, Nuts

Preparation time: 10 minutes;

Cooking time: 30 minutes; Serve: 4

Ingredients:

- 8 skinless chicken thighs
- 2 chopped onions
- 25 ml of coconut cream + 100 ml of coconut milk
- 4 tbsp coconut powder + 1 handful of dried fruit mix+ 5 dried apricots, diced + a few cashew nuts and almonds
- Fine salt + pepper

Direction:

1. Put the onions, chopped with the chicken thighs, in the air fryer (without oil). Add salt and pepper. Program 10 minutes at 200°C.

2. Stir alone with a wooden spoon.

3. Add coconut cream and milk, coconut powder, dried fruits, and apricots. Get out if necessary. Continue cooking by programming 20 minutes at 200°C. You don't have anything to do; it cooks alone, without any problem.

4. With the tongs, remove the bowl and serve hot with rice, vegetables, Chinese noodles............... A delight. Perfect kitchen

Nutrition Value (Amount per Serving):

- Calories 320.4
- Fat 11.6 g
- Carbohydrate 9.0 g
- Sugars 2.1 g
- Protein   44.0 g
- Cholesterol 102.7 mg

Forest Guinea Hen

Preparation time: about 15 minutes;

Cooking time: 1 h 15 - 1 h 30; Serve: 4

Ingredients:

- A beautiful guinea fowl farm weighing 1 to 1.5 kilos
- 100g of dried or fresh porcini mushrooms according to the season
- 8 large potatoes Béa
- 1 plate

- 2 cloves of garlic
- 1 shallot
- Chopped parsley
- A pinch of butter
- Vegetable oil
- Salt and pepper

Direction:

1. Put the dried mushrooms in water to rehydrate them or simply clean them if they are fresh porcini mushrooms. Peel the potatoes and cut them finely. Chop the garlic and parsley and set aside.

2. Prepare the guinea fowl by cutting the neck and removing all the giblets inside. Garnish with stuffed dough, garlic cloves and parsley.

3. Place guinea fowls in the air fryer at 200°C without oil of sufficient capacity. Simply add the butter knob and a tablespoon of cooking oil. Allow approximately one hour of cooking per kilo, so you will have to check after a certain period.

4. When the guinea fowl is ready, prepare the porcini mushrooms in the oil-free fryer by adding the shallot. This preparation is very fast, and you should not forget salt and pepper.

5. When everything is ready, place each of the preparations in the air fryer, sprinkle with the cooking juices and cook for another 15 minutes.

6. Serve hot to enjoy all the flavors of the dish.

Nutrition Value (Amount per Serving):

- Calories 110
- Fat 2.5g
- Carbohydrate 0g

- Sugars 0g
- Protein 21g
- Cholesterol 63mg

Fried and Crispy Chicken

Preparation time: 15 minutes;

Cooking time: 35-40 minutes; Serve: 4

Ingredients:

- 4 chicken breasts
- 1 tbsp olive oil
- 1 tbsp breadcrumbs
- 1 tbsp of a spice mixture
- Salt
- 250g of potatoes per person

Direction:

1. Cut chicken breasts into 4 slices

2. Mix them with the other ingredients so that the chicken is perfectly covered with the preparation.

3. Peel and cut the potatoes in the same way as the fries, trying to make a regular cut to cook better.

4. Place the strips in the air fryer without oil and cook at 200°C for 15 to 20 minutes to get a crispy chicken.

5. For French fries, wait 30 minutes to cook.

Nutrition Value (Amount per Serving):

- Calories 227
- Carbohydrates 23g
- Fat 18g
- Sugars 0g
- Protein 12g
- Cholesterol 63mg

Orange Turkey Bites

Preparation time: 10-20;

Cooking time: 15-30; Serve: 8

Ingredients:

- 750 g turkey
- 1 shallot
- 2 oranges
- Thyme to taste
- 1 tsp oil
- Salt and pepper to taste

Direction:

1. Cut the turkey into pieces and peel the oranges, cutting the skin into strips.

2. Put the chopped shallot, the orange peel, the thyme, and the oil in the basket of the preheated air fryer at 150 for 5 minutes. Brown all for 4 min.

3. Add ½ glass of water, lightly floured turkey, salt, and pepper; simmer for 6 more minutes.

4. Then add the orange juice and cook at 200°C for 15 minutes until a thick juice is obtained.

5. Serve garnished with some thyme leaves and slices of orange.

Nutrition Value (Amount per Serving):

- Calories 80
- Fat 5g
- Carbohydrates 1g
- Sugar 0g
- Protein 7g
- Cholesterol 25mg

Chicken Thighs with Potatoes

Preparation time: 0-10;

Cooking time: 45-60; Serve: 6

Ingredients:

- 1kg chicken thighs
- 800g of potatoes in pieces
- Salt to taste
- Pepper to taste
- Rosemary at ease
- 1 clove garlic

Direction:

1. Preheat the air fryer at 180°C for 15 minutes.

2. Place the chicken thighs in the basket and add the previously peeled and washed potatoes, add a clove of garlic, rosemary sprigs, salt, and pepper.

3. Set the temperature 200°C and cook everything for 50 min. Mix 3-4 times during cooking (when they are well browned on the surface) and chicken 1-2 times.

Nutrition Value (Amount per Serving):

- Calories 419.4
- Fat 9.5 g
- Carbohydrate 44.8 g
- Sugars 2.0 g
- Protein 39.1 g
- Cholesterol 115.8 mg

Chicken Blanquette With Soy

Preparation time: 10-20;

Cooking time: 15-30; Serve:

Ingredients:

- 600g Chicken breast
- 300g Potatoes
- 100g Bean sprouts
- 150g Broth
- 50g Onion
- 1tsp Olive oil
- 25g Soy sauce

Direction:

1. Cut the meat and potatoes into pieces.
2. Pour the sliced oil and onion into the bottom of the tank, close the lid.
3. Set the air fryer at 150ºC to brown for 5 minutes.
4. Add the floured chicken, potatoes, broth, salt, and pepper and cook for another 13 minutes.
5. Then pour the sprouts and the soy sauce and cook for another 10 minutes.

Nutrition Value (Amount per Serving):

- Calories 250
- Carbohydrates 19g
- Fat 11g
- Sugars 7g
- Protein 16g
- Cholesterol 0mg

Fish Sticks

Cooking time: 15-30;

Serve: 6

Ingredients:

- 18 pieces Fish patties

Direction:

1. Remove the mixing paddle from the tank.

2. Heat the air fryer at 150°C for 5 minutes

3. Cook everything for 20 min.

Nutrition Value (Amount per Serving):

- Calories 281
- Total Fat 15 g
- Carbohydrates 23.9 g

- Sugars 2.8 g
- Protein 12.5 g
- Cholesterol 36 mg

Vegetarian Curry with Pumpkin and Chickpeas

Preparation time: 20-30;

Cooking time: 15-30; Serve: 6

Ingredients:

- 600g pumpkin, cleaned
- 300g chicken weights already cooked
- 1 tsp oil
- 1 tsp paprika
- 1 tsp curry
- ½ onion
- 1 clove garlic
- 1 tsp tomato puree
- 200 ml of broth
- 1 tsp turmeric
- 480g basmati rice

Direction:

1. Remove the skin of the pumpkin and the seeds inside. Cut it into small pieces, the same size as the chickpeas to have the same cooking time.

2. Pour the chopped onion and garlic, oil, and spices (paprika - curry - turmeric - saffron) in the basket.

3. Set the temperature to 150°C and brown all for 4 min.

4. Add the pumpkin and brown for 6 min. additional.

5. Then pour the chickpeas, tomato puree, broth and cook for 10 min. additional.

6. Meanwhile, boil basmati rice in saltwater, drain and serve with vegetarian curry.

Nutrition Value (Amount per Serving):

- Calories 249.6
- Fat 11.7 g
- Carbohydrate 27.8 g
- Sugars 9.6 g
- Protein 8.1 g
- Cholesterol 0.0 mg

Turkey Diced with Ginger, Apples and Vegetables

Preparation time: 10-20;

Cooking time: 30-45; Serve: 4

Ingredients:

- 600g turkey breast
- 150g carrots
- 100g of celery
- 50g onion
- 200g of potatoes
- Ginger to taste
- Flour at discretion
- 200ml broth
- 1 tsp olive oil
- Leave at discretion
- Black pepper to taste
- 1 apple

Direction:

1. Preheat the air fryer at 150°C for 5 minutes.

2. Cut the meat and vegetables into small pieces.

3. Pour the sliced oil and onion into the bottom of the basket and cook for 5 minutes.

4. Add carrots, celery, potatoes, and broth, then cook for another 15 minutes.

5. Add the floured turkey, salt, and pepper, then cook for another 15 minutes (if necessary, add some water).

6. Add the apple pieces and ginger at the end and continue cooking for another 5 minutes.

Nutrition Value (Amount per Serving):

- Fat 13.6g
- Carbohydrates 2.3g
- Sugars 0g
- Protein 42.4g
- Cholesterol 124.9mg Value (Amount per Serving):

Ligurian Rabbit

Preparation time: 10-20,

Cooking time: 45-60, 6 people, Calories: 440

Ingredients:

- 1 kg of rabbit pieces
- 150g green olives
- 2 tbsp pine nuts
- 100ml broth
- 1 shallot
- 1 clove garlic
- 1 rosemary branch
- 1 glass of red wine
- 1 tsp olive oil
- 2-3 bay leaves
- Salt to taste

Direction:

1. Put the chopped onion, oil, and garlic in the basket. Set the temperature to 200^0C and brown for 2 min.

2. Add meat, red wine and cook for another 8 min.

3. Finally add the green olives, pine nuts, broth, herbs, salt and pepper and simmer for another 50 min. (until the rabbit becomes tender, the meat should easily detach from the bone) turning 2-3 times (if the bottom is too dry, add the broth).

Nutrition Value (Amount per Serving):

- Calories 795
- Fat 8g
- Carbohydrates 0g
- Sugars 0g
- Protein 20.8g
- Cholesterol 82mg

Frozen Chicken Nuggets

Cooking time: 15-30;

Serve: 8

Ingredients:

- 750 g of frozen chicken nuggets
- Fine salt to taste

Direction:

1. Pour the chicken nuggets in the basket
2. Cook for 18 min at 200°C.
3. Salt and serve.

Nutrition Value (Amount per Serving):

- Calories 33
- Fat 1g
- Carbohydrates 2.8g
- Sugar 0g
- Protein 3.3g
- Cholesterol 9mg

Chicken with Cacciatore (Chicken Hunter)

Preparation time: 10-20,

Cooking time: 30-45; Serve: 6

Ingredients:

- 1 kg of chicken pieces
- 1 onion:
- 2 carrots
- 3 celery stalks
- 1 clove garlic
- 1 glass of red wine
- 400 g peeled tomatoes
- 50 g of olives
- Salt, pepper, parsley to taste

Direction:

1. Clean the chicken and place it inside the basket previously greased with the cooking spray.

2. Set the temperature to 180°C and cook the chicken pieces for 15 minutes.

3. Add the celery mince, carrots, onions, garlic, red wine, salt, pepper, and simmer for an additional 5 minutes.

4. Then pour the tomato and olives and finish simmering for additional 20 minutes stirring chicken and sauce.

5. Once cooked, add a handful of chopped parsley, and serve hot with mash or polenta.

Nutrition Value (Amount per Serving):

- Calories 233
- Fat 7g
- 10g carbohydrates
- Sugars 2.2g
- Protein 34.7g
- Cholesterol 98.5mg

Devil Chicken

Preparation time: 10-20,

Cooking time: 45-60; Serve: 4

Ingredients:

- 1 kg of whole chicken
- Salt to taste
- Black pepper to taste
- Chili pepper

Direction:

1. Thoroughly clean the chicken and cut it along the white. Flatten it well on the work surface and then massage with oil and spices.

2. Cook the chicken for 35 minutes at 200°C.

3. Turn the chicken and cook another 25 minutes.

Nutrition Value (Amount per Serving):

- Calories 429.7
- Fat 17.3 g
- Carbohydrate 19.5 g
- Sugars 5.1 g
- Protein   51.1 g
- Cholesterol 155.0 mg

Chicken with Pineapple

Preparation time: 10 - 20,

Cooking time: 15 – 30; Serve: 6

Ingredients:

- 600g chicken breast
- 350 g canned pineapple
- 50 ml pineapple juice
- 1 tbsp of starch
- ½ tbsp ginger
- ½ tbsp curry
- 15 ml soy sauce
- Salt to taste
- Pepper to taste
- Flour (sufficient quantity)

Direction:

1. The floured chicken cut into small pieces, salt, and pepper in the basket previously greased.

2. Simmer for 8 minutes at 180^0C (If, at the end of cooking, the chicken pieces stick together, separate them with a wooden spoon).

3. Add the pineapple into small pieces, ginger and curry and simmer for added 3 minutes.

4. Finally, add water, soy sauce and diluted starch to pineapple juice. Simmer for another 6 minutes until the sauce has thickened.

5. Ideal accompanied with basmati rice.

Nutrition Value (Amount per Serving):

- Calories 222
- Fat 7.1g
- Carbohydrates 11g
- Sugars 9.7g
- Protein 27g
- Cholesterol 85mg

Chicken Curry

Preparation time: 10-20,

Cooking time: 15-30; Serve: 6

Ingredients:

- 600g chicken breast
- 1 onion
- 2 carrots
- 150 ml
- 200 ml of fresh cream

- 100 ml of milk
- Salt to taste
- 2 spoons of curry
- Flour 00 (sufficient quantity)

Direction:

1. Chop the onion in a food processor and cut the carrots into cubes or slices.

2. Spray the basket and distribute the onion and carrots evenly in the basket.

3. Brown for 5 minutes at 150°C.

4. Add the floured chicken, cut into small pieces, the broth, salt, and simmer for another 5 min.

5. Finally pour the fresh cream, the milk and finish cooking for another 15 min. Ideal accompanied with basmati rice.

Nutrition Value (Amount per Serving):

- Calories 243
- Fat 11g
- Carbohydrates 7.5g

- Sugars 2g
- Protein 28g
- Cholesterol 74mg

Chicken with Yogurt and Mustard

Preparation time: 10 - 20,

Cooking time: 15 – 30; 6

Ingredients:

- 500 g chicken breast
- 100 g of white yogurt
- 40 g mustard
- 1 shallot
- Salt to taste
- Pepper to taste

Direction:

1. Place the chopped shallot inside the basket previously greased.

2. Brown for 3 minutes at 150^0C

3. Add the chicken pieces, salt, pepper and cook for another 15 minutes at 180^0C.

4. Then pour the mustard and yogurt and cook for another 5 minutes.

Nutrition Value (Amount per Serving):

- Calories 287.1
- Fat 8.9g
- Carbohydrate 4.3 g
- Sugars 1.7 g
- Protein   43.6 g
- Cholesterol 99.9 mg

Almond Chicken

Preparation time: 10 - 20,

Cooking time: 15 – 30; 6

Ingredients:

- 500 g chicken breast
- 130g crushed almonds
- ½ onion
- 1 tbsp grated fresh ginger
- 60 g of soy sauce
- Water (sufficient quantity)

Direction:

1. Pour the almonds into the basket.

2. Roast the almonds for 5 minutes at 150°C.

3. Remove the almonds and pour the chopped onion and ginger, the oil into the tank and brown for about 2 minutes.

4. Add lightly floured chicken, salt, pepper and cook for additional 13 minutes.

5. Pour the soy sauce, a ladle of hot water, the roasted almonds and simmer for additional 5 minutes.

Nutrition Value (Amount per Serving):

- Calories 458
- Fat 34g
- Carbohydrates 22g
- Sugars 7.3g
- Protein 20g
- Cholesterol 24mg

Mushroom Chicken

Preparation time: 10-20,

Cooking time: 15-30; Serve: 6

Ingredients:

- 500 g chicken breast
- Mushroom 300g
- 100 g of fresh cream
- 1 shallot

Direction:

1. Cut the chicken into pieces and sliced mushrooms. Spray the basket and chopped shallot into the basket. Set the temperature to 150°C and lightly brown for 5 minutes.

2. Add the mushrooms and cook for additional 6 minutes.

3. Finally pour the chicken, salt, pepper, and simmer for another 10 minutes.

4. Then add the fresh cream and cook for 5 min. until the sauce has thickened.

Nutrition Value (Amount per Serving):

- Calories 220
- Fat 14g
- Carbohydrates 11g
- Sugar 4g
- Protein 12g
- Cholesterol 50mg

Pepper Chicken

Preparation time: 10-20;

Cooking time: 45-60; Serve: 6

Ingredients:

- 1 kg of chicken pieces
- 500 g of red and yellow peppers
- Salt to taste
- 50g onion

Direction:

1. Pour the chopped onion into the bowl with the chopped peppers and chicken. Add salt and pepper.

2. Set the temperature to 150°C.

3. Cook everything for about 50 minutes, mixing 3 to 4 times during cooking, both meat and peppers.

Nutrition Value (Amount per Serving):

- Calories 281
- Fat 12g
- Carbohydrates 21g
- Sugars 3.4g
- Protein 23g
- Cholesterol 102mg

Stuffed Chicken and Baked Potatoes

Preparation time: 10-20,
Cooking time: 45-60; Serve: 4

Ingredients:

- 800 g boneless chicken
- 300 g minced meat
- 150 g sausage
- 80 g French toast
- 1 tbsp chopped parsley

Direction:

1. Bone the chicken (or bone directly by the butcher).

Prepare the filling:

2. Put in a food processor the meat, the sausage, the French toast bathed in milk to soften it, the parsley, the eggs, the grated cheese, the salt, the pepper and mix until obtaining a homogeneous and compact mixture.

3. Fill the boneless chicken and tie it well with a kitchen rope so that the filling does not come out.

4. Place the chicken inside the bowl, add the chopped potatoes, oil, salt, and pepper.

5. Set the air fryer to 160°C. Cook everything for 60 minutes over mix the potatoes 2-3 times to cook evenly and turn the chicken about once in the middle of cooking.

Nutrition Value (Amount per Serving):

- Calories 223.8
- Fat 6.5 g
- Carbohydrate 19.8 g
- Sugars 1.9 g
- Protein   21.2 g
- Cholesterol 48.8 mg

Tandoori Chicken

Preparation time: more than 30,

Cooking time: 15 – 30; Serve: 4

Ingredients:

- 600 g chicken pieces
- 125 g whole yogurt
- 1 tbsp curry
- 3 tsp of spices for roasted meats

Direction:

1. Place all ingredients in a bowl, flame well and let stand for 1 hour in the refrigerator.

2. Place the pieces of meat in the basket and set the temperature to 160°C

3. Cook the meat for 30 minutes, turning it 1-2 times to brown the chicken on both sides.

Nutrition Value (Amount per Serving):

- Calories 263
- Fat 12g
- Carbohydrates 6.1g
- Sugars 3.7g
- Protein 31g
- Cholesterol 135mg

Crispy Chicken Fillets in Brine in Pickle Juice

Preparation time: 10 minutes;

Cooking time: 12 minutes; Serve: 4

Ingredients:

- 12 chicken offers (1 ¼ pounds in total)
- 1 ¼ cups pickled dill juice
- 1 large egg
- 1 large egg white
- ½ tsp kosher salt
- Freshly ground black pepper
- ½ cup seasoned breadcrumbs, regular or gluten free
- ½ cup seasoned breadcrumbs, regular or gluten free
- Olive oil spray

Direction:

1. Place the chicken in a shallow bowl and cover with the pickle juice (enough to cover completely). Cover and marine for 8 hours in the refrigerator.

2. Drain the chicken and dry it completely with a paper towel (discard the marinade). In a medium bowl, beat the whole egg, egg white, salt, and pepper. In a shallow arch, combine the breadcrumbs.

3. Dip the chicken in the egg mixture, piece by piece, then in the breadcrumbs, pressing lightly. Remove excess breadcrumbs and place it on a work surface. Spray generously both sides of the chicken with oil.

4. Preheat the fryer to 400°F.

5. Working in batches, place a single layer of chicken in the fryer basket. Cook 10 to 12 minutes, turning halfway through cooking, until cooked, crispy and golden brown. (For a toaster-style air fryer, the temperature stays the same; cook for about 10 minutes.)

Nutrition Value (Amount per Serving):

- Calories: 244kcal
- Carbohydrates 10g
- Protein: 37g
- Fat: 6g
- Cholesterol 150mg
- Sugar 1g

Chapter 5

Beef, Pork, Lamb Recipes

Perfect Garlic Butter Steak

Preparation: 20 min

Cooking time: 12 min.

Ingredients:

- 2 Ribeye steaks
- Salt
- Pepper
- Olive oil
- Garlic butter:

- ½ cup softened butter
- 2 tbsp chopped fresh parsley
- 2 garlic cloves, minced
- 1 tsp Worcestershire sauce
- ½ tsp salt (optional)

Direction:

1. Prepare the garlic butter by mixing all the ingredients together.
2. Place in parchment paper. Roll up and put in the fridge.
3. Let the steaks sit for 20 minutes at room temperature.
4. Brush with a little oil, salt, and pepper.
5. Preheat your hot air fryer to 400°F (200°C).
6. Cook for 12 minutes, turning halfway through cooking. Serve.
7. Place the garlic butter on the steaks and let sit for 5 minutes.
8. Enjoy!

Nutrition Value (Amount per Serving):

- Calories 250
- Fat 10g
- Carbohydrates 2g

- Sugars 1g
- Protein 36g
- Cholesterol 100mg

Crispy Pork Medallions

Preparation time: 20 minutes;

Cooking time: 5 minutes; Serve: 2

Ingredients:

- 1 pork loin, 330 g, cut into 6 or 7 slices of 4 cm
- 1 tsp Dijon mustard
- 1 tsp oil
- Salt, pepper and paprika
- Asian marinade
- 1 tsp salt reduced tamari sauce
- 1 tsp olive oil
- 1 clementine juice
- 1 pinch cayenne pepper
- 2 cloves garlic, pressed
- Crunchy coating
- 1/3 cup breadcrumbs
- ½ orange zest
- 2g freshly grated Parmesan cheese

Direction:

1. Prepare the marinade first. In a bowl, combine all the ingredients. Lightly salt the medallions, pepper, and sprinkle with paprika. Place these in the marinade and turn them several times to impregnate them completely. Cover with plastic wrap and marinate for 1 hour at room temperature.

2. Prepare the coating by combining the breadcrumbs, the orange zest, and the Parmesan cheese in a deep dish.

3. When the maceration time has elapsed, remove the marinade medallions, and dry them on absorbent paper. Spread with mustard, then move on to the crunchy layer. Brush lightly with oil.

4. Heat the air fryer to 350°F. Place the medallions in the fryer basket. Cook 5 minutes, stir, and then return to the fryer for another minute. Serve immediately.

Nutrition Value (Amount per Serving):

- Calories 222
- Carbohydrates 13g
- Fat 6g
- Protein 24g
- Sugars 0h
- Cholesterol 74mg

Nemos Beef with Dry Pepper Lactose Free

Preparation time: 30 minutes;

Cooking time: 20-25 minutes; Serve: 5

Ingredients:

- 250g of minced meat
- 1 handful of rice noodles
- 25 rice leaves
- 1 small onion
- 1 clove garlic
- 1 cube of chicken broth
- Roasted Sesame Oil
- 2 tsp dried pepper
- 1 tbsp soy sauce
- 1 tsp ground ginger

Direction:

1. Finely chop the onion and garlic and mix with the minced meat. Add half of the dried pepper, being careful to crush it beforehand. Add the ginger powder and soy sauce. Brown the preparation in roasted sesame oil, making sure you only have small pieces of minced meat.

2. Bring a pan of boiling water to which you will add chicken broth. Dip the rice noodles in it for only 3 minutes.

3. Add them to the ground beef preparation and then add the rest of the dried pepper.

4. Lightly moisten the rice leaves, place the filling in the middle and close them to create a perfect nem.

5. Place the spring rolls in the air fryer without oil previously heated at 150°C and cook for 10 to 15 minutes, according to taste.

Nutrition Value (Amount per Serving):

- Calories 203
- Carbohydrates 7g
- Fat 15g
- Protein 12g
- Sugars 5g
- Cholesterol 0mg

Pork and Parsni With Thai, Marinated with Honey and Soy

Preparation time: 20 minutes;

Cooking time: 30 minutes; Serve: 2

Ingredients:

- 2 pork ribs to choose from the tenderloin
- 1 large parsnip
- 1 coriander leaf
- 1 sprig fresh chopped parsley
- Salt
- For the marinade:
- 2 tbsp olive oil
- 2 tbsp soy sauce
- The juice of half a lemon
- 1 tbsp of honey, preferably flavored with orange blossom
- 1 tsp of specific spices for wok preparation
- 1 tsp of Asian spice mix
- Coriander powder

Direction:

1. Prepare the marinade by mixing all the ingredients in a large bowl. Mix to obtain a very homogeneous mixture.

2. Dip the pork chunks in the marinade, turning them over to make sure it covers the meat ribs perfectly. Prepare the parsnip by peeling and washing it, and then cut it into small dice.

3. Use a large plate to place the pieces of pork and parsnips covered with marinade. Pour the parsnips into the bowl and mix. Let stand for at least 1 hour before cooking.

4. Set the air fryer at 160°C without oil for 30 minutes and cook the parsnips.

5. At the end of the 10 minutes of cooking, add the pieces of pork or proceed to a traditional baking in the oven with 10 minutes on each side being careful to keep the cooking juices.

Nutrition Value (Amount per Serving):

- Calories 179
- Carbohydrates 11g
- Fat 13g
- Sugars 6g
- Protein 1g
- Cholesterol 0mg

Pork Fillet Mignon

Preparation time: 5 minutes;

Cooking time: 12 minutes; Serve: 3

Ingredients:

- 6 medallions of 100g to 150g cut in a pork loin
- Olive oil
- Salt and pepper

Direction:

1. Cut six pork medallions the same size as the pork loin you own.

2. Salt and pepper to your liking.

3. Use a cooking tool to spray a very small amount of olive oil.

4. Place your pork medallions on the air fryer previously preheated at 150°C and cook for 12 minutes.

Nutrition Value (Amount per Serving):

- Calories 125
- Fat 3.4g
- Carbohydrates 0g
- Sugars 0g
- Protein 22g
- Cholesterol 62mg

Lamb with Potatoes

Preparation time: 10-20 minutes;

Cooking time: 30 - 45 minutes; Serve: 2

Ingredients:

- 1 kg Lamb milk in pieces
- 600g Fresh potatoes
- 5 spoons Sunflower oil
- Salt and pepper
- 2 spoons Sage, rosemary, thyme
- ½ glass White wine

Direction:

1. Remove the mixing paddle from the tank.

2. Put the pieces of lamb, oil, sage, rosemary, and thyme in the cooking pot. Close the cover, set the thermostat to position 4, press the lower resistance power key and press the on / off key; brown for 4 min.

3. Add the wine and simmer for another 6 min.

4. Preheat the air fryer at 150°C for 5 minutes.

5. Finally pour the potatoes cut into pieces, salt, pepper and cook for 35 min. Extra by mixing the potatoes manually 2-3 times during cooking.

Nutrition Value (Amount per Serving):

- Calories 372.0
- Fat 12.3 g
- Carbohydrate 34.1 g
- Sugars 1.9
- Protein   31.5 g
- Cholesterol 86.7 mg

Veal Blanquette With Peas

Preparation time: 10-20;

Cooking time: 45-60; Serve: 2

Ingredients:

- 600g Veal meat
- 250g Frozen peas
- ½ Onions
- ½ glass White wine
- 1 tsp Oil
- 250 ml Broth

Direction:

1. Chop the onion and put it inside the tank with the oil. Close the lid

2. Brown for 5 min setting the air fryer at 150°C.

3. Add lightly floured meat, white wine, and simmer for 10 minutes.

4. Then add frozen peas, broth, salt, pepper, and simmer for 35 minutes. additional depending on the desired degree of cooking.

Nutrition Value (Amount per Serving):

- Calories 418
- Carbohydrates 24g
- Fat 14g
- Sugars 0g
- Protein 49g
- Cholesterol 357mg

Beef Stroganoff

Preparation time: 10-20;

Cooking time: 15 – 30; Serve: 6

Ingredients:

- 1000 g beef
- 500g onion
- Mushrooms 500g
- 150g sour cream
- 50 g butter
- 100 g of broth
- Salt, pepper to taste
- 2 tbsp paprika
- Flour

Direction:

1. Cut the onion into very thin slices, then clean the mushrooms well and cut them into slices, finally cut the meat into strips about 5 cm long.

2. Place the butter, onion, and mushrooms on the baking sheet.

3. Preheat the air fryer at 200C for 5 minutes. Simmer for 10 min.

4. Add the floured meat, paprika, broth, salt, pepper, and simmer for another 10 minutes.

5. Finally pour the cream and finish cooking for another 5 minutes or until ready.

Nutrition Value (Amount per Serving):

- Calories 391
- Fat 23g
- Carbohydrates 21g
- Sugars 3.2g
- Protein 25g
- Cholesterol 115mg

Meatballs with Tomatoes and Peas

Preparation time: 10 – 20;

Cooking time: 15 - 30, 6 people.

Ingredients:

- 425 g minced meat
- 1 egg
- 25 g grated cheese
- Salt to taste
- To taste breadcrumbs
- Parsley chopped to taste
- 150 g of frozen peas
- 400 g of tomatoes cut into large pieces
- 1 tsp oil
- 2 shallots

Direction:

1. Put the minced meat, the egg, the grated cheese, the salt, the parsley, the breadcrumbs in a bowl and mix until you get a consistent mixture. Form the meatballs (with these doses you will get 15-18 meatballs).

2. Chop the shallots and pour them into the basket greased with the oil. Close. Set the air fryer at 150°C and brown for 3 min.

3. Add the meatballs and simmer for an additional 7 minutes.

4. Then add the frozen peas, tomato, salt and pepper and simmer for another 18 minutes.

Nutrition Value (Amount per Serving):

- Calories 40
- Fat 2.9 g
- Carbohydrates 0.9 g
- Sugars 0.5 g
- Protein 2.7 g
- Cholesterol 15 mg

Cevapi

Preparation time: more than 30;

Cooking time: 15 – 30; Serve: 4

Ingredients:

- 150g of onion
- 350g ground beef
- 150g minced pork
- Leave at discretion
- Pepper at discretion
- Red paprika at discretion

Direction:

1. Mix all the ingredients in a bowl (the onion must be finely chopped) and knead well; form rolls 4 to 5 cm long and let stand in the refrigerator for at least 1 hour.

2. Place the cevapi in the basket of the air fryer. Set the temperature to 150^{0}C.

3. Cook the cevapis (8 at a time) for about 13 to 15 minutes, turning them in the middle of cooking.

Nutrition Value (Amount per Serving):

- Calories 63
- Fat 4.84g
- Carbohydrates 0.25g
- Sugars 0.02g
- Protein 4.19g
- Cholesterol 17mg

Milanese Chop

Preparation time: 10 – 20;

Cooking time: 15 – 30; Serve: 2

Ingredients:

- 2 veal chops
- 1 egg
- 70 g of breadcrumbs
- Salt to taste
- 1 tsp oil

Direction:

1. Beat the egg in a bowl and prepare the breadcrumbs on a flat plate.

2. Pass each chop in the egg and then in breadcrumbs. Press the meat firmly into the pie. Put in the refrigerator for at least half an hour.

3. Pour the oil into the basket. Place the two chops.

4. Set the air fryer to 150^0 and cook the meat for 10 minutes and then turn the chop.

5. Cook for 5 minutes additional.

6. Serve the chops still hot, covering the bone with aluminum foil to facilitate tasting.

Nutrition Value (Amount per Serving):

- Calories 231
- Carbohydrates 8g
- Fat 9g
- Sugars 0g
- Protein 27g
- Cholesterol 97mg

Lemon Chops

Preparation time: 0-10;

Cooking time: 0-15; Serve: 2

Ingredients:

- 4 slices of pork
- 40g butter
- Flour to taste
- 1 lemon juice
- Salt to taste

Direction:

1. Preheat the air fryer at 180°C for 5 minutes.

2. Flour the pork slices. Place the butter in the basket and brown for 2 minutes.

3. Add the previously floured and salted pork slices, simmer for 3 another minutes. Turn them on themselves.

4. Add the lemon juice and simmer for 3another minutes.

5. Remove the slices and add a pinch of butter to the tank to thicken the juice. Mix the juice with a wooden spoon and pour the scallops over it.

6. Serve decorating the dish with lemon julienne.

Nutrition Value (Amount per Serving):

- Calories 242.4
- Fat 15.7 g
- Carbohydrate 0.7 g
- Sugars 0.0 g
- Protein   23.2 g
- Cholesterol 65.9 mg

Amatriciana

Preparation time: 0-10 minutes;

Cooking time: 15-30 minutes; Serve: 4

Ingredients:

- 200g Pork cheek
- 1 Medium onion
- 400g Peeled tomatoes
- 3 spoons Oil
- 1 Chile
- Salt

Direction:

1. Chop the onion and cut the pork cheek (removing the hard shell). Put everything in the basket, adding the oil.

2. Close the cover, set the air fryer to 3 minutes at 150°C to brown. Then pour the tomato, pepper, and salt.

3. Cook for an additional 17 minutes, or until desired cooking is achieved.

Nutrition Value (Amount per Serving):

- Calories 321
- Fat 9g
- Carbohydrate 49g
- Sugars 50g
- Protein 14g
- Cholesterol 20mg

Pork Chops with Chicory Treviso

Preparation time: 10-20;

Cooking time: 0-15; Serve: 2

Ingredients:

- 4 pork chops
- 40g butter
- Flour to taste
- 1 chicory stalk
- Salt to taste

Direction:

1. Cut the chicory into small pieces. Place the butter and chicory in pieces on the basket of the air fryer previously preheated at 180°C and brown for 2 min.

2. Add the previously floured and salted pork slices (directly over the chicory), simmer for 6 minutes turning them over after 3 minutes.

3. Remove the slices and place them on a serving plate, covering them with the rest of the red chicory juice collected at the bottom of the basket.

Nutrition Value (Amount per Serving):

- Calories 504
- Fat 33
- Carbohydrates 0g
- Sugars 0g
- Protein 42g
- Cholesterol 130mg

Venetian Liver

Preparation time: 10-20;

Cooking time: 15-30; Serve: 6

Ingredients:

- 500g veal liver
- 2 white onions
- 100g of water
- 2 tbsp vinegar
- Salt and pepper to taste

Direction:

1. Chop the onion and put it inside the pan with the water. Set the air fryer to 180°C and cook for 20 minutes.

2. Add the liver cut into small pieces and vinegar, close the lid, and cook for an additional 10 minutes.

3. Add salt and pepper.

Nutrition Value (Amount per Serving):

- Calories 131
- Fat 14.19 g
- Carbohydrates 16.40 g
- Sugars 5.15 g
- Protein 25.39 g
- Cholesterol 350.41 mg

Vegetable Cane

Preparation time: 10-20 minutes,

Cooking time: more than 60 minutes; Serve: 4

Ingredients:

- 2 calf legs
- 4 carrots
- 4 medium potatoes
- 1 clove garlic
- 300ml Broth
- Leave to taste
- Pepper to taste

Direction:

1. Place the ears, garlic, and half of the broth in the greased basket.

2. Set the temperature to 180^0C.

3. Cook the stems for 40 minutes, turning them in the middle of cooking.

4. Add the vegetables in pieces, salt, pepper, pour the rest of the broth and cook for another 50 minutes (time may vary depending on the size of the hocks).

5. Mix the vegetables and the ears 2 to 3 times during cooking.

Nutrition Value (Amount per Serving):

- Calories 7.9
- Fat 0.49g
- Carbohydrate 0.77g
- Sugar 0.49g
- Protein 0.08mg
- Cholesterol 0mg

Milanese Veal Legs

Preparation time: 10-20 minutes,

Cooking time: more than 60 minutes;

Serve: 4

Ingredients:

- 1kg beef leg
- 1 onion
- 1 glass of white wine
- 150g hot broth
- Taste Flour

- Salt, pepper to taste
- 1 bunch of parsley
- ½ grated lemon
- 1 clove garlic

Direction:

1. Place the chopped onion in the basket. Brown for 4 minutes at 150⁰C.

2. Add the lightly floured ears the white wine, season with salt and pepper and simmer for 6 minutes.

3. Turn the spikes, add the broth, and cook for another 50 minutes turning the meat 1-2 times.

4. At this point, add the chopped parsley, a grated peel of half a lemon and a clove of garlic and continue cooking for the remaining 10 minutes.

5. Serve hot with the juice that has formed in the cooking vessel.

Nutrition Value (Amount per Serving):

- Calories 499
- Fat 22.54g
- Carbohydrate 38.25g

- Sugars 2.27g
- Protein 34.23g
- Cholesterol 160mg

Veal, speck, and cheese paupiettes

Preparation time: 10-20 minutes,

Cooking time: 15-30 minutes;

Serve: 6

Ingredients:

- 12 slices of veal
- 6 speck slices
- 12 slices of provola
- Salt to taste
- Pepper to taste

Direction:

1. Place half a slice of stain and one of provola on each slice of veal; Roll each slice and close them with toothpicks.

2. Pour the oil and place the paupiettes in the basket, season with salt and pepper.

3. Set the air fryer to 180°C.

4. Cook the paupiettes for 15 minutes, turning them around after about 8 to 9 minutes.

Nutrition Value (Amount per Serving):

- Calories 261
- Carbohydrates 0g
- Fat 11g
- Sugar 0g
- Protein 30g
- Cholesterol 0mg

Fried Pork

Preparation time: 10 – 20 minutes,

Cooking time: 0 – 15 minutes;

Serve: 4

Ingredients:

- 300 g pork loin
- 2 egg yolks
- 4 tsp Worcestershire sauce:
- Salt to taste
- Taste Flour
- Gusto breadcrumbs

Direction:

1. Put the egg yolk, Worcestershire sauce and some flour (to thicken the sauce) in a bowl.

2. Cut the meat into pieces, lightly salt, and then pass it first in the sauce (previously prepared) and in breadcrumbs.

3. Grease the basket of the air fryer.

4. Preheat the air fryer for 1 minute at 200°C.

5. Add the pork and cook for 10 minutes, turning the meat halfway through cooking.

Nutrition Value (Amount per Serving):

- Calories 178
- Fat 11.89g
- Carbohydrates 0g
- Sugars 0g
- Protein 16.66g
- Cholesterol 51mg

Roast Pork with Vegetables

Preparation time: 10-20 minutes,

Cooking time: more than 60 minutes;

Serve: 8

Ingredients:

- 1 kg of pork loin
- 4 carrots
- 3 potatoes
- 1 onion
- 1 clove garlic
- 250 ml broth
- Salt and pepper to taste

Direction:

1. Place the tenderloin in the center of the tank, as well as the vegetables in small pieces, salt, pepper and pour a little broth.

2. Set the temperature to 160°C. Simmer for 1 hour and 30 minutes. Mix the vegetables occasionally and turn the loin halfway through cooking. Add some broth as necessary to keep the meat tender.

Nutrition Value (Amount per Serving):

- Calories 487.3
- Fat 16.7 g
- Carbohydrate 40.3 g
- Sugars 1.1 g
- Protein 44.9 g
- Cholesterol 95.3 mg

Saltimbocca Roman Veal

Preparation time: 10 – 20 minutes,

Cooking time: 0 – 15 minutes;

Serve: 4

Ingredients:

- 70-80 g See
- 16 slices of raw ham
- 16 sage leaves
- 20 g butter
- Salt to taste
- Pepper to taste

Address:

1. Place the meat slices on a sheet of parchment paper. Arrange the ham slices on the meat, put the washed sage leaf, roll, and close with a toothpick.

2. Place the butter in the basket at 150⁰C. Melt the butter for 2 min.

3. Add the meat and simmer for 6 minutes.

Nutrition Value (Amount per Serving):

- Calories 323
- Fat 18g
- Carbohydrates 1.7g
- Sugars 0.4g
- Protein 29g
- Cholesterol 124mg

Sautéed Meat with Potatoes

Preparation time: 10-20 minutes,

Cooking time: 30-45 minutes;

Serve: 6

Ingredients:

- 750g beef
- 350 g of potatoes
- 200 ml of hot broth
- 250 g of tomato coulis
- 1 onion
- Salt to taste
- Pepper to taste

Direction:

1. Chop the onion and put it in the basket previously greased.
2. Set the temperature to 150°C.
3. Brown the onion for 3 to 4 minutes and then add the pieces of meat, broth, salt, and pepper.
4. Cook the meat for 20 minutes and add the potatoes and the tomato coulis.
5. Cook for another 20 to 25 minutes, mixing the sautéed with a wooden spoon 3 to 4 times during cooking to prevent it from drying out too much.

Nutrition Value (Amount per Serving):

- Calories 317
- Carbohydrates 13g
- Fat 18g
- Sugars 1g
- Protein 24g
- Cholesterol 73mg

Sautéed Pork with Peppers

Preparation time: 10 – 20 minutes,

Cooking time: 15 – 30 minutes;

Serve: 6

Ingredients:

- 600 g pieces of pork taken from the loin or shoulder
- 200 g of peppers
- 1 shallot
- Salt to taste
- Pepper to taste

Direction:

1. Preheat the air fryer at 150°C for 5 minutes. Spray the basket.

2. Chop the shallot and cut the peppers into strips Place the shallot and oil in the basket then brown for 2 minutes.

3. Add the peppers and simmer for another 8 minutes.

4. Finally pour the pieces of pork, salt, pepper, and simmer for another 10 minutes.

Nutrition Value (Amount per Serving):

- Calories 334.2
- Fat 11.5 g
- Carbohydrate 31.8 g
- Sugars 2.0 g
- Protein 24.5 g
- Cholesterol 59.2 mg

Chapter 6

Vegan and Vegetarian Recipes

Frying Potatoes

Preparation time: 5 minutes;

Cooking time: 40 minutes;

Serve: 4

Ingredients:

- 5 to 6 medium potatoes
- Olive oil in a spray bottle if possible
- Mill salt
- Freshly ground pepper

Direction:

1. Wash the potatoes well and dry them.

2. Brush with a little oil on both sides if not with the oil

3. Crush some ground salt and pepper on top.

4. Place the potatoes in the fryer basket

5. Set the cooking at 190°C for 40 minutes, in the middle of cooking turn the potatoes for even cooking on both sides.

6. At the end of cooking, remove the potatoes from the basket, cut them in half and slightly scrape the melting potato inside and add only a little butter, and enjoy!

Nutrition Value (Amount per Serving):

- Calories 365
- Fat 17g
- Carbohydrates 48g
- Sugars 0.3g
- Protein 4g
- Cholesterol 0mg

Avocado Fries

Preparation time: 5 minutes

Cooking time: 10 minutes;

Serve: 1

Ingredients:

- 1 egg
- 1 ripe avocado

- ½ tsp salt
- ½ cup of panko breadcrumbs

Direction:

1. Preheat the air fryer to 400°F (200°C) for 5 minutes.

2. Remove the avocado pit and cut into fries. In a small bowl, whisk the egg with the salt.

3. Enter the breadcrumbs on a plate.

4. Dip the quarters in the egg mixture, then in the breadcrumbs.

5. Put them in the fryer. Cook for 8-10 minutes.

6. Turn halfway through cooking.

Nutrition Value (Amount per Serving):

- Calories 390
- Fat 32g
- Carbohydrates 24g

- Sugars 3g
- Protein 4g
- Cholesterol 0mg

Crispy French Fries

Preparation time: 5 minutes;

Cooking time: 10 minutes;

Serve: 2

Ingredients:

- 2 medium sweet potatoes
- 2 tsp olive oil
- ½ tsp salt
- ½ tsp garlic powder
- ¼ tsp paprika
- Black pepper

Direction:

1. Preheat the hot air fryer to 400°F (200°C)
2. Spray the basket with a little oil.
3. Cut the sweet potatoes into potato chips about 1 cm wide.
4. Add oil, salt, garlic powder, pepper and paprika.
5. Cook for 8 minutes, without overloading the basket.
6. Repeat 2 or 3 times, as necessary.

Nutrition Value (Amount per Serving):

- Calories 240
- Fat 9g
- Carbohydrates 36g
- Sugars 1g
- Protein 3g
- Cholesterol 0mg

Frying Potatoes with Butter

Preparation time: 5 minutes;

Cooking time: 10 minutes;

Serve: 2

Ingredients:

- 2 Russet potatoes
- Butter
- Fresh parsley (optional)

Direction:

1. Spray the basket with a little oil.
2. Open your potatoes along.
3. Make some holes with a fork.
4. Add the butter and parsley.
5. Transfer to the basket. If your air fryer to a temperature of 198°C (390°F).
6. Cook for 30 to 40 minutes.
7. Try about 30 minutes. Bon Appetite!

Nutrition Value (Amount per Serving):

- Calories 365
- Fat 17g
- Carbohydrates 48g
- Sugars 0.3g
- Protein 4g
- Cholesterol 0mg

Homemade French Fries

Preparation time: 5 minutes;

Cooking time: 10 minutes;

Serve: 2

Ingredients:

- 2.5 lb. sliced and sliced potato chips
- 1 tbsp olive oil
- Salt and pepper to taste
- 1 tsp salt to season or paprika

Direction:

1. Put the fries in a bowl with very cold water.
2. Let it soak for at least 30 minutes.
3. Drain completely. Add the oil. Shake
4. Put them in the fryer bowl. Cook for 15 to 25 minutes. Set to 380°F (193°C).
5. Set the time according to your preferences or the power of your fryer to 23 minutes.

Nutrition Value (Amount per Serving):

- Calories 118
- Fat 7g
- Carbohydrates 27
- Sugars 1g
- Protein 2
- Cholesterol 0mg

Mini pepper/tomato/shallot/goat cheese tartlets

Preparation time: 10 minutes;

Cooking time: 15 minutes;

Serve: 4-6

Ingredients:

- 1 pure butter puff pastry

- 3 peppers+ 2 tomatoes + 1 shallot + 1 degermed garlic clove

- 1 whole egg + 2 tbsp salad seeds (squash, sunflower, sesame ......)

- 3 tablespoons cheese in cubes + ½ goat cheese log + 50 g grated emmental cheese

- 6/8 mini silicone molds (round, square, heart ....)

- Salt + pepper 5 berries

Direction:

1. Put the grid / cubes in the 11 in 1 mandolin and cut all the vegetables (cleaned) into small pieces.

2. Beat the egg in an omelet and add the cut vegetables, the cubed cheese, the seeds, salt, and pepper.

3. Unroll the puff pastry and cut circles (squares of hearts ...) and darken the mini molds. Prick the bottom with a fork.

4. Garnish with the egg/vegetable preparation and add a little goat cheese and grated emmental cheese on top.

5. Place the molds on the fryer grid, close the hood, and program the "15-minute pie" function at 150°C.

6. When it is well cooked, remove the grid with the tongs. Serve hot or warm with a salad.

Nutrition Value (Amount per Serving):

- Calories 152g

- Fat 9g

- Carbohydrates 10g

- Sugars 10g

- Protein 4g

- Cholesterol 0mg

Almond Apples

Preparation time: 10 minutes;

Cooking time: 45 minutes;

Serve: 5-6

Ingredients:

- 600 g of peeled potatoes
- 2 egg yolks
- 2 eggs
- 60g of almond powder
- Salt,
- Pepper
- frying oil
- 30g of butter
- 50g of almond chips
- 50g of breadcrumbs
- 50g of flour

Direction:

1. Peel the potatoes (if you feel like it, instead of throwing the husks, baked shell chips, it's a delight).

2. Cut the potatoes into cubes and cook them in salted water (starting with cold water) approximately 15 minutes after boiling.

3. Drain and puree with a potato masher. Add salt and pepper.

4. Add the egg yolks, butter, and almond powder, mix well.

5. Place in the refrigerator for a quarter of an hour, then roll balls into the palm of your hand. Then, roll them rolling successively in flour, beaten eggs in an omelet, then in a mixture of breadcrumbs and flaked almonds.

6. Let cool for 15 minutes.

7. Put them in the air fryer at 180°C for 15 minutes. Then place the almond apples on a paper towel.

Nutrition Value (Amount per Serving):

- Calories 284.0
- Fat 19.1 g
- Carbohydrate 27.9 g
- Sugars 13.8 g
- Protein 5.0 g
- Cholesterol 0.0 mg

French fries without dry

Ingredients:

- 500g of French fries
- 1 tbsp oil

Preparation:

1. Peel and cut the potatoes, using a knife or a "fried cut".

2. Rinse with water and dry the fries.

3. Put them in a bowl and add the oil spoon, mix well.

4. Preheat the air fryer to 160°C. Put the fries in the basket for 15 minutes.

5. Pour the fries in the bowl, mix, and pass the fryer to more than 200°C.

6. Put the fries back in the basket and cook again for about 10 minutes. Look carefully because the overhead comes quickly!

Nutrition Value (Amount per Serving):

- Calories 118
- Fat 7g
- Carbohydrates 27
- Sugars 1g
- Protein 2
- Cholesterol 0mg

Bugnes Lyonnaises

Preparation: 30 minutes;

Rest: 2 hours;

Cook: 15 minutes

Ingredients:

- 250 g flour
- ½ packet of yeast
- 50g of powdered sugar
- 50g butter
- 2 eggs
- 1 tsp rum
- 1 pinch of salt
- Frying oil

Direction:

1. Soften the butter; beat the eggs with a fork.

2. Place the flour in a bowl; add the salt, the butter, the beaten eggs, the aroma.

3. Mix until you have a consistent paste. Form a ball and let stand at least 2 hours in the fridge.

4. Heat the fryer oil at 150°C for 15 minutes.

5. Stretch the dough to a thickness of 5 mm. Cut into strips of 10 cm by 4 cm and make an incision in the center of 5 cm.

6. Pass a corner of the strip in the incision to tie a knot or leave it as is.

7. Dip the bugnes in the fryer, flip them 1 time and drain once cooked on absorbent paper.

8. Sprinkle with icing sugar or icing sugar and serve hot.

Nutrition Value (Amount per Serving):

- Calories 140
- Carbohydrate 6 g
- Fat 13 g
- Protein 1 g
- Sodium 29 mg
- Sugar 1 g

Green salad with roasted pepper

Preparation time: 5 minutes;

Cooking time: 10 minutes;

Serve: 2

Ingredients:

- 1 red pepper
- 1 tbsp lemon juice
- 3 tbsp yogurt
- 2 tbsp olive oil
- Freshly ground black pepper
- 1 romaine lettuce, cut into large strips
- 50g arugula leaves

Direction:

1. Preheat the Air Fryer to 200°C.

2. Place the pepper in the basket and insert it into the Air Fryer. Set the timer for 10 minutes and roast the pepper until the skin is slightly burned.

3. Then cut the pepper into quarters and remove the seeds and skin. Cut the pepper into strips.

4. Prepare vinaigrette in a bowl with 2 tablespoons of pepper juice, lemon juice, yogurt, and olive oil. Add pepper and salt according to your taste.

5. Mix the lettuce and arugula leaves in the vinaigrette and garnish the salad with the pepper strips.

Nutrition Value (Amount per Serving):

- Calories 47.3
- Fat 0.4 g
- Carbohydrate 10.8 g
- Sugars 2.0 g
- Protein   1.8 g
- Cholesterol 0.0 mg

Fat Free Crispy Fries

Preparation time: about 15 minutes;

Cook time: 10 to 35 minutes;

Serve: 4

Ingredients:

- 500g of special fries
- 1 tbsp olive oil
- 1 freezer bag
- Salt + pepper

Direction:

1. Peel the potatoes, cut them with a potato chip cutter, rinse them with clean water and dry them well with a cloth.

2. It is important to cut all the potatoes evenly; otherwise you may have some overcooked and not enough fries.

3. Place the sliced fries in a freezer bag, add 1 tablespoon of oil, close the bag, and stir everything.

4. Place the French fries in the basket, close it, and close the lid of the fryer and set to 230°C to 35 minutes.

5. At the end of cooking, remove the basket with the tongs and remove the fries. Add salt and pepper.

Nutrition Value (Amount per Serving):

- Calories 118
- Fat 7g
- Carbohydrates 27
- Sugars 1g
- Protein 2
- Cholesterol 0mg

Marinated Potatoes with Chimichurri Sauce

Preparation time: 20 minutes;

Cooking time: 45 minutes;

Serve: 4

Ingredients:

- 1kg to 1.2kg of potatoes
- 2 tablespoons chimichurri sauce

Direction:

1. Depending on the taste, you can peel the potatoes, but the real potatoes are prepared with the skin.

2. Wash the potatoes before cutting them.

3. Cut them in quarters to get the shape of the potatoes and place them in a freezer bag.

4. Add the sauce and use the solid closure of the sachet to keep it closed.

5. Mix everything by handling the bag in all directions. Potatoes should be well impregnated with the preparation.

6. Pour all the preparation in the air fryer without oil.

7. Set the air fryer at 180⁰C for 45 minutes and serve immediately after the end of cooking.

Nutrition Value (Amount per Serving):

- Calories 367
- Sugars 2.0 g
- Fat 18.4 g
- Protein 5.7 g
- Carbohydrate 45 g
- Cholesterol 0mg

Homemade Gluten Free Spicy Chips

Preparation time: 25 minutes;

Cooking time: 30 minutes;

Serve: 1

Ingredients:

- 500g of potatoes to choose from among those with firm meat
- 1 tbsp vegetable oil
- 1 pinch of salt
- 1 mixture of texmex spices

Direction:

1. Peel the potatoes and cut them into slices approximately 2 millimeters thick. Preferably use a mandolin for a very fine and regular cut.

2. Rinse the potatoes to get rid of their starch and let them stand for 15 minutes in a bowl of cold water.

3. Drain the potatoes and dry them with a paper towel by simply sliding them. Avoid rubbing them as they could break.

4. Pour the potatoes in the fryer and cover them with the necessary tablespoon of oil.

5. Set the air fryer at 150°C for 30 minutes.

6. Be sure to stir the fries with a wooden utensil every ten minutes to make sure they cook perfectly.

7. Wait 5 minutes before the end of cooking to add salt and spices.

Nutrition Value (Amount per Serving):

- Calories 150
- Cal
- 17%
- Carbohydrates 15g
- Fat 32g
- Protein 1g
- Sugars 3g
- Cholesterol 0mg

Funghetto Eggplant (Golden Neapolitan)

Preparation time: 0-10 minutes;

Cooking time: 15-30 minutes;

Serve:

Ingredients:

- 600g Eggplant
- 100g Broth
- 1 Garlic clove
- Salt
- Pepper
- 3 spoons Olive oil
- Parsley

Direction:

1. Wash the eggplants, dry them, and cut them into 1.5 cm cubes.
2. Place the mixing blade in the tank
3. Pour oil and peeled garlic, close the lid.
4. Set the air fryer to 150°C to brown for about 2 min.
5. Add eggplant, broth, salt and pepper and simmer for another 23 min.
6. Finally, before serving, sprinkle with chopped fresh parsley.

Nutrition Value (Amount per Serving):

- Calories 142
- Fat 12.9g
- Carbohydrate 5.20g
- Protein 1.9g
- Sugars 0g
- Cholesterol 0.1mg

Fried Bananas

Preparation time: 0-10 minutes;

Cooking time: 0 – 15 minutes;

Serve: 3

Ingredients:

- 3 Bananas
- 2 Eggs
- Breadcrumbs
- Flour at discretion
- Salt
- 1 tsp Oil

Direction:

1. Peel the bananas and cut them into sections of approximately 2 to 3 cm.

2. Pass them first in the flour, then in the egg beaten with salt and then in the breadcrumbs.

3. Heat the air fryer at 180^0C for 10 minutes. Then, place the breaded bananas.

4. Cook the bananas for 8 to 10 minutes, turning them 2 to 3 times during cooking to match the Dorado.

5. Serve warm.

Nutrition Value (Amount per Serving):

- Calories 262.4
- Fat 12.1 g
- Carbohydrate 33.9 g
- Sugars 20.7 g
- Protein 1.3 g
- Cholesterol 30.5 mg

Sautéed air mushrooms and parsley

Preparation time: 10 – 20 minutes;

Cooking time: 15 – 30 minutes;

Serve: 6

Ingredients:

- 600 g mushrooms
- 1 clove garlic
- 1 tsp olive oil

- Parsley
- Leave at discretion
- Black pepper at discretion

Direction:

1. Clean the mushrooms well and chop them.
2. Place the garlic and oil inside the basket close. Set the temperature to 150°C.
3. Brown for 2 minutes.
4. Add the mushrooms and cook for another 15 minutes.
5. Add (at discretion) salt and pepper, parsley, and finish cooking for another 3 minutes.

Nutrition Value (Amount per Serving):

- Calories 130
- Fat 7g
- Carbohydrates 17g

- Sugars 4g
- Protein 4g
- Cholesterol 0mg

Cauliflowers au gratin

Preparation time: 20-30 minutes;

Cooking time: 15-30 minutes;

Serve: 6

Ingredients:

- 800g cauliflower
- ½ liter of Béchamel
- 4 slices of cheese
- Parmesan to taste

Direction:

1. Separately, cook the cauliflowers in water. Meanwhile, prepare ½ liter of bechamel (dose: 500 ml of milk, 50 g of flour, 50 g of butter, salt, and nutmeg).

2. Pour some bechamel into the basket. Arrange the cauliflower flowers, covered with the slices of cheese and cover with the béchamel sauce. Sprinkle with Parmesan cheese.

3. Set the air fryer to 150°C. Simmer for about 20 minutes or according to the degree of gratin desired.

Nutrition Value (Amount per Serving):

- Calories 285
- Sugars 2.5g
- Fat 19g
- Protein 14g
- Carbohydrates 17g
- Cholesterol 55mg

Peach Clafoutis

Preparation time: 20 – 30 minutes;

Cooking time: 30 – 45 minutes;

Serve: 10

Ingredients:

- 300 g flour
- 150g butter
- 150g of sugar
- 4 eggs
- 1 sachet of baking powder
- 500g peaches in syrup
- 1 lemon
- 3-4 tbsp milk
- Icing sugar at discretion

Direction:

1. Melt the butter in the microwave; Work the butter, sugar, and eggs in a bowl.

2. Add flour, baking powder, grated lemon peel and milk. Work everything with an electric mixer until you get a smooth and homogeneous mixture.

3. Butter and flour the tank and pour the mixture inside, smearing well.

4. Place a whole peach in the center and place the others (cut into quarters) next to each other following the circumference of the mold.

5. Set the air fryer on the lower heating temperature.

6. Bake the cake for 45 minutes.

7. Let cool and remove it from the tank; sprinkle with icing sugar.

Nutrition Value (Amount per Serving):

- Calories 148
- Carbohydrates 14g
- Fat 8g
- Sugars 6 g
- Protein 4g
- Cholesterol 102mg

Zucchini thinly sliced

Preparation time: 0-10 minutes;

Cooking time: 15-30 minutes;

Serve: 6

Ingredients:

- 600g zucchini
- 1 clove garlic
- 100 ml of water
- 1 tsp olive oil
- Parsley Taste
- Salt to taste
- Pepper to taste

Direction:

1. Wash and turn the zucchini, then dry them and cut them into rings. Add the oil and peeled garlic to the basket.

2. Set the temperature to 150^0C.

3. Brown for about 2 minutes, then remove the garlic from the tank and pour the zucchini with the water, season with salt and pepper and close the lid.

4. Simmer for 23 minutes. At the end of cooking, add the chopped parsley, a drizzle of oil and serve.

Nutrition Value (Amount per Serving):

- Calories 21
- Fat 0.2g
- Carbohydrates 3.9g
- Sugars 3.1g
- Protein 1.5g
- Cholesterol 0mg

Couscous with Vegetables

Preparation time: 10-20 minutes;

Cooking time: 30-45 minutes; Serve: 8

Ingredients:

- 50g carrot
- Eggplant 250g
- 50g cherry tomatoes
- 1 shallot
- 150g broth
- 250g zucchini
- Salt to taste

- 1 clove garlic
- Chili pepper
- 375g couscous
- 400 ml of water
- Butter taste
- 1 ml of olive oil

Direction:

1. Peel the garlic, cut the chili into pieces, chop the shallot and place everything on the baking sheet, distributing it well through the bottom; add the oil. Before you start cooking, wash, and cut eggplants, zucchini, carrots, and small diced tomatoes (the latter should be reserved as they will be added to couscous when they are cold).

2. Set the air fryer to 150^{0}C and brown for 3 minutes. Add carrots, broth, and simmer for another 6 min. Finally pour the eggplant and zucchini, salt and pepper and simmer for another 25 minutes.

3. In addition to preparing the semolina by putting the water in a saucepan, boil, pour a small spoonful of salt. Add the couscous in the rain, oil, mix and stop the fire. Let swell for 3 min. Add a pinch of butter and cook again for another 3 min. mixing regularly with a fork to shell properly.

4. As soon as the vegetables have cooled, add the small tomatoes, and pour everything into a bowl with the couscous.

Nutrition Value (Amount per Serving):

- Calories 219.6
- Fat 4.0 g
- Carbohydrate 40.3 g

- Sugars 0.0 g
- Protein 6.5 g
- Cholesterol 0.0 mg

Rillette mushroom crusts

Preparation time: more than 30,

Cooking time: 15 - 30,

Calories: 273

Ingredients:

- 400g mushrooms
- 1 shallot
- 40g nuts without shell
- 150g of butter
- Parsley at discretion
- 1 tsp olive oil
- Bread slices

Direction:

1. Cut the shallot finely and pour it into the greased basket previously preheat at 150°C for 5 minutes.

2. Let brown for 2 minutes.

3. Add sliced mushrooms, salt, and cook for 20 minutes.

4. At the end of cooking, mix the mushrooms, soft butter and nuts until a homogeneous mixture is obtained.

5. Put everything in the fridge for 1 hour.

6. Remove the preparation paddle from the basket (be careful, it will be hot), place the slices of bread inside and toast them for 4 to 5 minutes or until golden brown.

7. Fill each crouton with the rillette.

Nutrition Value (Amount per Serving):

- Calories 190
- Fat 1.5g
- Carbohydrates 36g
- Sugars 3g
- Protein 7g
- Cholesterol 0mg

Mediterranean Bream

Preparation time: 10-20 minutes;

Cooking time: 15-30 minutes;

Serve: 2

Ingredients:

- 2 gold
- 200g cherry tomatoes
- 100g of black olives
- 1 clove garlic

- Thyme to taste
- Leaves to taste
- Pepper to taste
- 1 tsp peanut oil

Direction:

1. First, remove the golden scales. Clean them and gut them. Salt and pepper inside the belly, add a clove of garlic and two sprigs of thyme.

2. Grease the basket with the oil.

3. Cut the tomatoes in half and add them to the basket with the black olives and capers; salt everything

4. Set the temperature to 150^0C and cook for 25 minutes.

Nutrition Value (Amount per Serving):

- Calories 248
- Carbohydrates 22g
- Fat 12g

- Sugars 3g
- Protein 8g
- Cholesterol 0mg

Draniki

Preparation time: 10-20 minutes;

Cooking time: 15-30 minutes;

Serve: 2

Ingredients:

- 4 medium potatoes
- ½ onion
- 1 carrot
- 1 egg
- 100g flour
- Leaves to taste
- 1 tsp oil

Direction:

1. Peel the potatoes, the onion and the carrot and wash them well.

2. Using a food processor cut all vegetables in julienne and place them in a large bowl.

3. Add the egg, salt, and flour (the doses of the latter may vary depending on the degree of moisture present in the vegetables) and mix well.

4. Cover the bottom of the basket with baking paper and pour a little of the mixture with a tablespoon and spread well.

5. Fill the useful space inside the tank (about 5 to 6 empanadas at a time).

6. Set the air fryer to 180°C.

7. Cook for 10 to 12 minutes depending on the degree of browning desired.

8. After finishing the mixture, remove the baking paper, grease the bottom of the tank, and brown the previously cooked empanadas for another 2 minutes on each side.

Nutrition Value (Amount per Serving):

- Calories 84
- Carbohydrates 16g
- Fat 2g
- Sugars 0g
- Protein 3g
- Cholesterol 0mg

Chips

Preparation time: 10-20 minutes;

Cooking time: 30-45 minutes;

Serve: 8

Ingredients:

- 1500g of fresh potatoes
- Fine salt to taste
- 1 tsp peanut oil

Direction:

1. Peel the potatoes and cut them into sticks of approximately 1 cm per side.
2. Put the cut potatoes in water for a few minutes and rinse thoroughly.
3. Drain and clean well with a paper towel.
4. Pour the potatoes and the correct amount of oil in the pan.
5. Cook for 37/40 minutes at 180^{0}C. Salt then serve.

Nutrition Value (Amount per Serving):

- Calories 365
- Fat 17g
- Carbohydrates 48g
- Sugars 0.3g
- Protein 4g
- Cholesterol 0mg

French Fries with Paprika

Preparation time: 10-20 minutes,

Cooking time: 15-30 minutes;

Serve: 8

Ingredients:

- 700g of carrots
- 1 tsp sweet paprika
- 1 tsp oil

Direction:

1. Peel the carrots and cut them into sticks.

2. Add carrots and paprika in the basket. Set the temperature to 180°C.

3. Cook the carrots for about 20 minutes (time may vary depending on the size of the carrots).

Nutrition Value (Amount per Serving):

- Calories 299
- Carbohydrates 33g
- Sugars 3g
- Fat 16g
- Protein 7g
- Cholesterol 163 mg

Frozen French Fries

Cooking time: 15-30 minutes;

Serve: 8

Ingredients:

- 1000g Standard French fries (10 X 10) mm frozen
- Fine salt to taste

Direction:

1. Preheat the air fryer at 150°C.

2. Let cook for 27 minutes: salt and serve.

Nutrition Value (Amount per Serving):

- Calories 150.0
- Fat 0.0 g
- Carbohydrate 20.0 g
- Sugars 0.0 g
- Protein   2.0 g
- Cholesterol 0.0 mg

Beans in sauce

Preparation time: 0-10 minutes,

Cooking time: 15-30 minutes;

Serve: 8

Ingredients:

- 500g canned beans
- 300g of tomato puree
- ½ carrot
- 1 onion

- ½ sprig of rosemary
- Salt and pepper to taste
- 1 tsp olive oil

Direction:

1. Prepare a chopped carrot and onion and place it inside the cooking tray with rosemary. Grease the basket with the oil.

2. Set the air fryer to 150°C and brown for 4 min.

3. Add the drained beans from your vegetable water and rinse thoroughly, simmer for another 3 min.

4. Add the tomato, ½ glass of water, salt and pepper and continue cooking for another 13 minutes.

Nutrition Value (Amount per Serving):

- Calories 270
- Fat 1g
- Carbohydrates 53g

- Sugars 14g
- Protein 14g
- Cholesterol 0mg

Spicy Potatoes

Preparation time: 10-20 minutes;

Cooking time: 30-45 minutes;

Serve: 8

Ingredients:

- 1250g of fresh potatoes
- 10g sweet paprika
- Tomato puree
- 2 tbsp vinegar
- Salt and pepper to taste

Direction:

1. Peel the potatoes and cut them into 1 cm cubes on each side. Put the potatoes in the water for a few minutes and rinse them well. Drain and clean with a paper towel.

2. Pour the potatoes, rosemary, and the exact amount of oil inside the tank, salt, and pepper.

3. Set the air fryer to 160°C and cook for 25 min.

4. Add the paprika, tomato puree and vinegar, then finish cooking and simmer for another 10 minutes.

5. Prepare the "tapas" by piercing the potatoes with toothpicks.

Nutrition Value (Amount per Serving):

- Calories 250
- Carbohydrates 33g
- Fat 11g
- Sugars 0g
- Protein 4g
- Cholesterol 0mg

Frozen Potatoes

Cooking time: 15-30 minutes;

Serve: 8

Ingredients:

- 1000 g of potatoes in frozen rooms
- Fine salt to taste

Direction:

1. Cook for 30 minutes at 160⁰C.

2. Salt and serve

Nutrition Value (Amount per Serving):

- Calories 18.2
- Fat 0.0g
- Carbohydrate 4.1g
- Protein 0.6g
- Cholesterol 0mg

Potatoes (Unpeeled) And Yogurt Sauce

Preparation time: 10 – 20 minutes,

Cooking time: 30 – 45 minutes;

Serve: 4

Ingredients:

- 750 g of fresh potatoes
- 1 pepper
- 1 onion
- Salt taste
- Basil at ease

- 50 g lean yogurt
- 50 g of mayonnaise
- 20 g tomato sauce
- 1 pinch sweet paprika

Direction:

1. Wash the potatoes and let them soak in cold water and baking soda for 15 minutes and then brush them well with water.

2. Cut them in quarters and put them in the basket previously greased.

3. Set the air fryer to 150°C.

4. Cook the potatoes for 15 minutes and then add the chopped pepper and sliced onion; Salt.

5. Cook for another 15 minutes and then add the fresh basil cut from the menu.

6. Cook for another 15 minutes.

7. If you want to accompany the potatoes with the yogurt sauce, simply mix all the ingredients until you get a creamy sauce.

Nutrition Value (Amount per Serving):

- Calories 49.1
- Fat 2.5 g
- Carbohydrate 2.4 g

- Sugars 1.7 g
- Protein 4.1 g
- Cholesterol 5.2 mg

Frozen New Potatoes

Cooking time: 30-45 minutes;

Serve: 8

Ingredients:

- 1200 g of frozen new potatoes
- Fine salt to taste

Direction:

1. Pour the potatoes in the basket.
2. Cook for 38 minutes at 180°C.
3. Salt and serve.

Nutrition Value (Amount per Serving):

- Calories 89
- Carbohydrates 19g
- Fat 0g
- Sugars 0g
- Protein 2g
- Cholesterol 0mg

Potatoes, Beets and Carrots

Preparation time: 10-20 minutes,

Cooking time: 30-45 minutes;

Serve: 6

Ingredients:

- 300g beet
- 300 g of carrots
- 300 g of potatoes
- 2 cloves of garlic
- Rosemary to taste
- Salt to taste
- Pepper to taste

Direction:

1. Clean, wash all vegetables (beets, carrots, and potatoes) and cut them into pieces of 2 to 3 cm.

2. Put the garlic clove, chopped vegetables, rosemary and spray the basket; Season with salt and pepper.

3. Cook for about 35 minutes at 150°C.

Nutrition Value (Amount per Serving):

- Calories 170.5
- Fat 7.1 g
- Carbohydrate 26.5 g
- Sugars 9.5 g
- Protein   3.4 g
- Cholesterol 0.0 mg

Frozen Onion Rings

Cooking time: 15-30 minutes;

Serve: 6

Ingredients:

- 15 pieces onion rings: 15 pieces
- Fine salt to taste

Direction:

3. Cook everything for 15 minutes at 180°C.

Nutrition Value (Amount per Serving):

- Calories 220
- Sugar 5g
- Fat 11g
- Protein 4g
- Carbohydrates 27g
- Cholesterol 0mg

Sautéed Potatoes and Pumpkin

Preparation time: 10 – 20 minutes,

Cooking time: 15 – 30 minutes;

Serve: 4

Ingredients:

- 450 g of potatoes
- 550 g pumpkin
- 20 g of breadcrumbs
- Coarse salt

Direction:

1. Preheat the air fryer to 180°C for 5 minutes.

2. Thoroughly clean the pumpkin and potatoes and cut them into large pieces. Pour all ingredients into the basket.

3. Cook for 30 minutes or until you get the crispy you want.

Nutrition Value (Amount per Serving):

- Calories 30
- Fat 0.1g
- Carbohydrates 8g
- Sugars 3.2g
- Protein 1.2g
- Cholesterol 0mg

Rice spaghetti with vegetables

Preparation time: 10 – 20 minutes;

Cooking time: 15 – 30 minutes;

Serve: 4

Ingredients:

- 100 g of celery
- 150 g of carrots
- 150g kale
- 2 scallions
- 2 tbsp soy sauce
- 100 g of bean sprouts
- 200 g of rice spaghetti

Direction:

1. Spray the basket of the air fryer. Cut all the vegetables in julienne and put the celery, chives, and carrots in the basket.

2. Set the air fryer to 150°C. Cook for 10 minutes.

3. Add the sprouts and soy sauce and cook for another 10 minutes.

4. Meanwhile, cook the rice spaghetti in salted water and boil and serve with the previously prepared sauce.

Nutrition Value (Amount per Serving):

- Calories 235.0
- Fat 10.9 g
- Carbohydrate 34.7 g
- Sugars 6.4 g
- Protein   13.9 g
- Cholesterol 0.5 mg

Strapatsada

Preparation time: 10-20 minutes;

Cooking time: 15-30 minutes;

Serve: 4

Ingredients:

- ½ onion
- 1 red pepper
- 100g mushrooms
- 300 g of tomatoes

- 6 eggs
- Fine salt to taste
- Black pepper to taste

Direction:

1. Cut the mushrooms (washed) and onions in julienne.

2. Distribute everything in the tank with the oil.

3. Set the temperature to 180^{0}C and Cook for 12 minutes.

4. Add the tomatoes (skinless) cut into pieces, salt, and cook for another 8 minutes.

5. Remove the trowel (take care that it is hot!) And distribute the vegetables at the basket.

6. In a bowl, beat the eggs with salt and pepper and pour all over the vegetables. Cook another 7 to 8 minutes.

Nutrition Value (Amount per Serving):

- Calories 380
- Carbohydrates
- Fat 30g

- Sugars 6g
- Protein 19g
- Cholesterol 370g

Chicory Strudel

Preparation time: 10-20 minutes;

Cooking time: 30-45 minutes;

Serve: 6

Ingredients:

- 1 puff pastry
- Red chicory
- 100 g of stravecchio cheese
- 100 g of cow mozzarella
- 3 slices of Italian stuffed piglet

Direction:

1. Unroll the puff pastry, cover with a layer of cheese shavings, add the pieces of raw chicory and diced mozzarella.

2. Cover the whole with slices of stuffed piglet and close the puff pastry to form a stake.

3. Place the lining on the baking paper inside the basket.

4. Set the temperature to 160°C and cook for 35 minutes.

5. Very good with cheese sauce.

Nutrition Value (Amount per Serving):

- Calories 210
- Carbohydrates 30g
- Fat 5g
- Sugars 10g
- Protein 9g
- Cholesterol 0mg

Toast with Eggplant Caviar

Preparation time: 10-20 minutes,

Cooking time: 15-30 minutes;

Serve: 8

Ingredients:

- Eggplants 450g
- 1 tbsp concentrated tomatoes
- 100 g almonds
- 1 shallot
- 25 g of Parmesan
- 15 basil leaves
- Bread slices

Direction:

1. Cut the shallot finely and pour it into the basket previously greased with the spray.

2. Brown for 2 minutes at 160°C.

3. Add chopped eggplants, tomato puree diluted in 100 ml of water, salt and cook for 23 minutes.

4. Chill the eggplants after cooking. Place the almonds in the basket and roast them for 4 to 5 minutes.

5. Mix eggplant with almonds, parmesan, and basil separately until a homogeneous compound is obtained.

6. Remove the preparation paddle from the tank (be careful, it will be hot), place the slices of bread inside and roast them for 4 to 5 minutes or until golden brown.

7. Fill each crust with the previously prepared sauce.

Nutrition Value (Amount per Serving):

- Calories 91.8
- Fat 6.1 g
- Carbohydrate 9.2 g
- Sugars 0.0 g
- Protein 1.5 g
- Cholesterol 1.3 mg

Provencal Tomatoes

Preparation time: 10 – 20 minutes,

Cooking time: 15 – 30 minutes;

Serve: 4

Ingredients:

- 4 tomatoes
- 80 g of breadcrumbs
- 1 clove garlic
- 2 marjoram branches

- 1 rosemary branch
- Parsley chopped to taste
- Salt to taste
- Butter to taste

Direction:

1. Remove the top of the tomatoes and drain them. Separately, place all other ingredients (except butter) in a bowl and mix them; The mixture must be quite sandy.

2. Fill the tomatoes and then place them in the basket by adding the butter.

3. Set the temperature to 160°C and cook for 20 minutes depending on the size of the tomatoes.

4. It can be served both cold and hot.

Nutrition Value (Amount per Serving):

- Calories 69
- Carbohydrates 8g
- Fat 2g

- Sugars 2g
- Protein 3g
- Cholesterol 7g

Potato Omelet

Preparation time: 10 – 20 minutes,

Cooking time: 15 – 30 minutes;

Serve: 6

Ingredients:

- 600 g of potatoes
- ½ onion

- 6 eggs
- Salt, pepper to taste

Direction:

1. Peel the potatoes and cut them into squares of approximately 1 cm; Peel the onion and cut it into slices that are not very thin.

2. Pour the onion, oil and potatoes in the basket Cook for 25 minutes at 160⁰C.

3. Distribute potatoes and onion well in the bottom of the basket. Then pour the previously made egg, salt, and pepper mixture. Continue cooking for another 5 minutes.

Nutrition Value (Amount per Serving):

- Calories 193
- Carbohydrates 27g
- Fat 5g

- Sugars 1g
- Protein 10g
- Cholesterol 185 mg

Vol Au Vent with Mushrooms

Preparation time: 10 - 20 minutes,

Cooking time: 15 – 30 minutes;

Serve: 6

Ingredients:

- 1 roll of puff pastry
- Whole milk to taste
- 100 g of air sautéed mushrooms and parsley
- Brie to taste

Direction:

1. Unroll the puff pastry, prick the bottom with a fork and cut 18 discs about 7 cm in diameter. Place 6 discs in the bowl covered with baking paper.

2. Make a hole of approximately 3 cm in the other 12 discs and place them two at a time in the large discs. Brush with milk so that they adhere well to each other.

3. Set the temperature to 160°C

4. Cook for 15 to 17 minutes. Rotate the baking paper after 10 minutes for best results.

5. Fill the vol au vent with a preparation of mushrooms sautéed in air and parsley and cover with a piece of cheese.

6. Serve still hot

Nutrition Value (Amount per Serving):

- Calories 94
- Fat 6.4g
- Carbohydrates 6.7g
- Protein 1.7g

Spanish Potatoes

Preparation time: 10 minutes;

Cooking time: 57 minutes;

Serve: 2

Ingredients:

- 400 g potato
- Water
- 1 tbsp olive oil
- Salt

Direction:

1. Peel and cut the potato in julienne about 0.5 CM thick.

2. Prepare a bowl with very cold water, if necessary, add ice. Place the cut potatoes for at least 30 minutes to make them starch.

3. Dry each potato with an absorbent napkin and place in another dry bowl.

4. When they are all dry, sprinkle with oil or brush with olive oil and season with salt and whatever you like (sweet paprika, oregano, etc.).

5. In this case place in a fryer without oil at temperature 160^{0}C for 17 minutes.

6. Set the fryer at 180^{0}C another 10 minutes and that's it.

Nutrition Value (Amount per Serving):

- Calories 77
- Fat 0.09g
- Carbohydrate17.47g
- Sugars 0.78g
- Protein2.02g
- Cholesterol 0mg

Green Salad with Roasted Pepper

Preparation time: 15 minutes;

Cooking time: 10 minutes;

Serve: 4

Ingredients:

- 1 red pepper
- 1 tbsp lemon juice
- 3 tbsp yogurt
- 2 tbsp olive oil
- Freshly ground black pepper
- 1 romaine lettuce in wide strips
- 50 g arugula leaves

Direction:

1. Preheat the air fryer to 200°C.

2. Place the pepper in the basket and place it in the air fryer. Set the timer to 10 minutes and roast the pepper until the skin is slightly burned.

3. Place the pepper in a bowl and cover it with a lid or with transparent film. Let stand 10 to 15 minutes.

4. Next, cut the pepper into four parts and remove the seeds and skin. Cut the pepper into strips.

5. Mix a dressing in a bowl with 2 tablespoons of the pepper juice, lemon juice, yogurt, and olive oil. Add pepper and salt to taste.

6. Pour the lettuce and arugula leaves into the dressing and garnish the salad with the pepper strips.

Nutrition Value (Amount per Serving):

- Calories 77.9
- Fat 0.4 g
- Carbohydrate 19.3 g
- Sugars 4.6 g
- Protein 2.7 g
- Cholesterol 0.0 mg

Garlic Mushrooms

Preparation time: 10 minutes;

Cooking time: 10 minutes;

Serve: 2

Ingredients:

- 1 slice of white bread
- 1 crushed garlic clove
- 1 tbsp chopped parsley
- Freshly ground black pepper
- 1 tbsp olive oil
- 12 mushrooms

Direction:

1. Preheat the air fryer to 200°C.
2. Grate the slice of bread until it is thin in the kitchen robot and mix it with the garlic, parsley, and season to taste. Finally, pour the olive oil.
3. Remove the mushroom stems and fill the caps with the breadcrumbs.
4. Place the mushrooms in the basket and place it in the air fryer. Set the timer to 10 minutes. Bake until golden brown and crispy.
5. Serve them on a tray.

Nutrition Value (Amount per Serving):

- Calories 139
- Fat 11.6g
- Carbohydrates 6.1g
- Sugars 3.5g
- Protein 4.7g
- Cholesterol 30.4mg

Roasted Potatoes with Paprika and Greek Yogurt

Preparation time: 10 minutes;

Cooking time: 20 minutes;

Serve: 4

Ingredients:

- 800 g of white potatoes
- 2 tbsp olive oil
- 1 tbsp spicy paprika
- Freshly ground black pepper
- 150 ml Greek yogurt

Direction:

1. Preheat the air fryer to 180°C. Peel the potatoes and cut them into cubes of 3 cm. Dip the cubes in water for at least 30 minutes. Dry them well with paper towels.

2. In a medium-sized bowl, mix 1 tablespoon of olive oil with the paprika and add pepper to taste. Coat the potato dice with the spiced oil.

3. Place the potato dice in the fryer basket and place it in the air fryer. Set the timer to 20 minutes and fry the dice until golden brown and ready to take. Spin them occasionally.

4. In a small bowl, mix the Greek yogurt with the remaining tablespoon of olive oil and add salt and pepper to taste. Spread the paprika over the mixture. Serve the yogurt as a sauce with the potatoes.

5. Serve the potato dice on a tray and salt them. They will be delicious with ribs or kebabs.

Nutrition Value (Amount per Serving):

- Calories 225.1
- Fat 13.8 g
- Carbohydrate 24.2 g
- Sugars 9.7 g
- Protein   2.5 g
- Cholesterol 0.0 mg

Mini peppers with Goat Cheese

Preparation time: 10 minutes;

Cooking time: 8 minutes;

Serve: 4

Ingredients:

- 8 mini peppers
- ½ tbsp olive oil
- ½ tbsp dried Italian herbs
- 1 tsp freshly ground black pepper
- 100 g soft goat cheese in eight portions

Direction:

1. Preheat the air fryer to 200°C.

2. Cut the top of the mini peppers and remove the seeds and the membrane.

3. Mix the olive oil in a deep dish with the Italian herbs and pepper. Pour the portions of goat cheese in the oil.

4. Press a serving of goat cheese against each mini pepper and place the mini peppers in the basket next to each other. Insert the basket in the air fryer and set the timer to 8 minutes. Bake the mini peppers until the cheese is melted.

5. Serve mini peppers in small dishes such as snacks or snacks.

Nutrition Value (Amount per Serving):

- Calories 17
- Fat 1g
- Carbohydrates 1g
- Sugar 1g
- Protein 0g
- Cholesterol 60mg

Chapter 7

Desserts

Cake with cream and strawberries

Preparation time: 10 minutes;

Cooking time: 15 minutes;

Serve: 2

Ingredients:

- 1 pure butter puff pastry to stretch
- 500g strawberries (clean and without skin)
- 1 bowl of custard
- 3 tbsp icing sugar baked at 210°C in the air fryer

Direction:

1. Unroll the puff pastry and place it on the baking sheet. Prick the bottom with a fork and spread the custard. Arrange the strawberries in a circle and sprinkle with icing sugar.

2. Cook in a fryer setting a 210°C for 15 minutes.

3. Remove the cake from the fryer with the tongs and let cool.

4. When serving sprinkle with icing sugar

5. And why not, add some whipped cream.

Nutrition Value (Amount per Serving):

- Calories 212.6
- Fat 8.3 g
- Carbohydrate 31.9 g
- Sugars 17.4 g
- Protein   2.3 g
- Cholesterol 21.4 mg

Caramelized Pineapple and Vanilla Ice Cream

Preparation time: 0-10;

Cooking time: 15-30;

Serve: 4 people

Ingredients:

- 4 slices Pineapple
- 20g Butter
- 50g Cane sugar
- Ice cream/vanilla cream

Direction:

1. Heat the Air Fryer at 150°C for 5 minutes. Let it brown for 15-30 minutes. Then, take it out and top with the cream.

Nutrition Value (Amount per Serving):

- Calories 648
- Fat 36.4g
- Carbohydrates 73.2g
- Sugar 61.6g
- Protein 9.5g
- Cholesterol 94mg

Apple Pie

Preparation time: 20-30;

Cooking time: 45-60;

Serve: 3

Ingredients:

- 600g Flour
- 350g Margarine
- 150g Sugar
- 2 Eggs
- 50g Breadcrumbs

- 3 Apples
- 75g Raisins
- 75g Sugar
- 1tsp Cinnamon

Direction:

2. Put the flour, sugar, eggs, and margarine nuts in the blender just outside the refrigerator.

3. Mix everything until you get a compact and quite flexible mixture. Let it rest in the refrigerator for at least 30 minutes.

4. Preheat the air fryer at 150^0C for 5 minutes.

5. Spread 2/3 of the mass of broken dough in 3-4 mm thick covering the previously floured and floured tank and making the edges adhere well, which should be at least 2 cm.

6. Place the breadcrumbs, apple slices, sugar, raisins, and cinnamon in the bottom; cover everything with the remaining dough and make holes in the top to allow steam to escape.

7. Cook for 40 minutes and then turn off the lower resistance.

8. Cook for another 20 minutes only with the upper resistance on. Once it has cooled, put it on a plate and serve.

Nutrition Value (Amount per Serving):

- Calories 411
- Fat 19.38g
- Total Carbohydrate 57.5g

- Sugars 50g
- Protein3.72g
- Cholesterol0mg

Apple Rotation

Preparation time: 10 – 20 minutes,

Cooking time: 15 – 30 minutes;

Serve: 6

Ingredients:

- 1 roll of rectangular puff pastry
- 220g of apples
- 50g of sugar
- 100g raisins
- 50g pine nuts
- To taste breadcrumbs
- Cinnamon powder to taste

Direction:

1. Put the raisins in warm water for at least 30 min. Meanwhile, peel the apples, remove the kernel, and cut them into thin slices. Pour the apples into a large bowl and add the dried raisins.

2. Add the cinnamon, sugar, and pine nuts, gently mix the ingredients and let stand.

3. Meanwhile, spread the puff pastry on a work surface with parchment paper. Sprinkle with the breadcrumbs, leaving a 2-3 cm border around. Place the mixture in the center of the dough and close the coating along.

4. Be careful not to tear the dough, close the sides tightly so that the contents do not come out during cooking.

5. Place the liner on the air fryer and Cook over low temperature for about 25 min. When finished cooking, sprinkle the strudel with icing sugar and serve warm sliced.

Nutrition Value (Amount per Serving):

- Calories 411
- Fat 19.38g
- Total Carbohydrate 57.5g
- Sugars 50g
- Protein3.72g
- Cholesterol0mg

Stuffed brioche crown

Preparation time: more than 30 minutes;

Cooking time: 30 – 45 minutes;

Serve: 8

Ingredients:

- 250g Manitoba flour
- 250g flour 00
- 200 ml of warm milk
- 100 ml of warm water
- 50 ml of olive oil
- 25g baker's yeast
- 1 tbsp sugar
- 1 tsp fine salt
- 250g cooked ham
- 8 slices of emmental
- Poppy seeds
- 1 tbsp of water
- 1 tsp olive oil

Direction:

1. Prepare the brioche crown and let it grow in a lightly floured and closed container with food wrap for about an hour.

2. Once the survey is finished, spread the dough with a rolling pin, forming a narrow rectangle. First place the ham and then the cheese, leaving about 2 cm of free edge around.

3. Roll everything up to get a cylinder. Cut approximately 2 cm slices and place them in the basket covered with baking paper by placing them side by side to form a crown.

4. Let the preparation rise for another hour before cooking. In the end, brush with a mixture of warm water and oil over the entire surface of the crown and sprinkle with poppy seeds.

5. Preheat the air fryer at 180°C for 5 minutes. Cook for 40 minutes.

Nutrition Value (Amount per Serving):

- Calories 516
- Fat 32g
- Carbohydrates 39g
- Sugars 7g
- Protein 17g
- Cholesterol 0mg

Fried Cream

Preparation time: 10-20 minutes;

Cooking time: 15-30 minutes;

Serve: 8

Ingredients:

For the cream:

- 500 ml of whole milk
- 3 egg yolks
- 150 g of sugar
- 50 g flour
- 1 envelope Vanilla Sugar

Ingredients for the pie:

- 2 eggs
- Unlimited Breadcrumbs
- 1 tsp oil

Direction:

1. First prepare the custard; once cooked, pour the cream into a dish previously covered with a transparent film and level well. Let cool at room temperature for about 2 hours.

2. Grease the basket and distribute it all over.

3. When the cream is cold, place it on a cutting board and cut it into dice; Pass each piece of cream first in the breadcrumbs, covering the 4 sides well in the beaten egg and then in the pie.

4. Place each part inside the basket. Set the temperature to 150°C.

5. Cook for 10 to 12 minutes, turning the pieces after 6 to 8 minutes.

6. The doses of this cream are enough to make 2 or even 3 kitchens in a row.

Nutrition Value (Amount per Serving):

- Calories 355
- Fat 18.37g
- Carbohydrates 44.94g
- Sugars 30.36g
- Protein 4.81g
- Cholesterol 45mg

Apple, cream, and hazelnut crumble

Preparation time: 10-20 minutes;

Cooking time: 15-30 minutes;

Serve: 6

Ingredients:

- 4 golden apples
- 100 ml of water
- 50g cane sugar
- 50g of sugar

- ½ tbsp cinnamon
- 200 ml of fresh cream
- Chopped hazelnuts to taste

Direction:

1. In a bowl, combine the peeled apples, cut into small cubes, cane sugar, sugar, and cinnamon.

2. Pour the apples inside the basket, add the water. Set the air fryer to 180°C and simmer for 15 minutes depending on the type of apple used and the size of the pieces.

3. At the end, divide the apples in the serving glasses, cover with previously whipped cream and sprinkle with chopped hazelnuts.

Nutrition Value (Amount per Serving):

- Calories 828.8
- Fat 44.8 g
- Carbohydrate 120.6 g

- Sugars 54.2 g
- Protein 4.4 g
- Cholesterol 29.5 mg

Fregolotta (Venetian puff pastry pie) with hazelnuts

Preparation time: 10-20,

Cooking time: 15-30, 8 people, Calories: 347

Ingredients:

- 200g of flour
- 150g of sugar
- 100 g melted butter

- 100g hazelnuts
- 1 egg
- ½ sachet of yeast

Direction:

1. Do not finely chop the hazelnuts. In a large bowl, pour all the ingredients (the butter once melted should be cooled before using), mix lightly, without the dough becoming too liquid.

2. Place parchment paper on the bottom of the basket and pour the mixture into it. Spread it evenly.

3. Set the air fryer to 180°C and simmer for 15 minutes and then turn the cake.

4. Cook for an additional 5 minutes.

5. Let cool and sprinkle the cake with icing sugar.

Nutrition Value (Amount per Serving):

- Calories 465
- Carbohydrates 37g
- Fat 25g

- Sugars 3g
- Protein 20g
- Cholesterol 0mg

Frozen Treats

Cooking time: 15-30 minutes;

Serve: 8

Ingredients:

- 14 frozen pieces

Direction:

1. Place the handles, placing them on the parchment paper and place them on the basket.

2. Set the temperature to 150°C.

3. Cook everything for 25 min.

Nutrition Value (Amount per serving):

- Calories 111
- Fat 20 g
- Carbohydrates 21 g

- Sugars 45g
- Protein 7g
- Cholesterol 0mg

Roscon Of Reyes (Spanish King's Cake)

Preparation time: 10-20 minutes;

Cooking time: 30-45 minutes;

Serve: 4

Ingredients:

- 2 puff pastries
- 100g almond flour
- 1 egg
- 75g of sugar
- 50g butter
- 1 vial of almond aroma
- 1 porcelain bean

Direction:

First, prepare the filling:

1. In a bowl mix the flour, egg, sugar, butter at room temperature and almond extract.

2. Stretch a puff pastry with the baking paper inside the basket. Prick with a fork and spread the filling well.

3. Place the bean inside, choosing an external position for the cake.

4. Cover with the second roll of puff pastry and weld the edges well. Brush the surface with an egg yolk diluted with milk and decorate with small incisions.

5. Set the temperature to 180°C. Bake the pie for 25 minutes

6. Turn the baking paper half a turn and cook for another 10 minutes.

7. Tradition says that the person who finds the hidden bean becomes the "king" of the day.

Nutrition Value (Amount per Serving):

- Calories 1426
- Fat 10.54g
- Carbohydrates 56.54g
- Sugar 23.51g
- Protein 6.58g
- Cholesterol 29mg

Nut cake

Preparation time: 10-20 minutes,

Cooking time: 30-45 minutes;

Serve: 10

Ingredients:

- 250 g of walnuts
- 150g Maïzena
- 4 medium eggs
- 200g of butter (room temperature)

- 1 sachet of yeast
- 1 sachet of vanilla sugar
- 200g of sugar

Direction:

1. Chop the nuts with 50 g of sugar. Using a food processor, beat the butter with the remaining sugar until you get a shiny and foamy mixture.

2. Add the eggs one by one, making sure the mixture is still soft, then add the vanilla.

3. Add the chopped nuts with the sugar and then the cornstarch that will sift with the yeast.

4. Butter and flour the basket, then pour the mixture in the center.

5. Set the air fryer at 180^0C.

6. Cook for 45 minutes (turn off the lower heating element 40 minutes later). Let cool before serving.

Nutrition Value (Amount per Serving):

- Calories 440
- Fat 20.48g
- Carbohydrate 62.22g

- Sugars 49.65g
- Protein 3.72g
- Cholesterol 53mg

Italian cake

Preparation time: 10-20 minutes;

Cooking time: 30-45 minutes;

Serve: 8

Ingredients:

- 250g of potato starch
- 150g of flour 00 (flour 55)
- 250g of sugar
- 6 eggs
- 50 g butter
- 1 sachet of yeast
- Powdered sugar

Direction:

1. Melt the butter in a small saucepan and let it cool.

2. Beat the eggs with the fine sugar until you get a light and frothy mixture. Add the flour, starch, sifted yeast, melted butter and mix until a homogeneous mixture is obtained.

3. Butter and flour the basket and pour the preparation into it.

4. Set the temperature to 180ºC and cook the cake for 35 min.

5. Remove the cake from the bowl, let it cool and sprinkle with icing sugar.

Nutrition Value (Amount per Serving):

- Calories 440
- Carbohydrates 40g
- Fat 30g
- Sugars 28g
- Protein 4g
- Cholesterol 65mg

Marble cake

Preparation time: 10-20 minutes;

Cooking time: 45-60 minutes; Serve: 10

Ingredients:

- 190g Butter
- 1g bag of vanilla sugar
- 12g baking powder
- 375g Flour
- 22g cocoa powder
- 4g medium eggs
- 225g of sugar
- 165 ml of milk
- Salt (a pinch)

Direction:

1. Put the previously softened butter into small pieces in a bowl with the sugar, mount the ingredients until a white and foamy cream forms.

2. Add the eggs at room temperature, one by one, the salt and beat about 5 minutes until you get a mixture without lumps. Add the flour (except 30 g that will keep aside), the yeast and vanilla sugar sifted alternately with the milk.

3. Mix the ingredients well, then divide them evenly and add the remaining flour in a bowl and the sifted cocoa in another.

4. Butter and flour the basket and first place the transparent mixture divided into three separate parts. Do the same with the dark mixture by filling the remaining gaps between the light mixture.

5. To get the veined effect, rotate a fork from top to bottom through the two colors of the mixture.

6. Set the air fryer to 180°C and cook for 40 minutes and then turn off the lower resistance.

7. Cook for another 10 min. Control the baking of the cake with the tip of a knife.

Nutrition Value (Amount per Serving):

- Calories 195
- Fat 7.6g
- Carbohydrates 28g
- Sugars 14g
- Protein 3.5g
- Cholesterol 47mg

Genoves Cake

Preparation time: 10-20 minutes;

Cooking time: 30-45 minutes;

Serve: 10

Ingredients:

- 6 eggs
- 190g of sugar
- 150g of flour 00 (flour 55)
- 75g potato starch
- 2g vanilla sugar

Direction:

1. In a bowl, beat the eggs with the sugar until you get a light and smooth mixture. Add the sifted flour, starch and vanilla sugar and mix with a whisk until a homogeneous mixture is obtained.

2. Butter and flour the basket, then pour the mixture.

3. Set the air fryer to 180°C and simmer for 35 minutes.

Nutrition Value (Amount per Serving):

- Calories 74
- Fat1.83g
- Carbohydrate10.91g
- Sugars 5.08g
- Protein 3.83g
- Cholesterol 74mg

Frozen Sorrentino gnocchi

Cooking time: 0 – 15 minutes;

Serve: 2

Ingredients:

- 550 g Sorrentino gnocchi

Direction:

5. Pour the gnocchi in the basket and cook for 13 minutes at 150°C mixing once halfway through cooking.

Nutrition Value (Amount per Serving):

- Calories 170
- Carbohydrates 30g
- Fat 2g

- Sugars 11g
- Protein 6g
- Cholesterol 5mg

Khachapuri (Georgian bread)

Preparation time: more than 30 minutes;

Cooking time: 15 – 30 minutes;

Serve: 4

Ingredients:

- 500g of flour
- 450g whole yogurt
- ½ tsp baking soda
- ½ tsp salt
- 150 g ricotta
- 100g provokes smoked
- 150g Greek feta cheese
- 4 tbsp fine parsley

Direction:

1. Prepare the khachapuri dough by mixing all the ingredients until a smooth and homogeneous mixture is obtained. Divide the dough into 8 equal parts.

2. Form 8 balls cover them with a clean cloth. Let them rest in a warm place and away from drafts. After about 1 hour of lifting, start spreading the dough.

3. Meanwhile, prepare the filling by grating provokes smoked and the feta cheese and then mix with the ricotta and parsley.

4. Spread the 8 balls by hand in circles of 10 to 15 cm, fill 4 circles with the previously prepared filling and close with the other 4. Now roll the 4 khachapuri with a roller until you get a diameter of the size of the basket.

5. Grease the bottom of the basket and place 1 khachapuri. Also grease the surface and prick with a fork.

6. Set the air fryer to 180ºC and cook each khachapuri for 15 minutes.

Nutrition Value (Amount per Serving):

- Calories 556
- Fat 33g
- Carbohydrates 37g
- Sugars 3.6g
- Protein 28g
- Cholesterol 181mg

Sweet and Sour Onions

Preparation time: 10-20 minutes,

Cooking time: 30-45 minutes;

Serve: 8

Ingredients:

- 600g of borretano onions
- 30g butter
- 30g of sugar
- 50g of Modena balsamic vinegar

Direction:

1. First peel and wash the onions.

2. Add the butter and set the air fryer to 160°C

3. Melt the butter for 2 minutes.

4. Add the sugar and vinegar and cook for another 3 minutes.

5. Then pour the onions and cook them for 30 minutes or to the desired cooking point (this may vary depending on the size of the onions).

6. They can be served as an appetizer or to accompany meat dishes.

Nutrition Value (Amount per Serving):

- Calories 80
- Carbohydrates 17g
- Fat 1g
- Sugars 12g
- Protein 1g
- Cholesterol 0mg

Frozen Paella

Cooking time: 15-30 minutes;

Serve: 2

Ingredients:

- 600 g of paella

Direction:

1. Pour the paella in the basket and set the temperature to 150^0C.

2. Cook for 15 minutes, mixing once in the middle of cooking.

Nutrition Value (Amount per Serving):

- Calories 315
- Carbohydrates 0g
- Fat 9g

- Protein 0g
- Sugar 0g
- Cholesterol 0mg

Spice Bread

Preparation time: 10 – 20 minutes;

Cooking time: 0 – 15 minutes;

Serve: 10

Ingredients:

Ingredients for 30 - 35 cookies:

- 350g flour
- 160g of sugar
- 150g of butter
- 1 egg
- 1 pinch of salt

- 150g of honey
- 2 tsp cinnamon
- ¼ tsp nutmeg
- 2 tsp ginger
- ½ tsp of clove (powder)

Direction:

1. Put all the ingredients in a blender (the butter should be cold as soon as it comes out of the fridge).

2. Mix everything until you get a compact and sufficiently elastic mixture. Let it rest in the refrigerator for about 2 hours.

3. Then spread a 4 mm thick puff pastry with the rolling pin. Use templates to cut the dough in several ways.

4. Bake the cookies for 7 minutes at 180°C, and then rotate the baking paper.

5. Cook for additional 5 minutes, after cooling. Decorate to your liking.

Nutrition Value (Amount per Serving):

- Calories 100
- Fat 0g
- Carbohydrates 21g

- Sugar 6g
- Protein 3g
- Cholesterol 0mg

Rolls

Preparation time: 20 – 30 minutes;

Cooking time: 30 – 45 minutes;

Serve: 4

Ingredients:

- 20 ml of water
- 350 g flour
- 4 g of sugar
- 6 g of salt
- 10 g fresh yeast

Direction:

1. Put the flour in a large bowl (or on a pastry board), form a hole in the center and pour all the ingredients. Knead everything until you get a ball that you must knead for at least 10 minutes or until it becomes soft and elastic.

2. Cover with a slightly damp cloth and let it grow in a warm room without drafts for at least two hours. The mass should double in volume.

3. When the dough has risen, place it on a floured surface, cut several pieces (according to the size of the bread you want to obtain) and form the bread with your hands.

4. Place the rolls in the basket covered with parchment paper.

5. Set the temperature to 160⁰C and simmer for 30 minutes.

Nutrition Value (Amount per Serving):

- Calories 96
- Fat 1.7g
- Carbohydrates 18g
- Sugars 3.1g
- Protein 3.1g
- Cholesterol 0mg

Small Frozen Pizzas

Cooking time: 15-30 minutes;

Serve: 8

Ingredients:

- 14 pieces Small frozen pizzas

Direction:

1. Place the small pizzas, place them on the parchment paper, close the lid, place the thermostat in position 3, press the power key of the lower heating element and press the on / off key.

2. Cook everything for 20 minutes at 180°C.

Nutrition Value (Amount per Serving):

- Calories 350.0
- Fat 16.0 g
- Carbohydrate 38.0 g

- Sugars 3.0 g
- Protein   16.0 g
- Cholesterol 30.0 mg

Small Slippers With Flour

Preparation time: more than 30 minutes,

Cooking time: 15 – 30 minutes; Serve: 4

Ingredients:

- 200 ml of water
- 250 g flour
- 250 g Manitoba flour
- 12 g fresh beer yeast
- 10 g of salt

- 5 g of sugar
- 250 g mozzarella
- 150 g of tomato coulis
- Oregano to taste
- Salt to taste

Direction:

1. Pour the flours into a bowl, form a well and then add the other ingredients in the center.

2. Knead by hand until you get soft and flexible dough. Form a ball with this dough and then let it grow in a previously floured bowl.

3. Cover with a clean cloth, let stand in a warm place away from drafts. After about 1 hour of lifting, separate the small slipper by dividing the dough into 8 equal parts to obtain 8 circles.

4. Fill each slipper with the desired ingredients, close the dough to form a crescent and weld the ends well with a fork.

5. Grease the basket and place 4 small turnovers (brush each rotation with a little tomato sauce).

6. Set the air fryer to 150⁰C.

7. Cook for another 15 to 20 minutes and then put the other 4 empanadas for cooking.

Nutrition Value (Amount per Serving):

- Calories 455
- Fat 1.2g
- Carbohydrates 95.4g

- Sugars 0.3g
- Protein 12.9g

Peas with Bacon

Preparation time: 10 – 20 minutes,

Cooking time: 30 – 45 minutes;

Serve: 8

Ingredients:

- 750 g of frozen peas
- 100 g smoked bacon
- 2 shallots
- Salt and pepper to taste
- 200ml broth

Direction:

1. Preheat the air fryer to 160°C for 5 minutes.
2. Pour the chopped onion, bacon, oil in the basket
3. Brown for 5 min.
4. Add the peas, broth, salt, pepper, and simmer for additional 30 minutes.

Nutrition Value (Amount per Serving):

- Calories 129.6
- Fat 6.0 g
- Carbohydrate 13.6 g
- Sugars 3.3 g
- Protein   6.0 g
- Cholesterol   7.7 mg

Fresh Pizza

Preparation time: 10-20 minutes,

Cooking time: 30-45 minutes;

Serve: 1

Ingredients:

- 70ml of water
- 125 g flour
- 3g salt
- 7 g fresh yeast
- 100 g of tomato
- 100 g mozzarella
- Oregano to taste

Direction:

1. Pour the flour into a bowl, form a well, and then add the other ingredients in the center.

2. Knead with your hands until you get soft and flexible dough. Form a ball with this dough, and then let it grow in a previously floured bowl.

3. Cover with a clean cloth and let stand at room temperature, away from drafts. After about 1 hour of lifting, start spreading the dough

4. Preheat the air fryer to 150°C for 5 minutes.

5. Grease the bottom and spread the pizza dough. Cover with tomato coulis. Add a pinch of salt and oregano.

6. After 15 minutes cook add the diced mozzarella

7. Approximately after 10 minutes, turn the pizza half a turn

8. Cook for an additional 7 minutes.

Nutrition Value (Amount per Serving):

- Calories 290
- Carbohydrates 36g
- Fat 11g
- Sugars 0g
- Protein 11g
- Cholesterol 15mg

Frozen Pizza

Cooking time: 15-30 minutes;

Serve: 1

Ingredients:

- 1 piece Frozen Pizza

Direction:

1. Cook for 20 minutes at 180°C turning after 15 minutes.

Nutrition Value (Amount per Serving):

- Calories 576
- Fat 26g
- Carbohydrates 62g
- Sugars 7.7g
- Protein 22g
- Cholesterol 30mg

Poivronnade

Preparation time: 10-20 minutes,

Cooking time: 45-60 minutes;

Serve: 8

Ingredients:

- 750g Peppers
- 220g onion
- 300 g of tomato puree
- Broth 175g
- Salt and pepper to taste

Direction:

2. First, prepare the ingredients: chop the onion and cut the peppers into strips.

3. Put the onion and oil inside the basket at 150°C and brown for 5 min.

4. Add peppers, broth, salt, pepper, and simmer for 20 minutes.

5. Then add the tomato and finish cooking for an additional 30 minutes.

Nutrition Value (Amount per Serving):

- Calories 118
- Carbohydrates 5g
- Fat 10g
- Sugars 0g
- Protein 1g
- Cholesterol 0mg

Stuffed Peppers

Preparation time: 10 – 20 minutes,

Cooking time: 30 – 45 minutes;

Serve: 4

Ingredients:

- 2 Peppers
- 150 g minced meat
- 75 g Sausage
- 40 g French toast
- 1 spoon chopped parsley

- 1 egg
- 50 g grated cheese
- 1 garlic clove
- Salt and pepper to taste
- Butter to taste

Direction:

Prepare the filling:

1. Place all the ingredients, except the peppers, in a food processor (the bread must be soaked in milk to soften it) and mix until a homogeneous and compact compound is obtained.

2. Cut the peppers in half lengthwise, remove the white filaments and seeds.

3. Place the four halves of peppers inside the tray and fill them with the previously prepared mixture. Put in each of them pieces of butter.

4. Set the air fryer to 150°C and cook for 45 minutes depending on the size of the peppers.

Nutrition Value (Amount per Serving):

- Calories 444
- Fat 24g
- Carbohydrates 30g

- Sugars 8.2g
- Protein 29g
- Cholesterol 121mg

Baked Apples with Cinnamon

Preparation time: 0-10 minutes;

Cooking time: 15-30 minutes;

Serve: 4

Ingredients:

- 4 golden apples
- 1 roll of rectangular puff pastry
- 100 g apricot jam
- Raisins (sufficient quantity)
- Cinnamon (sufficient quantity)
- Sugar taste

Direction:

1. Peel the apples and remove the core. Unwind the puff pastry and cut it transversely to obtain 4 mini rectangles. Put the apples in the center and fill the hole with jam and some raisins.

2. Sprinkle with cinnamon and sugar (optional) and close with the edges of the puff pastry, pressing well to seal the apple inside. Brush the surface with a little milk to make them color during cooking.

3. Cook for 30 minutes or until desired browning is obtained, at 180°C.

Nutrition Value (Amount per Serving):

- Calories 173
- Fat 3.2g
- Carbohydrates 39g
- Sugars 32g
- Protein 0.8g
- Cholesterol 7.8mg

Baked Potatoes

Preparation time: 0-10 minutes,

Cooking time: more than 60 minutes;

Serve: 4

Ingredients:

- 4 whole potatoes (230 g each)
- 4 slices of cheddar cheese
- 20 g butter
- 4 slices of bacon
- Salt to taste
- Pepper to taste

Direction:

1. Wash potatoes well, brushing them gently to remove all traces of dirt without damaging the skin.

2. Cover each potato with oil and cover with a handful of salt (this will make the skin crisp).

3. Place the potatoes in the basket of the pan on parchment paper.

4. Set the air fryer to 160°C. Simmer for 60 min. (the time varies according to the size of the potatoes used), therefore, it will be useful to verify from time to time that the cooking is perfect.

5. After cooking, cut the potatoes crosswise and dig a little inside. Cover each potato with a piece of butter, a slice of bacon and a slice of cheese.

6. Sprinkle with black pepper and always brown with the thermostat in position 4 for another 3 minutes.

Nutrition Value (Amount per Serving):

- Calories 160.9
- Fat 0.2g
- Carbohydrates 36.6g
- Sugar 2g
- Protein 4.3g
- Cholesterol 160mg

Potatoes with Small Bacon

Preparation time: 10-20 minutes,

Cooking time: 30-45 minutes;

Serve: 8

Ingredients:

- 1250 g of fresh potatoes(peeled)
- 100 g smoked bacon
- Salt and pepper to taste
- 1 sprig rosemary

Direction:

1. Peel the potatoes and cut them into quarters. Put the potatoes in the water for a few minutes and rinse them well. Drain and clean with a paper towel.

2. Pour the potatoes, rosemary in the basket previously greased, season with salt and pepper.

3. Set the temperature to 150°C and cook for 15 minutes.

4. Add the bacon and finish cooking, simmer for another 20 minutes.

Nutrition Value (Amount per Serving):

- Calories 180
- Fat 6g
- Carbohydrates 30g
- Sugars 5g
- Protein 3g
- Cholesterol 60mg

Butter and bread pudding (dessert)

Preparation time: 10-20 minutes,

Cooking time: 15-30 minutes;

Serve: 4

Ingredients:

- 5/6 slices of honey bread
- 30 g butter
- 20 g raisins
- 400 ml of milk

- 4 egg yolks
- 90 g of sugar
- Cinnamon to taste
- 1 vanilla pod

Direction:

1. Remove the crust from the slices of bread and spread the butter on each slice, place them in the container previously buttered.

2. Pour the raisins over the bread. Separately, beat the eggs and sugar with an electric mixer and then add the milk (previously heated with the vanilla pod) until a very homogeneous mixture is obtained.

3. Pour the mixture over the slices of bread, being careful to distribute it evenly. Sprinkle with sugar and cinnamon.

4. Cook at 160°C for 30 minutes or until desired browning is achieved.

5. Serve hot with whipped cream or jam.

Nutrition Value (Amount per Serving):

- Calories 313
- Fat 15g
- Carbohydrates 36g

- Sugars 13g
- Protein 8.6g
- Cholesterol 98mg

Risotto with Porcini Mushrooms

Preparation time: 0-10 minutes,

Cooking time: 15-30 minutes;

Serve: 6

Ingredients:

- 320 g of basmati rice
- 200 g of porcini mushrooms
- 1250ml of broth
- 1 clove garlic
- Parsley to taste
- Grated cheese to taste
- Butter to taste

Direction:

1. Grease the basket and add the garlic clove.

2. Set the temperature to 150°C and brown for 2 minutes.

3. Remove the garlic, add the porcini mushrooms and simmer for another 5 minutes.

4. Add the rice, half the amount of the broth and simmer for another 10 minutes.

5. Pour the rest of the broth and finish cooking for another 13 minutes. Mix 2-3 times with a ladle at the end of cooking.

6. At the end of cooking, add the chopped parsley and mix with butter and grated cheese, serve.

Nutrition Value (Amount per Serving):

- Calories 365.0
- Fat 19.3 g
- Carbohydrate 30.5 g
- Sugars 1.7 g
- Protein   17.5 g
- Cholesterol 50.8 mg

Speck and Cheese Roll

Preparation time: 10 – 20 minutes,

Cooking time: 0 – 15 minutes;

Serve: 6

Ingredients:

- 1 roll of puff pastry
- 6 speck slices
- 4 slices of provola (spun cheese)

Direction:

1. Unroll the puff pastry and spread the speck slices.

2. Place the cheese slices on the speck and roll the puff pastry until you get a roll. Weld well.

3. Cut the roll into slices and place it inside the mold lined with baking paper.

4. Set the temperature to 180°C.

5. Cook the rolls for 13 minutes or according to the desired degree of cooking.

Nutrition Value (Amount per Serving):

- Calories 96
- Carbohydrates 8g
- Fat 4g
- Sugars 1g
- Protein 4g
- Cholesterol 6mg

Pesto Rolled and Brie

Preparation time: 10 – 20 minutes,

Cooking time: 0 – 15 minutes;

Serve: 6

Ingredients:

- 1 roll of puff pastry
- 100 g Genovese pesto
- 100 g of brie

Direction:

1. Unroll the puff pastry and spread the pesto.

2. Cut the cheese into thin slices and cover the pesto. Roll the puff pastry until you get a roll. Weld well.

3. Cut the roll into slices and place it inside the mold lined with baking paper.

4. Set the temperature to 160^{0}C.

5. Cook the rolls for 13 minutes or according to the desired degree of cooking.

Nutrition Value (Amount per Serving):

- Calories 483
- Carbohydrates 0g
- Fat 19g
- Sugars 0g
- Protein 35g
- Cholesterol 60mg

Santiago's Cake

Preparation time: 10-20 minutes;

Cooking time: 30-45 minutes;

Serve: 8

Ingredients:

- 250 g of almonds:
- 160 g of sugar
- 6 eggs
- Grated orange rind
- Grated lemon rind
- 5 drops of almond flavor

Direction:

1. In a food processor, chop the almonds until you get flour

2. With an electric mixer, beat the egg yolks with the sugar; add the grated lemon peel, the almond extract and the previously made flour.

3. Separately, beat the egg whites and fold them gently with the rest of the ingredients.

4. Remove the mixing paddle from the tank.

5. Butter and flour the tank and pour the mixture inside.

6. Set the temperature to 180^0C.

7. Bake the cake for 35 minutes.

8. For the final touch, cut a cardboard Santiago cross, place it in the center of the cake and sprinkle with icing sugar. By removing the cross, you will get the design on the cake.

Nutrition Value (Amount per Serving):

- Calories 295.2
- Fat 16.5 g
- Carbohydrate 29.9 g
- Sugars 26.2 g
- Protein 10.1 g
- Cholesterol 142.5 mg

Cream and Pine Nuts Cake

Preparation time: more than 30 minutes,

Cooking time: 45-60 minutes; Serve: 10

Ingredients:

- 250 g flour
- 125 g butter
- 110 g of sugar
- 2 eggs (1 whole and egg yolk)
- Salt to taste
- 500ml pastry cream
- 120 g of pine nuts

Direction:

1. Remove the flour, sugar, eggs, butter nuts from the refrigerator and a pinch of salt in the blender.

2. Mix everything until you get a compact and quite flexible mixture. Let it rest in the refrigerator for at least 30 minutes.

3. Butter and flour the basket. Spread the mass of broken dough with a thickness of ¾ cm and place it at the bottom of the basket, carefully cutting the edge.

4. Prick with a fork and spread the custard with a spoon.

5. Finish the cake by covering it completely with pine nuts.

6. Set the air fryer to 180°C.

7. Cook for 40 minutes and then turn off the lower resistance.

8. Cook another 15 minutes. Cool the cake well before turning it over to turn it off.

Nutrition Value (Amount per Serving):

- Calories 191
- Fat 19g
- Carbohydrates 3.7g
- Sugars 1g
- Protein 3.9g

Ricotta Cake

Preparation time: 10 minutes;

Cooking time: 40 minutes;

Serve: 10

Ingredients:

- 250 g flour
- 200 g of sugar
- Eggs
- 350 g ricotta
- 120 g melted butter
- 1 sachet of yeast
- 50 g of chocolate chips

Direction:

1. Add ricotta with sugar, add eggs and melted butter. Add the sifted flour with the yeast and finally the chocolate chips.

2. Butter and flour the basket and pour the mixture inside, smearing well.

3. Set the temperature to 180°C and bake the cake for 40 minutes.

4. Let cool and remove it from the basket; sprinkle with icing sugar.

Nutrition Value (Amount per Serving):

- Calories 269
- Fat 9.9g
- Carbohydrates 39g
- Sugars 21g
- Protein 6g
- Cholesterol 64mg

Ricotta Cake and Chocolate Chips

Preparation time: 10-20 minutes, Cooking time: 45-60 minutes; Serve: 10

Ingredients:

For the dough:

- 380g flour
- 165 g of sugar
- 185 g of butter
- 2 eggs
- 1 egg yolk

- 1 pinch of salt

Ingredients for filling:

- 600 g ricotta
- 1 lemon zest
- 100 g of chocolate chips

Direction:

1. Put the flour, sugar, eggs, butter in pieces just outside the refrigerator and a pinch of salt in a blender. Mix everything until you get a compact and sufficiently elastic mixture. Let it rest in the fridge for at least half an hour.

2. Grease and flour the basket. Unroll the mass of broken dough to a thickness of 3-4 mm and cover the bottom and walls. In a bowl, beat the ricotta with the eggs, the sugar, and the lemon zest until you get a smooth and smooth mixture. Finally, add the chocolate chips.

3. Pour everything inside the baking sheet covered with broken dough and slightly bend the edges inwards.

4. Set the temperature to 180°C.

5. Cook for 40 minutes and then turn off the lowest resistance. Cook for another 10 minutes. Cool well before removing from the baking sheet.

Nutrition Value (Amount per Serving):

- Calories 143.7
- Fat 7.8 g
- Carbohydrate 17.3 g

- Sugars 11.5 g
- Protein   3.0 g
- Cholesterol 28.7 mg

Amandine Pistachio Cake

Preparation time: more than 30 minutes,

Cooking time: 30 – 45 minutes; Serve: 8

Ingredients:

For the broken dough:

- 250 g flour
- 110 g of sugar
- 125 g butter
- 2 eggs
- Salt to taste

Direction:

Broken dough:

1. Remove flour, sugar, eggs, butter nuts from the refrigerator and a pinch of salt in the blender.

2. Mix everything until you get a compact and quite flexible mixture. Let it rest in the refrigerator for at least 30 minutes.

Almond cream:

3. Put the chopped almonds, sugar in a blender, and mix everything, then add the flour, eggs and mix well. Separately, cut the pistachios and cut them into large pieces.

4. Butter and flour the bottom of the basket. Unroll the broken dough leaving an edge that may contain almond cream. Prick with a fork and spread the jam.

5. Spread the almond cream and distribute the chopped pine nuts and pistachios.

6. Cook for 45 minutes at 180°C

7. Let cool and sprinkle with icing sugar.

Nutrition Value (Amount per Serving):

- Calories 242
- Carbohydrates 35g
- Fat 9g
- Sugars 21g
- Protein 3g
- Cholesterol 61mg

Asparagus and Sheep Cheesecake

Preparation time: 10-20 minutes,

Cooking time: 15-30 minutes;

Serve: 6

Ingredients:

- 250g asparagus
- 6 medium eggs
- ½ white onion
- 30 g grated Roman sheep cheese
- Breadcrumbs to taste
- Salt to taste
- Pepper to taste

Direction:

1. Peel the asparagus tail with a peeler. Cut the tip and boil them in salted water for about 5 to 7 minutes.

2. Cut 3 asparagus, the slightly larger ones in length and set them aside. Cut all others into pieces.

3. Beat the eggs in a bowl with salt and pepper. Add the pecorino and the chopped onion and mix well. Then add the asparagus into pieces and mix gently.

4. Butter the basket and cover with breadcrumbs

5. Pour the egg mixture into the basket. Arrange the asparagus cut lengthwise to beautify the cake.

6. Cook for 15 minutes at 180°C.

Nutrition Value (Amount per Serving):

- Calories: 548.5
- Fat 41.7 g
- Carbohydrate 22.9 g
- Sugars 4 g
- Protein 21.5 g
- Cholesterol 252.2 mg

Cherry tomato and mozzarella cake

Preparation time: 10 – 20 minutes,

Cooking time: 15 – 30 minutes;

Serve: 4

Ingredients:

- 1 roll of puff pastry
- ½ yellow pepper
- 100 g mozzarella
- 5 cherry tomatoes
- 2 eggs
- 20 g Parmesan
- 50 ml of milk
- Salt and pepper to taste

Direction:

1. Beat the eggs, milk, Parmesan in a bowl with a little salt and pepper.

2. Unroll the puff pastry (leaving the baking paper) and then prick the bottom with a fork.

3. Arrange the chopped mozzarella, pepper, and sliced tomatoes; pour the prepared preparation.

4. Fold the edges of the dough in and cut the excess baking paper with scissors (keep the ends cut so you can easily rotate and extract the cake).

5. Set the temperature to 160°C and cook another 15 minutes.

6. Turn to 180°C and cook for another 12 minutes (using the baking paper).

Nutrition Value (Amount per Serving):

- Calories 277.8
- Fat 23.5 g
- Carbohydrate 5.1 g
- Sugars 0.6 g
- Protein 13.3 g
- Cholesterol 44.8 mg

Tasty Chicory and Mota Cake

Preparation time: 10-20 minutes,

Cooking time: 15-30 minutes;

Serve: 6

Ingredients:

- 1 roll of puff pastry
- 200 g of cooked chicory
- 120 g speck in pieces
- 100 ml of fresh cream
- 2 eggs
- 20 g grated cheese:
- 50 ml of milk:
- Salt to taste
- Pepper to taste

Direction:

1. Beat the eggs, cream, grated cheese, and milk in a bowl with a little salt and pepper.

2. Unroll the puff pastry with parchment paper and prick the bottom with the teeth of a fork.

3. Put the speck in pieces and cooked chicory (see recipe "Treviso chicory sauce") in the tank. Add the previously prepared liquid mixture.

4. Fold the edges of the dough and with scissors cut the excess baking paper (keeping some points that will be used to rotate the quiche easily)

5. Cook the cake for 15 minutes at 180° (using parchment paper). Turn and cook for an additional 8 minutes.

Nutrition Value (Amount per Serving):

- Calories 6.7
- Fat 0.1g
- Carbohydrate 1.4g
- Sugars 2g
- Protein 0.5g
- Cholesterol 0.0mg

Frozen Salty Cake

Cooking time: 30-45 minutes;

Serve: 6

Ingredients:

- 1 piece of frozen salted cake

Direction:

1. Preheat the air fryer at 160⁰C for 5 minutes. Place the savory cake in the basket.

2. Cook everything for 45 minutes, turning it to 180°C (using parchment paper) after about 30 minutes.

Nutrition Value (Amount per Serving):

- Calories 250
- Fat 13g
- Carbohydrate 32g
- Sugars 22g
- Protein 2g
- Cholesterol 20mg

Toad in the hole

Preparation time: 10-20 minutes,

Cooking time: 30-45 minutes;

Serve: 4

Ingredients:

- 8 sausages
- 8 slices of bacon
- 100 g onion
- Thyme to taste

Ingredients for donut dough:

- 130 g flour
- 2 g baking powder

- 1 whole egg
- 1 egg-yolk
- 200 ml of milk
- 100 ml of water
- Salt to taste
- Pepper to taste

Direction:

1. Prepare the donut dough. Beat all the ingredients together until you get a homogeneous mixture without lumps. Cover with the film and let stand for about 10 minutes.

2. Chop the onion and pour it into the tank with the oil; Wrap each sausage with a slice of bacon and place on the onions with a few sprigs of fresh thyme. Pour 100 ml of water.

3. Cook for 15 minutes at 160°C.

4. Turn the sausages and cook for 10 minutes. At the end of cooking, pour the donut dough over the sausages, turn off the bottom element and close.

5. Cook for 15 to 20 minutes depending on the degree of cooking desired.

6. Serve the toad in the still hot hole with a side sauce

Nutrition Value (Amount per Serving):

- Calories 366
- Fat 23.8g
- Carbohydrates 20.4g

- Fiber 3.4g
- Protein 11.9g
- Cholesterol 160 mg

Asparagus, Cheese and Speck Pie

Preparation time: 10-20 minutes,

Cooking time: 30-45 minutes;

Serve: 6

Ingredients:

- 150 g of green asparagus
- 150 g of water:
- 1 roll of broken dough
- 100 g of diced mota
- 100 g of Italian cow's milk cheese
- 3 eggs
- 100 ml of milk
- Salt to taste
- Pepper to taste

Direction:

1. Clean the asparagus. Cut them into small pieces and place them in the basket with the water.

2. Set the air fryer to 150°C.

3. Cook for about 15 minutes.

4. Remove the asparagus from the tank once cooked and wait for them to cool

5. Unroll the broken dough (leaving the baking paper) and then prick the bottom with a fork.

6. Arrange the diced speck and cheese and asparagus, then pour the prepared preparation.

7. Fold the edges of the dough in and cut the excess baking paper with scissors (keep the ends cut so you can easily rotate and extract the cake).

8. Cook another 25 minutes.

Nutrition Value (Amount per Serving):

- Calories 260
- Fat 17g
- Carbohydrates 18g
- Protein 7g

Mushroom, Egg and Mozzarella Cake

Preparation time: 10 minutes;

Cooking time: 50 minutes;

Serve: 6

Ingredients:

- 2 rolls of puff pastry: 2
- 300 g mushrooms
- 1 onion

- Parsley to taste
- 150 g mozzarella
- 3 eggs

Direction:

1. Clean the mushrooms well and chop them.

2. Spray the basket of the air fryer. Pour the chopped onion in the basket

3. Brown for 2 minutes at 160°C.

4. Add the mushrooms and cook for another 15 minutes. Add (at discretion) salt and pepper, parsley, and finish cooking for another 3 minutes. Meanwhile, prepare hard boiled eggs.

5. In a bowl, mix the mushrooms with the crushed eggs and the chopped mozzarella, salt, and pepper.

6. Unroll the broken dough (leaving the baking paper) and then prick the bottom with a fork.

7. Arrange the egg and mushroom mixture and close with the other dough roll. Weld the edges well.

8. Brush the surface of the dough with egg yolk and prick the steam out.

9. Bake the cake for 30 minutes.

Nutrition Value (Amount per Serving):

- Calories 345.0
- Fat 28.6 g
- Carbohydrate 2.0 g

- Sugars 1.1 g
- Protein   20.4 g
- Cholesterol 464.1 mg

Roasted pears

Preparation time: 5 minutes;

Cooking time: 20 minutes;

Serve: 2

Ingredients:

4 portions

- 4 pears with rind well washed
- 50 g Raisins
- 2 tbsp jam without sugar
- 1 tsp honey
- 1 pinch cinnamon powder

Direction:

1. Pears are washed, hollowed out by extracting the heart.
2. Separate the pulp
3. Mix the jam chosen with the pulp of pears, honey and raisins and cinnamon
4. Fill the pears with that mixture
5. Place the pears in the fryer
6. In the bowl place a glass of water
7. Cook for 20 minutes at 180°C
8. Serve them alone or accompanied with a scoop of vanilla ice cream.

Nutrition Value (Amount per Serving):

- Calories 101
- Fat 0.3g
- Carbohydrates 27g
- Fiber 5.5g
- Sugars 17g
- Protein 0.6g

Gluten-Free Yogurt Cake

Preparation time: 10 minutes;

Cooking time: 40 minutes;

Serve: 2

Ingredients:

- 1 Greek yogurt
- 3 eggs
- 150 g sugar
- 100 g cream
- 50 g sunflower oil
- 50 g butter
- 200 g gluten free flour
- Salt
- 1 on yeast

Direction:

1. Put the eggs, yogurt, and sugar in the basket. Mix well. Add the rest of the ingredients and mix.

2. Put the dough in the sponge cake container, previously brushed with oil. Preheat the fryer and put the mold with the dough for 40 minutes at 170°C.

3. When it cools, unmold, and decorate to taste.

Nutrition Value (Amount per Serving):

- Calories 361.2
- Fat 10.9 g
- Carbohydrate 59.2 g
- Sugars 31.2 g
- Protein   9.6 g
- Cholesterol 53.1 mg

Rösti (Swiss Potatoes)

Preparation time: 10 minutes;

Cooking time: 15 minutes;

Serve: 4

Ingredients:

- 250 g peeled white potatoes
- 1 tbsp chopped chives
- Freshly ground black pepper
- 1 tbsp olive oil
- 2 tbsp sour cream
- 100 g smoked salmon

Direction:

1. Preheat the air fryer to 180°C. Grate the thick potatoes in a bowl and add three quarters of the scallions and salt and pepper to taste. Mix it well.

2. Grease the pizza tray with olive oil and distribute the potato mixture evenly throughout the pan. Press the grated potatoes against the pan and spread the top of the potato pie with olive oil.

3. Place the pizza tray in the fryer basket and place it in the air fryer. Set the timer to 15 minutes and fry the rösti until it has a pretty brown color on the outside and is soft and well done inside.

4. Cut the rösti into 4 quarters and place each quarter on a plate. Garnish with a tablespoon of sour cream and place the slices of salmon on the plate next to the rösti. Spread the rest of the scallions on sour cream and add a touch of ground pepper.

Nutrition Value (Amount per Serving):

- Calories 123.3
- Fat 6.9 g
- Carbohydrate 7.2 g
- Sugars 0.3 g
- Protein 7.5 g
- Cholesterol 27.4 mg

Thai Fish Cake with Mango Sauce

Preparation time: 20 minutes;

Cooking time: 14 minutes;

Serve: 4

Ingredients:

- 1 ripe mango
- 1 tsp and a half of red chili paste
- 3 tbsp fresh cilantro or parsley
- 1 lime juice and zest
- 500 g of white fish fillets
- 1 egg
- 1 chopped chive
- 50 g ground coconut

Direction:

1. Peel the mango and cut it into small dice. Mix the mango dice in a bowl with ½ teaspoon of red chili paste, 1 tablespoon of cilantro and the juice and zest of a lime.

2. Beat the fish in the kitchen robot and mix it with 1 egg, 1 teaspoon of salt and the rest of the lime zest, red chili paste and lime juice. Mix everything with the rest of the cilantro, chives and 2 tablespoons of coconut.

3. Place the rest of the coconut on a deep plate. Divide the fish mixture into 12 portions, shape them in round cakes and coat them with the coconut.

4. Place six fish cakes in the basket and place it in the air fryer at 180°C. Set the timer to 7 minutes and fry the cakes until golden brown and ready to drink. Fry in the same way the rest of the fish cakes.

5. Serve with mango sauce.

Nutrition Value (Amount per Serving):

- Calories 361
- Fat 22.8g
- Carbohydrate 13.8g
- Sugars 8.7g
- Protein 25.8g
- Cholesterol 93.9mg

Conclusion

Throughout this book, we have learned a lot about owning and using an air fryer. We can confidently say that the air fryer is one of the best inventions of kitchen appliances.

Healthy food should not be a fad or an impossibility to choose; it should be part of everyone's life. Of course, this does not mean that you must give up enjoying the kitchen; neither of the many dishes that can be prepared healthy. To get it there are certain appliances that can help you and a lot: for example, an air fryer.

In our earlier chapters, you could see that with an air fryer, you will cook different foods in a similar way as a traditional one would. But thanks to its special operation, you can do it without using a single drop of oil. In this way, you can prepare exquisite dishes without added fats and with a considerably lower caloric intake.

Now you know some of the many functions and recipes of an air fryer. We hope that this eBook has helped you discover some interesting features.

Having an air fryer is a great option. You can enjoy a healthier meal and save a good part of the oil expense, all without giving up enjoyable, fried foods

Please enjoy the different recipes that we have listed for you in this cookbook.

CPSIA information can be obtained
at www.ICGtesting.com
Printed in the USA
LVHW070614121020
668553LV00008B/62